SCIENCE  AND  CULTURE  SERIES

JOSEPH  HUSSLEIN,  S.J.,  Ph.D.,  GENERAL  EDITOR

# ALMS FOR OBLIVION

# ALMS FOR OBLIVION

*Books, Men and Biography*

## GEORGE CARVER

THE BRUCE PUBLISHING COMPANY
*Milwaukee*

To

E. S. C.

Time hath, my lord, a wallet
at his back,
Wherein he puts alms
for oblivion.

— *Shakespeare*

# Preface by the General Editor

A study has here been made of twenty-four representative men of letters who during the past twelve centuries have contributed, in some significant way, to the development of biography as a recognized form of English literature. Beginning with Anglo-Saxon days their line stretches down to us, though purposely no living biographers have been included.

The book, without question, is of exceptional literary moment and of no slight value to every student of English letters; but its general appeal extends to a far wider circle.

To each author a separate chapter is here devoted. And what lends particular human interest is the invariable sketch of the biographer's own life, together with an equally fascinating account of what might be called an introduction to the guest of the day, the person described in the biography.

From an academic point of view the book distinctly assumes the belles-lettres form. It largely dispenses with the usual trappings of scholarship, although a bibliography is provided, and so is rendered more widely acceptable, while scholars will in turn be attracted by the leisured and informal literary comment that crowds these pages.

If emphasis is occasionally shifted from the critical and historical to the more purely social aspect of things, this is no more than conformable to our modern preoccupation with living issues.

Biography naturally strives to lay bare, as far as possible, the very soul of the person portrayed: his aims, motives, longings, and ambitions, no less than to describe his visible achievements. The decay of biography, where that too frequently has set in with excessive "fictional" treatment on the part of modern popular writers, is clearly manifested in the wanton interpretation and often direct distortion of the characters treated. In such instances fancy or prejudice rather than objective truth prevail.

Obviously, not all biographers chosen for this volume are proposed as commendable from every point of view, even when highly excellent in their specific art. Expressions, therefore, of literary appreciation by the author of this book must not necessarily be interpreted as a commendation also of the religious and moral attitude of all that is contained in any particular volume under discussion here, or in one that is perhaps incidentally mentioned in a laudatory way. Yet such cautions are not meant to imply that religious and moral aspects have not been strongly and even frequently stressed by the author. Each biographer, on the other hand, is carefully rated according to the canons of his art and his distinctive contribution.

But, above all, biography should not fall far short of being a grammar for the living.

What perhaps may impress the reader is the tiny number of those whose memory, as enshrined in biographic form, has during the past twelve centuries actually survived the obliterating floods of the ages. All, to be sure, are not listed here, but their number becomes infinitesimally small when compared with the millions of human beings who have lived within that period in English-speaking lands.

Why, we may curiously inquire, were precisely these few men chosen for such exceptional remembrance? Some, doubtless, because of their special integrity of personality, like a Saint Thomas More; some, because of their achievements in a particular field, like a Sir Walter Scott; and lastly some, because of no towering merit of their own, but merely by reason of a personal attraction they exercised on the biographer, like a Sterling, a Savage, or a Nash.

Of the vast surplus of biographies published in recent years, how many will outlive a millennium? We can leave that for the reader to guess. But for ultimate justice to be done to all the countless unknown, unnamed, and disregarded we must wait for the last entry to be made in the Book of Life, the only and final Who's Who of all the ages.

JOSEPH HUSSLEIN, S.J., PH.D.,
*General Editor, Science and Culture Series*

Saint Louis University

# Contents

# 1—By Way of Definition

> *But as the joyful swans, that, singing sweet,*
> *Convey the medals to the fane,*
> *So they whose praises poets well repeat*
> *Are rescued from oblivion.* — Ariosto.

THE word *biography* was introduced into English during the
seventeenth century. "The New English Dictionary" gives
credit to Damascius for having first used its Greek equivalent —
about the year 500. It goes on to record that "biographist" was first
employed in England by Thomas Fuller in 1662; "biography" by
Dryden in 1683; "biographer" by Addison in 1715; and "biographical" by Oldys in 1738. Professor Donald A. Stauffer, of Princeton,
however, in a recent study, "English Biography Before 1700," takes
exception. He says:

> Before the publication of *The Worthies of England* and
> preceding Dryden by more than twenty years, both *biography*
> and *biographer* were known. *The Works of Mr. Richard
> Hooker* was published in 1662 with a prefatory life by Bishop
> Gauden. This life speaks of "Others (who warped away from
> the Church of England) and have ventured to be (*Biogra-
> phers*) writers of the lives of some English Divines." This mis-
> print shows the unfamiliarity and strangeness of the newly
> coined word, and Gauden's own explanatory phrase shows the
> term to be practically unknown. The anonymous *Life of . . .
> Dr. Thomas Fuller* (1661) and the *Flagellum: Or the Life and*

[ 1 ]

*Death . . . of O. Cromwell* (1663) use the word *biography* in its usual modern sense, without an explanatory synonym.[*]

It would seem, then, because the word became so recently a part of the language, that the concept itself had been lacking hitherto. As a matter of fact, Professor Stauffer found that the writing of "lives" had before 1700 included all aspects of what later came to be called biography — "the impersonal, political, ethical, malicious, encomiastic, romantic, mystical, satirical, documented, and subjective" — yet not until under the influence of the renaissance and the quickening effect of the widespread interest in classical literature was there a sufficiently well-focused conception of life writing to require an appropriate term. "Historiography" had early appeared, and "life writing" had likewise been used. But until after translations of classical models were made, during the sixteenth century, North's "Plutarch," for instance, Golding's "Caesar," Savile's "Agricola," Justin's "Pomperius," and the like, no awareness of life writing seems to have been vital enough to require a word to distinguish it from chronical and historical writing in general.

It becomes difficult, therefore, to find a definition for "biography" that will serve to cover all writing in the form. There have been many attempts made by lexicographers, but none is entirely satisfactory. Perhaps the best way to determine what it is, is to learn what various biographers in various periods have said in the accounts which they have given of the purpose and range of their own work — not a difficult matter, for biographers more than any other writers have commented freely upon why they undertook particular tasks and what they hoped to accomplish.

The earliest examples of life writing in England are the Latin "lives" of the saints. Restricted to accounts of holy men, they were written, patterned roughly after the gospel "lives" of Christ, for the purpose of "showing virtue her own feature." A tradition was established in connection with them which has been continued ever since. Its characteristic mood is panegyric, attained by citing the subject as an example of virtue, and stressing saintliness above

---

[*] Included by the courteous permission of the publishers of D. A. Stauffer's "English Biography Before 1700," the Harvard University Press.

all else. Among the hundreds of saints' "lives" composed during the centuries that fixed the tradition, three or four have survived as representative of typical accomplishment. But so nearly related are they in both range and purpose that what one writer has to say about his book may be taken in general as characteristic of the others. Pertinent comment occurs in Jonas' "Life of Columbanus," Bede's "St. Cuthbert," Eddius' "St. Wilfrid," although the statement most sharply concentrated, appears in Adamnan's "St. Columba" near the end of Book 1, and in the Reeves translation stands:

> Holy and apostolic men in general in order to avoid vain-glory strive as much as they can to conceal the wonders of God's secret workings within them; yet God sometimes, whether they will or no, maketh some of these known to the world and bringeth them into view by various means, wishing thus, as He doth, to honor the saints who honor Him.

From Adamnan to Izaac Walton, it may be said, extends the thread of ecclesiastical life writing, from the seventh century, that is (Adamnan died in 704), to the seventeenth. There are accounts, naturally, during these thousand years that do not fall into this category — many "lives" of rulers, for instance, began to appear, in keeping with the growing stress upon the "ways of wise government" as indicated by the rapidly increasing accumulation of books concerned with "morality, courtesy, and polity." The prevailing mood, none the less, was panegyric and the purpose throughout was didactic. The range alone was somewhat increased. In fact, Izaac Walton's comment, set down in his famous "Lives," sums up the whole matter, including the attitude of his own day. "Biography," he wrote:

> is an honor due to the virtuous dead and a lesson in magnanimity to those who shall succeed them.

Whether ecclesiastical or not, until very recently biography has been almost wholly concerned with moral teaching. How best to live in order to merit the rewards of heaven was its earliest preoccupation. Later a note of worldliness began to manifest itself, and the emphasis was changed to how best to live in order to merit the rewards of society. But before Walton's "Lives" began their separate appearances — they were published at intervals between 1640 and 1678 — Francis Bacon had issued his lament that biography (he referred to it, however, as "lives") was so little employed, since it so far "excelleth in profit and use." The remark occurs in connection with his analysis of history in "The Advancement of Learning." "History," he said,

> which may be called just and perfect history, is of three kinds, according to the subject which it propoundeth, or pretendeth to represent: for it representeth a time, a person, or an action. . . . The second excelleth in profit and use. . . . Lives, if they be well written, propounding to themselves a person to represent, in whom actions both greater and smaller, publick and private, have a commixture, must of necessity contain a more true, native, and lively representation.

As the renaissance progressed and the intellectual horizon widened, persons other than saints and rulers became increasingly popular as the subjects of biographers. The same purpose — commemoration and moral teaching — was sustained, but little by little the range was increased to include statesmen and literary men. Cavendish's "Wolsey," Roper's "More" (no doubt prepared as material for Harpsfield's "Life of Sir Thomas More"), and Speght's "Chaucer," were all written before 1600. Cavendish wrote to preserve the good name of his patron from the evil reports that sprang up immediately after his death; he had been a gentleman-in-waiting to the cardinal and so was conversant with his character and personality in more than ordinary degree. He was, however, equally interested in the moral application of careers like Wolsey's. Near the beginning of his book, he says:

> Since his death I have heard divers and sundry surmises and imagined tales, made of his proceedings and doings, which I myself have known to be most untrue. . . . Therefore, I commit the truth to Him who knoweth all things.

And toward the end he enlarges upon his purpose and sets forth the vanity of human greatness, the futility of ambition. He writes:

> Who list to rede and consider with indifference this history, may behold the wondrous mutability of vain honors, the

brittle assurance of abundance, the flattering of feigned friends, and the ticklish trust of worldly princes.

Cavendish considered Wolsey's attainment and his exercise of power more nearly in terms of their manifestations than of the character of Wolsey as a man, and the work becomes, hence, something of a warning against worldliness. Instead of erecting a model to be followed, he describes a way of life to be avoided. None the less the "Wolsey" is panegyric. Cavendish admired his patron above all other men, and he is not slow to say so. And in no less degree did William Roper admire his father-in-law, Sir — now Saint — Thomas More; only, his point of view differs widely from Cavendish's. Roper wrote panegyric in the usual manner recording the experience of his subject as an example of virtue to be followed and defining him as a personality to become enshrined in memory. His purpose is clearly explained in his introductory remarks:

> For that I am continually a resident in his house by the space of sixteen years and more, I thought it therefore my part to set forth such matters touching his life as I could at this present call to memory, among which are many notable things not meet to have forgotten . . . but which in my poor judgment seem worthy to be remembered.

Nicholas Harpesfield's "More," contemporary with the "Wolsey," is the first — from the more modern point of view — full-length literary biography in the language; and Speght's comment upon Chaucer has been of high significance to current scholarship.

About the middle of the seventeenth century both range and purpose were enlarged, as has been suggested, but new characteristics developed — illustrated by the work of two women — which contributed further significance. Hitherto the persons whose "lives" were written had been distinguished figures well known to the nation at large, and their fame was the chief reason for their selection as subjects. In not a few biographers, however, of which Margaret Newcastle and Lucy Hutchinson are typical, neither wide fame nor eminent virtue was the motivating force. Mrs. Hutchinson's "Life" of her husband, Colonel Hutchinson, one of Cromwell's best soldiers, was written solely that his children might have the means of remembering him. Nevertheless, the book is noteworthy because it is an authentic document presenting an account of a very vital personality and depicting much of the turmoil which surrounded him. The purpose is revealed in an early section of the work, the title of which is "Memoirs of the Life of Colonel Hutchinson":

> I am under a command [given by her husband] not to grieve at the common fate of desolate women, while I am studying which way to moderate my woe, and if it were possible to augment my love, can for the present find out none more just to your dear father nor consolatory to myself than the preservation of his memory; which I need not guild with such flattering conmmendations as the hired preachers do equally give to the truly and the titular honorable. A naked undressed narrative, speaking the simple truth of him will deck him with more substantial glory, than all the panegyrics the best pens could ever consecrate to the virtues of the best men.

The other biography of a husband by his wife is "The Life of the Duke of Newcastle" by Margaret, his duchess. Like the foregoing, it was a labor of love, but, unlike it, the book was written almost as much to satisfy the duchess' own taste for fame as to preserve the fame of the duke. Lady Margaret was something more, however, than a Restoration sensation-seeker. She wrote some sixteen books in fifteen years; and although some of her contemporaries, including Samuel Pepys, had harsh things to say about her, Charles Lamb called her "thrice noble." At all events she had a philosophy of history, within which she included a definite attitude toward biography. "Although there be many sorts of history," she wrote

> yet these are the chiefest (1) A general history. (2) A national history. (3) A particular history. . . . The third is the history of the life of a particular person . . . it is the most secure; because it goes not out of its own circle, but turns on its own axis, and for the most part keeps within the circumference of truth.

It was left for Thomas Fuller, however, to state specifically all previous purposes and to add two new ones, held perhaps by earlier

writers but not before acknowledged. Many had written in commemoration of an admired character and many more had written
to teach virtue. Not a few had endeavored by means of biography
to enhance their position in the world. And one or two had used
it as a means of finding consolation for bereavement. Thomas Fuller,
to these, added monetary gain and entertainment when he set down
his reasons for writing the "Worthies of England":

> First, to gain some glory to God. Secondly, to preserve the
> memories of the dead. Thirdly, to present examples to the
> living. Fourthly, to entertain the reader with delight. And
> lastly (which I am not ashamed publicly to profess) to procure
> some honest profit to myself.

Probably the most important work of the century, notwithstanding, from the point of view of theory and technique of biography,
was Dryden's "Plutarch," in which was included a comment that
has influenced biographers ever since.

> Biographia, [he wrote] or the history of particular men's
> lives . . . is inferior to history as being more confined in action,
> and treating of wars and counsels, and all other affairs of
> nations, only as they relate to him whose life is written. . . .
> In history you are conducted only into the rooms of state;
> in biography you are led in to the private lodgings of the
> hero: you see him in undress and are made familiar with his
> private actions and conversations. . . . The pageantry of life is
> taken away; you see the poor reasonable animal, as naked as
> ever nature made him; are made acquainted with his passion
> and his folly, and find the demi-god a man.

In this passage is set forth an idea the importance of which biography had overlooked for a thousand years. Any number of writers
had made feeble attempts to include informal material, but no one
before Dryden had given authoritative sanction to the practice.
With Dryden's statement and his use of informal detail — as far as
his limited sources of information concerning Plutarch made possible — the way was pointed toward the highest reaches the form
has yet attained: Boswell's "Life of Johnson."
Not until a hundred years had passed did Boswell's work appear,

however; and when it did, even then its contribution to the form might well be considered a matter of method rather than of range or purpose. In fact, the contribution throughout the eighteenth century concerned chiefly method. Even though, it is true, during the early years, biographers like Captain Alexander Smith were occupied with the "lives" of rogues, and rogues had not been given much attention; nevertheless, Smith's work, like that of his colleagues and imitators, was almost entirely commercial and had small influence upon authentic life writing. Somewhat later came the biographical lexicographers — although their way had been pointed out for them during the previous century — who stressed factual accuracy and contributed at least a modicum of objectivity to the practice of their forerunners. In the same category fell the antiquarians, who, reaching their climax in Edmund Malone, Boswell's friend and adviser, have left a permanent impress upon the tradition. An exception to the foregoing is the work of Roger North. As early as 1715 he had finished the "Lives" of his three brothers, a work which, although it added nothing new to biographical writing, served to emphasize the practice of Dryden by putting informal material more fully into use than Dryden himself had been able to do. Furthermore, North, in a manner, repeats the ideas of Dryden in his introduction to "The Lives of the Norths":

> It may be thought that I have here touched too much on the panegyric, but I have not formalized upon what I am fully possessed is most true. And if some things that are set down seem too trivial, let it be considered that the smaller incidents in the life of a busy man are often as useful to be known though not so diverting as the greater, and profit must share with entertainment. . . .
>
> If the history of a life hangs together with great importances, such as concern Church and State, and drops the peculiar economy and private conduct of the person that gives title to the work, it may be history and very good, but of anything rather than of that person's life . . . Scars and blemishes as well as beauties ought to be expressed; otherwise it is an outline filled up with lilies and roses.

Hence, Roger North underscores Dryden's ideas by advocating

the inclusion not only of informal detail but of blemishes and imperfections as well.

As the eighteenth century advanced, biographical devices were augmented by various additions, including careful research into primary sources, until by the accomplishment of Boswell the pattern was, for the time at least, fixed. Just prior to Boswell's work, however, appeared that of William Mason, from which the biographer of Johnson obtained perhaps more than a hint. Mason's account of his aims and methods is illuminating. He says, toward the end of his "The Poems and Letters of Thomas Gray With Memoirs of His Life and Writings":

> The method by which I have arranged the foregoing pages has, I trust, one degree of merit — that it makes the reader so well acquainted with the man himself, as to render it totally unnecessary to conclude the whole with his character. If I am mistaken in this point, I have been a compiler to little purpose; and I choose to be this rather than a biographer, that I might do the more justice to the virtues and genius of my friend. I might have written his life in the common form, perhaps with more reputation to myself; but, surely, not with equal information to the reader: for whose sake I have never related a single circumstance of Mr. Gray's life in my own words, when I could employ his for the purpose.

And Boswell, referring incidentally to Mason's work, describes his own plan, and in so doing defines his contribution to the form — the crystallization of the autobiographical method:

> Instead of melting down my material into one mass, and constantly speaking in my own person, by which I might have appeared to have more merit in the execution of the work, I have decided to adopt and enlarge upon the excellent plan of Mr. Mason in his Memoirs of Gray. Wherever the narrative is necessary to explain, connect, and supply, I furnish it to the best of my abilities; but in the chronological series of Johnson's life, which I trace as distinctly as I can, year by year, I produce, whenever it is in my power, his own minutes, letters, or conversation, being convinced that this mode is more lively, and will make my readers better acquainted with

him, than even those were who actually knew him, but could know him only partially; whereas, there is here an accumulation of intelligence from various points by which his character is more fully understood and illustrated.

Indeed I cannot conceive a more perfect mode of writing any man's life, than not only relating all the most important events of it in their order, but interweaving what he privately wrote, and said, and thought; by which mankind, are enabled, as it were, to "live o'er each scene" with him, as he actually advanced throughout the several stages of life. Had his other friends been as diligent and ardent as I was, he might have been entirely preserved. As it is, I will venture to say that he will be seen in this work more completely than any man who has ever yet lived.

In the meantime Johnson himself had had much to say about biography; but his comments serve to emphasize the value rather than add to the range and purpose of the form; as do likewise his actual biographical writings. He does, however, by precept, if less by practice, add to its growing prestige; and Boswell sets down a number of such precepts stated during conversation. Pertinent remarks on biography appear in No. 84 of the "Idler," which, like No. 60 of the "Rambler," is devoted to a discussion of biography:

> The mischievous consequences of vice and folly . . . are best discovered by those relations which are levelled with the general surface of life, which tell not how any man became great, but how he was made happy; not how he lost the favor of his prince, but how he became discontented with himself.

And he remarks further, in much the same strain, to Boswell while commenting upon Goldsmith's "Parnell" (something of similar import is to be found in No. 68 of the "Rambler"): "Nobody can write the life of a man but those who have eat and drunk and lived in social intercourse with him." In fact one might compile a body of comment made by Johnson about biography — as, in a manner, Professor Bergen Evans has done — which would serve more or less as a grammar of such writing, and which comment does serve, in the opinion of Mr. Harold Nicholson, Hogarth Lecturer on the subject of biography, as the best definition yet to appear.

One may say, therefore, that during the eighteenth century the form became of age in England and that in Boswell's "Johnson" it arrived at its maturity. Taken all in all, an ideal had been achieved, and Boswell's remark in the introduction to his celebrated work, that Johnson "will be seen in this work more completely than any man who has ever yet lived," is still unexceptionable. Nevertheless, something has been added by subsequent biographers.

The nineteenth century, rich though it was in the production of literary art in general, was poor in the quality of its biography, although in quantity it reached to excess. An anonymous comment in 1854, for instance, insisted that

> To write a life has ceased to be a distinction; and the highest glory that can now be awarded to departed worth, is that it may be sacred from the profane ink of the biographer.

The range remained much the same, but the purpose reverted to that of the early period, almost the whole emphasis being placed upon commemoration and moral teaching. The most notable works to appear as the century progressed were the "Scott" by John G. Lockhart, who alone at the time profited by Boswell's contribution to method; the "Nelson" by Robert Southey, who made use of England's great admiral to teach patriotism and to aid in building up the morale of the British navy; George Otto Trevelyan's "Macaulay"; James Anthony Froude's "Carlyle," which added disenchantment to the biographer's prerogatives and so helped to prepare the way for twentieth-century sensationalism; and Thomas Carlyle's "Sterling" — which aimed to teach "the monitions and moralities." Carlyle, incidentally, made some very pertinent observations on biography in his essay "Biography," in "Heroes and Hero Worship," and in other writings.

In "Heroes and Hero Worship," for instance, he says, "History is the biography of great men." And again: "History is the essence of innumerable biographies." And yet again — this time in his "Journal": "Biography is the only true history," an idea upon which he enlarges somewhat in the "Essay on Burns":

> If an individual is really of consequence enough to have his life and character recorded for public remembrance, we

have always been of opinion that the public ought to be made acquainted with all the inward springs and relations of his character. How did the world and the man's life, from his particular position, represent themselves to his mind? How did existing circumstances modify him from without; how did he modify these from within? With what endeavors and what efficacy rule over them; with what resistance and what suffering sink under them? In one word, what and how produced was the effect of society on him; what and how produced was his effect upon society? He who should answer these questions, in regard to any individual, would, we believe, furnish a model of perfection in Biography.

Furthermore, in the essay, "Biography," he bewails the innocuity into which the form had fallen in his day:

> Considering the multitude of mortals that handle the Pen in these days, and can mostly spell, and write without glaring violations of grammar, the question naturally arises: How is it, then, that no Work proceeds from them, bearing any stamp of authenticity and permanence; of worth for more than a day? . . . How is it that . . . no one can attain to the smallest mark of excellence, or produce ought that shall endure longer than 'Snowflake on the river' or the foam on penny beer? We answer: Because there is no Reality.

And his cry for Reality was justified. For in spite of the torrents of biographies which poured from the presses, if one excepts the works previously mentioned, such invaluable undertakings as the "Dictionary of National Biography," and a handful of writings in quality more or less comparable, nothing appeared which in distinguished manner added either to range or purpose. In fact, so stereotyped and conventional and yet so prevalent had the writing of biography become that James Russell Lowell, in his essay on Izaac Walton, published in 1889, wrote:

> The modern biographer has become so indiscriminate, so unconscious of the relative importance of a single life to the universe, so careless of the just limits whether of human interest or endurance, so communistic in assuming that all men are entitled to an equal share of what little time is left in the

world, that many a worthy, whom a paragraph from the right pen might have immortalized, is suffocated in the trackless swamps of two octavos.

And the wits of the 90's made sport of it, Oscar Wilde, for instance, remarking, "Whenever nowadays an eminent man dies, there enter those with the undertaker who forget they came to serve as mutes."

However, if the nineteenth century failed to augment the range and purpose of biography, certain trends established thus far during the twentieth have offset somewhat the failure. In the first place, in mere numbers of biographies written nothing has approached our record. In the year 1928, for instance, the total number of "lives" published exceeded that of novels. And, in the second place, the social changes which lay at the root of this excessive demand were such that only fresh aspects would satisfy. Hence, the so-called "new biography" appeared, based upon the old but extending the range and redacting somewhat the ancient purposes — as is evident from the introduction to the late Lytton Strachey's "Eminent Victorians." Strachey writes:

> The art of biography seems to have fallen on evil times in England. We have had, it is true, a few masterpieces. . . . With us the most delicate and humane of all the branches of the art of writing has been relegated to the journeyman of letters; we do not reflect that it is perhaps as difficult to write a good life as to live one. Those two fat volumes, with which it was our custom to commemorate the dead — who does not know them, with their ill-digested masses of material, their slip-shod style, their tone of tedious panegyric, their lamentable lack of selection, of detachment, of design? They are as familiar as the *cortege* of the undertaker, and wear the same air of funeral barbarism. One is tempted to suppose, of some of them, that they were composed by that functionary, as the final item of his job. The studies in this book are indebted, in more ways than one, to such works — works which certainly deserve the name of Standard Biography. For they have provided me not only with much indispensible information, but with something more precious — an example. How many lessons are to be learned from them! But it is hardly necessary to particularize. To preserve, for instance, a becoming brevity — a brevity which

excludes everything that is redundant and nothing that is significant — that, surely, is the first duty of the biographer. The second, no less surely, is to maintain his own freedom of spirit. It is not his business to be complimentary; it is his business to lay bare the facts of the case as he understands them. That is what I have aimed at in this book — to lay bare the facts of some cases as I understand them, dispassionately, impartially, and without ulterior intentions. To quote the words of a Master — "Je n'impose rien; je ne propose rien; j'expose."*

During the years since Strachey's appearance as the most widely read biographer in English, there has been, as before suggested, unprecedented productivity; but little has been added — if one except the growing tendency toward the creative that has resulted from Strachey's practice. Many writers have used him as a model; in more than a few instances he has been exploited to his ultimate conclusion, which is nothing less than detraction; so that now one may say that biography has run the full course from extollment to condemnation. There have been some, however, who, drawing their own lessons from Strachey's teaching, have "attacked old problems from new angles," have "thrown unexpected light into dark corners," and have approached new, "hitherto unexplored territory with a courage drawn from fresh standards." This last applies particularly to those who have sought material among men of science and of finance — the fields of interest latest to be included in the range of the form. And with these the continuity is broken. What men will choose next to emphasize in their ever shifting conception of ideal accomplishment, who can say?

Naturally no *quod erat demonstrandum* is possible when the proposition is concerned with fallible humanity. In the light of what many biographers have had to say about their work, however, one is enabled, at least partly, to recognize the goals which they have thus far set for themselves and, at least faintly, to perceive the impulses that have urged them on. They and their work, more particularly described, are the subjects discussed in the following pages.

---

* Included by the courteous permission of the publishers of Strachey's "Eminent Victorians," Harcourt, Brace and Company.

# 2—Adamnan and Saint Columba*

Let us now praise famous men. — Son of Sirach.

The worship of God is: honoring His gifts in other men, each according to his genius, and loving the greatest men best; those who envy and calumniate great men hate God. — Blake.

BIOGRAPHY in England received early impetus from a need of the Church. For a thousand years, during which time according to Sir Thomas Duffus Hardy's "Descriptive Catalogue" 1277 "lives" appeared, Bishop Asser's "Life of King Alfred," written in 893, was the only memorable "life" of a man not of the clergy; but even that is completely in harmony with the hagiographical tradition. And it was inevitable that during the early centuries clerics should have been emphasized.

Disturbingly vital to pagan civilization, Christianity swept through the society of antiquity, reviving hope among people oppressed by a decadent culture. Turning from its conquest of Greece and Rome, Christianity sought to cultivate the savage hordes to the north. To insure success it selected for its missionaries men at once the hardiest of body and the most fervent of spirit. These scattered among the Goths, the Franks, and the Celts, and by both precept and example taught, converted, civilized.

---

* Reprinted with the kind permission of the editor of "The Magnificat," in the pages of which this chapter first appeared.

In time, as they progressed, they required new methods and fresh materials with which to sustain the faith of their followers and to capture the interest of those who were slow to change their ways. Hence, with the life of Christ as an example, and taking advantage of men's impulse to commemorate, they recorded events in the lives of the most eminent among themselves, their accomplishments and traits of character — entirely for the purpose of propagating the faith.

It is not to be expected, therefore, that Adamnan's "Life of Saint Columba" is biography in the sense to which we have become accustomed, in spite of comments like that of Pinkerton, a Scottish historian not given to the praise of things Irish, that it is "the most complete piece of such writing that all Europe can boast of not only at so early a period, but even through the middle ages." Not until the eleventh century when the first example of modified hagiography, Eadmer's "Life and Conversation of Anselm," appeared, did a saint's "life" begin to assume anything like modern form. It was a work almost Boswellian in inclusiveness — as is suggested by its title. This was followed by a "life" of St. Godric, composed by a monk of Durham who accompanied Godric everywhere and recorded his conversation.

Adamnan, like hagiographers in general, looked upon details of character and personality as too trivial in themselves for inclusion; he dwelt only upon such acts of the saint as would serve to commemorate him and to establish him as an example of virtue. The book, therefore, is highly selective, concentrating as it does upon holy works; for the author pays scant attention to items like birth and ancestry, and none at all directly to personal characteristics. He focuses upon Columba's prophecies, his miracles, and his visions of angels. There is no lack of information to be drawn, however, by reading between the lines. Every section is rich in comment — no doubt by unconscious implication — upon places, time, occupations, modes of travel, customs, utensils, and manners. One learns of water mills, for instance, of war chariots equipped with swords, of ten varieties of boats, of feather beds, deer traps made of sharpened stakes, houses made of sawed planks, and of customs like that of diners reclining in Roman fashion upon couches. The result is literature, biography, and history, but all made subordinate to the main purpose: to set forth the career of a great saint in order that the reader might emulate his life.

The good abbot (Adamnan was ninth Abbot of Hy; Columba was the first) felt that he was the one appointed to reveal "God's secret workings within" Columba. It is notable among most enduring biographies that some intimate relationship has linked author with subject. It is only necessary to recall Boswell and Johnson, Trevelyan and Macaulay, Lockhart and Scott, and Carlyle and Sterling for confirmation. Adamnan and Columba had been similarly linked. The author was born only twenty-seven years after the death of his subject; he was related through his father to the clan of which Columba was a member; he followed the saint to Hy from the same part of Ireland, County Donegal. But most important psychologically must have been the prophecy concerning him which Columba left in the archives of the Abbey. It was this:

> Columba foretelling of Adamnan. He shall receive his name from my name. He shall make a law for women, from the noble widespread Ictian sea hither. He shall attract half the language of envy, for he will ordain a great law. A sapling who will wrest the sovereignty of Tara from Finnachta. Over Tara he shall not assume power. Thirty years in abbotship shall Adamnan sit, of high and illustrious power.

However, it was not merely because of his various relationships with Columba that Adamnan became the effective biographer he was. Probably no one at the time was better qualified than he by education, by aptitude in writing, or by appreciation of Columba's accomplishments. And it is not to be assumed that he was accorded a place in memory simply because he allied himself with a famous character; he deserves to have escaped oblivion on his own account and would have merited remembrance had he never undertaken the work that has come down to us.

His name, meaning "little Adam," is one seldom encountered in Irish records — it occurs only three or four times. He was the son of Ronan and Ronnat, born in the barony of Tirhugh in Donegal. At least here lived his clan and here remain several marks commemorating him. His father was distantly related to the reigning family, of which Columba was a member. His mother came of the Civel Enna group, whose home was the barony of Raphoe.

Because he came of a noble family he was entitled to an education, if he chose to study. To obtain it he had to attend the school at Aran perhaps, or at Clonard, Moville, or Clonmacnoise, flourishing schools of Ireland, all of which contributed men famous in tradition as furthering civilization. Unfortunately there are no records of his early training. We know only from his subsequent experience that he profited from what education was available. Only one anecdote — and that a doubtful one — has been discovered. It concerns Adamnan and Finnachta the Festive, the man whom Columba mentions in the prophecy just quoted, and who later became king in Ireland and with whom Adamnan became associated.

Finnachta, it seems, was one day riding toward the home of his sister to pay her a visit. On the way he almost rode over Adamnan, who was plodding along the way carrying a jar of milk on his shoulder. Adamnan stumbled in avoiding the horse, dropped the jar and broke it. Finnachta exclaimed, "Thou shalt receive protection from me, O Student," and he begged the boy not to be downcast.

"O good man," replied Adamnan, "I have cause for grief, for there are three students in one house, and three more of us who are younger to wait on them. And we act thus: one among us goes out in turn to collect food for the other five, and it is my turn today but what I have gathered has been spilt upon the ground; and what grieves me more, the borrowed jar is broken and I have not wherewith to pay for it."

The story has been thought little more than one fabricated for political purposes, perhaps in a measure to account for the favor which Adamnan came later to enjoy. However that may be, at least it gives us an interesting glimpse of student life in the seventh century.

It is probable, of course, that during his time as a student Adamnan's ambition to become a churchman developed. At all events he was admitted into the brotherhood by the Columban order, and his proficiency and attainments soon made him eligible for the headship. As was true of all leaders in his day, his abilities were various. His writings show him to have been learned in both Latin and Greek and they hint at some awareness of Hebrew.

His rapid rise in the affairs of Ireland was due in part to his appointment as *amchara,* or spiritual adviser, to Finnachta soon after the latter had been made king. The relationship was a particularly stormy one because Finnachta was the kind of man who would let little stand in the way of his ambitions. He had, in fact, come to the throne through having put his predecessor, a cousin, to death. Nevertheless, Adamnan remained *amchara* during the entire reign. However, he continually engaged in quarrels with Finnachta, in the beginning because of the way in which he had become king, and later over the title to the Island of Hy. This had been granted to Columba by his kinsman, King Connell, at the time of his supposed exile, and so rested in the abbotship, but Finnachta from time to time threatened to revoke the title. Concerning the island — which today is known as Iona — it is interesting to note Samuel Johnson's comment made to Boswell during their tour of the Hebrides:

> We were now treading that illustrious Island which was once the luminary of the Caledonian regions, whence savage clans and roving barbarians derived benefits of knowledge and the blessings of religion. . . . Far from me, and from my friends, be such frigid philosophy as may conduct one indifferent and immoved over any ground which has been dignified by wisdom, bravery, or virtue. That man is little to be envied, whose patriotism would not gain force upon the plain of Marathon, or whose piety would not grow warmer among the ruins of Iona.

In connection with it, too, one recalls Wordsworth's sonnet beginning:

> Homeward we turn. Isle of Columba's cell,
> Where Christian piety's soul-cheering spark
> (Kindled from Heaven between the light and dark
> Of time) shone like the morning-star, farewell!

As an administrator — he became Abbot of Hy in 679 — Adamnan proved to be of extraordinary ability. He was responsible for the making and the execution of a law exempting women from military service and protecting slaves from gross treatment. Besides this, and most important among his administrative accomplishments, he brought about a uniformity in the observance of Easter, a matter concerning which there had been, ever since the time of St. Patrick, disagreements resulting in armed disturbances and scores of deaths each year. This event is described in "Mac Firbis's Annals," as having taken place at a synod at Tara in 697:

> In this year the men of Erin consented to receive jurisdiction and one rule from Adamnan respecting the celebration of Easter on Sunday, the fourteenth of the moon of April; and the coronal tonsure of Peter was performed upon the clerics of Erin, for there had been great variance in Erin on these questions until then, inasmuch as some of the clerics of Erin were in the habit of celebrating Easter on Sunday, the four-teenth of the moon of April and had the coronal of Peter the Apostle following in the steps of Patrick; others following Columcille, celebrated Easter on the fourteenth of the moon of April no matter what the day, and had the tonsure of Simon Magus. A third party followed neither the sect of Patrick nor the sect of Columcille, so that the clerics of Erin held many synods and they were used to come to these synods with weapons, so that pitched battles used to be fought be-tween them and many used to be slain, so that many evils ensued to Erin from this, namely the Bear-Mor and the very great dearth and many diseases and injury to Erin by extern tribes. They continued even to the time of Adamnan. He was the ninth Abbot who succeeded after Columcille to the government.

So much for Adamnan the administrator. Of him as a personality there is little to be learned except what is to be derived by implication from his writings. One knows, for instance, that once when he had become angry with Finnachta, he called him *in righ crin liath cen detu*, "the old gray king without teeth"; and that he once tried to stir him to action by addressing him in these verses:

> Were I a king of reddened spears
> I would humble mine enemies;

> I would exalt my high places;
> My combats would be frequent.

Still another record shows him as "fasting against" an antagonist named Irgalach. The latter, it seems, resisted by "fasting against" Adamnan until Adamnan, inducing one of his followers to impersonate him, put Iraglach off his guard and so won the encounter. As an administrator, however, and as a personality he is interesting chiefly because an understanding of those qualities enables one better to understand the "Life of Saint Columba," for Adamnan's fame today is that of a biographer—a fame not unworthily attained.

He drew his materials for the "Life" from both oral and written sources. As he composed the work about 695, writing upon the site of Columba's activities, he had ready access to the tradition which had accumulated in the vicinity; in fact, there seems to have been a great body of this tradition, as he implies that one of his chief difficulties lay in selecting clearly applicable incident and detail from a mass of comment much of which was palpably false. Moreover, he had at hand the writings of Cumene the Fair, which he made use of for the greater part of Book III. In addition, he drew upon the poems that had been written in praise of the saint, especially the "Amhia"; upon the manuscripts in which Columba was mentioned; and upon the "Life" that St. Mura had written. All these sources were available to him, and he used them all, enlarging, improving—particularly the order of events—to such extent that comparison serves but to show the authenticity of his work.

As has been said, he pays small attention directly to biographical detail. His primary purpose in writing the book was to fix a pattern for his society to follow. Toward that end he chose only such matter as served directly. The final paragraph of the Second Preface, however, contains a rapid survey directly biographical:

> Saint Columba was born of noble parents; his father was Fedilmuth, son of Fegus, and his mother was Aethne, whose father can be called in Latin Filius Navis, but in the Scotic tongue Mac Nave. In the second year after the battle of Culedrebina [fought A.D. 561] and in the forty-second year of his age, Saint Columba, resolving to seek a foreign country

for the love of Christ, sailed from Scotia [Ireland] to Britain. From his boyhood he had been brought up in Christian training in the study of wisdom, and by the grace of God has so preserved the integrity of his body and the purity of his soul that, though dwelling on this earth, he appeared to live like the souls in Heaven. For he was angelic in appearance, graceful in speech, holy in work, with talents of the highest order and consummate prudence; he lived a soldier of Christ during thirty-four years in an island. He could never spend the space of even one hour without study or prayer or writing, or some other holy occupation. So incessantly was he engaged night and day in the unwearied exercise of fasting and watching, that the burden of each of these austerities would seem beyond the power of all human endurance. And still in all these he was beloved by all, for a holy joy ever beaming on his face revealed the joy and gladness with which the Holy Spirit filled his inmost soul.

This passage and one other, which sets forth the circumstances of the saint's death, comprise all that can be thought of as biographical in the strict sense. It is not necessary, however, that details be given directly. Almost every chapter communicates something of character. In Book I, for instance, occurs a passage which is much more effective in defining the saint's gentleness and simplicity of soul, the while relating the circumstances of one of the prophecies, than any amount of exposition would have been. The passage conveys also a sense of Columba's feeling of loneliness in a strange land, a feeling which, it is frequently apparent, he never entirely overcame:

At one time while the saint was living in the Ionan island, he called one of the brothers and addressed him thus: "In the morning of the third day from this thou must sit down and wait on the shore on the western side of the island, for a crane, which is a stranger from the northern region of Hibernia and hath been driven about by various winds, shall come, weary and fatigued, after the ninth hour, and lie down on the beach quite exhausted. Treat the bird tenderly, take it to some neighboring house, where it may be kindly received and carefully nursed and fed by thee for three days and three nights.

[ 22 ]

When the crane is refreshed with the three day's rest and is unwilling to abide any longer with us, it shall fly back with renewed strength to the pleasant part of Hibernia from which it originally hath come. This bird do I consign to thee with such special care because it cometh from our native place." The brother obeyed, and on the third day, after the ninth hour, he watched as he was bid for the arrival of the expected guest. As soon as the crane came and alighted on the shore, he took it up gentle in its weakness and carried it to a nearby dwelling, where in its hunger he fed it. On his return to the monastery in the evening, the saint, without inquiry, but as stating a fact, said to him, "God bless thee, my child, for thy kind attention to this visitor that shall not remain long on its journey, but return within three days to its home." As the saint predicted, so exactly did the event prove, for after being carefully nursed for three days the bird gently rose on its wings to a great height in the sight of its hospitable entertainer, and making for a little way its path through the air homeward, it directed its course across the sea to Hibernia, straight as it could fly, on a calm day.

Columba was one who pre-eminently deserves a place among those the art of whose lives has preserved them against oblivion. He was not only successful in furthering civilization at a time when baptism was beginning to be both a symbol and a realization of that state, but successful also in accomplishing his purpose in such a manner as to become indelibly etched upon the minds of those who followed him, so that they, in turn, passed on his memory to us.

The year 521 is usually given as the date of his birth, although the legends surrounding the event obscure it almost completely, in spite of Adamnan's record. His home was at Garton, at the time a wild, rugged, and remote district of Donegal. Fedilmuth was his father, a member of the ruling family and related to the ruler of Scotland. Muircertach, the saint's half-uncle, was on the throne when Columba was born, and six cousins followed one another as rulers during his life. His mother, Aethne, belonged to the clan of a provincial ruler. Columba, therefore, was himself eligible to rule. To this circumstance is sometimes attributed his immense influence, and the resulting fame of the monasteries he established. Such attribution is perhaps not unjust if it be limited to the protection he was able to rely upon for any of his undertakings; it seems entirely unjust, however, if it is used to account for his achievements — which could have been effected only by one of high endowment, as every record which has survived attests.

He was baptized Colum, "a dove"; but "cille," meaning "of the cell" was added to the name. He was also given a purely secular name, Crimthian, meaning "a wolf." After a childhood spent at Garton where his first teacher, Cruithnecan, taught him the alphabet by impressing a few letters at a time upon a cake (when Columba had learned the letters, he was permitted to eat the cake), and he was sent to study with St. Finnian, a famous bishop whose establishment lay to the south, at Moville. In time Columcille became deacon, and soon after having been ordained he performed his first miracle — as set forth by Adamnan — in the tradition of first miracles, by turning water into wine at the celebration of a mass for which the wine had not been provided. His time at Moville being accomplished, he proceeded southward to Leinster in order to study with Gemman, one of the best known and most highly regarded of the bards. His accomplishments as a singing poet were later to aid in no slight degree his missionary enterprises. There, according to Adamnan, he foretold a murder, a curious affair concerning a young girl and her would-be lover. The incident revealed his gentleness and his ever-ready sympathy, traits which appear again and again, in contrast to the many references to his aggressive nature.

Soon after his ordination — which took place at Clonard — he entered a monastery near Dublin; but a violent plague caused the community to scatter, and Columcille went north. In 544, when he was twenty-five years old, he founded at Derry his first church. His principal foundation in Ireland, however, was a monastery at Durrow; it is this establishment which is mentioned by Bede.

In the year 561 occurred the battle of Culedrebina, which not a few powerful persons believed Columcille to have caused. They called a synod at Teltown, in Meath, for the purpose of excommunicating him, but could not agree upon a sentence. St. Brendan of Birr, for instance, testified against any sentence; and St. Finnian, his former teacher at Moville, spoke for him before the synod, recalling an incident of Columba's youth — set down in Adamnan's account as follows:

> On one occasion Columba paid a visit to the venerable Bishop Finnio, who had once been his preceptor — a youth visiting a man of advanced years. When the old man saw him coming, he observed also an angel of the Lord accompanying him as he proceeded, and as it is handed down to us by well informed persons, he made it known to certain brethren who were standing by, saying to them, "Behold, look now to Columba as he draweth near; he hath been deemed worthy of having an angelic inhabitant of heaven to be his companion in his wanderings."

In spite of the failure of the synod to agree, Columcille, nevertheless, sailed from Ireland to Hy, taking with him a few soldiers and — after the manner of men of his station who patterned their acts upon the ministry of Christ — also twelve disciples. His enemies, naturally, spread abroad the report that he had instigated the battle and had been forced into exile. But it is a bit absurd to suppose that his going to Hy was anything but voluntary. His connections (his crowning in 574 of the Scottish King Aidon at Iona bears out the idea) were far too powerful for him to have been forced against his will into any course of action; and besides, Hy is only a day's sail from his native province, hardly a matter requiring extraordinary self-denial, despite Adamnan's recurring allusions to loneliness.

The Ionan monastery erected and the work of converting the island well under way, Columcille was free frequently to return to Ireland, where according to Adamnan, he took a vigorous part in both civil and religious affairs — further argument against the idea that he was exiled. Among other things, for example, he fought in the battle of Cuilfedha, which occurred in 587, near Clonard. According to an account of the battle in Keating's "History," a nobleman was killed at a feast by a man named Curran who fled to Columcille for sanctuary. Curran was taken and executed by Diarmid, the king of Ulster, for violating the law of the feast. In revenge for the affront to his right of sanctuary, Columcille gathered together the clan Neill of the North, and enlisting the aid of the king of Connaught, gained a victory over Diarmid. With this version of the story the "Annals of the Four Masters" is in substantial agreement.

A much more interesting story is told, however, in the "Black Book of Molaga." While accounting for the battle in a way more or less similar to the foregoing, it adds another possible reason for the affray. Columcille was in the habit of transcribing manuscripts, having overseen the making of some 300 copies of the New Testament in the course of his life. Once during a visit to St. Finnian he made a copy of the Psalms with Finnian's knowledge but without his consent. Upon its completion Finnian claimed the copy as "Son-book." The disputants laid the matter before Diarmid the king, who made the famous decision, "To every book belongs its son-book, as to every cow belongs her calf." And as a result the battle took place — after which Columcille seems to have obtained what he considered his property, for the manuscript was encased in silver and gold and became one of the chief relics of the saint.

One draws the inevitable conclusion from all the accounts of St. Columba that he was highly aggressive. Not only does Adamnan communicate this impression, but all the other writers give it as well. That he was no weakling goes without saying; but that he had any greater pugnacity than most of his contemporaries is difficult to credit. One must remember that in the British Isles during the sixth century — and for many centuries thereafter — life was hard in the extreme, a veritable survival of the fittest. If one survived he was worthy to survive, at least partly by reason of his might; and the conditions were particularly hard for one of high station. Officials held office because they were strong; if they were also well beloved by their people, so much the better. But before there was esteem there must have been something to create it — naturally strength was an obvious cause. Moreover, hard as life must needs be, it fostered high temper and sensitive dispositions. Everybody was called upon to take care of his own. Even women, it will be remembered, were expected to take part in battle as late as Adamnan's law. Besides military operations, there were also excommunications, "fastings against," and cursings, all frequently employed. Columcille had inherited the high bearing of his race and was by no means disposed to receive affronts in silence. Adamnan relates how once he pursued a plunderer with curses, following the man as he made off in a boat until the depth of the water forced him to desist. Upon another occasion he poured forth curses against a miser who, in the face of long established custom, had refused him hospitality. Once, too, he excommunicated some robbers who had despoiled a church. One of these robbers, according to Adamnan's account, was afterwards killed by an arrow discharged in the name of the saint.

His somewhat vindictive nature and his imperious manner, while they helped to create the great awe in which he was held, may also have been the cause of Bede's speaking of him with certain qualifications. He writes, for instance, at the end of his account of Columcille's settling among the Picts in order to convert them: "But whatever he was himself this we know for certain, that he left successors renowned for their continency." There is, however, small reason to believe that he did not deserve the high place to which he attained or to doubt the effectiveness of his administration; and there is still less reason to question the piety of his life, the essential purity of his spirit, and, hence, his fitness to serve as an example of virtue — good manners are superfluous where sanctity abides. Even at a distance of twelve hundred years, Adamnan's relation of the events during the last days of the saint's life and the account of his death itself must be looked upon as recording the passing of a great soul:

> Doirmit therefore entered the church, having missed the abbot and knowing well his ways, and cried out in a mournful voice, "Where art thou, Father?" And feeling his way in the darkness, as the brothers had not yet brought in the lights, he found the saint lying before the altar, and raising him up a little he sat down beside him, and laid his holy head upon his bosom. Meanwhile the rest of the monks ran in hastily in a body with their lights, and beholding their dying Father, burst into lamentations.

This passage and the high seriousness of its tone, together with the prophecy concerning the crane, serve in a manner to render the atmosphere of the whole. When one considers that atmosphere and the panorama of the events which it is used to sustain, he cannot fail to appreciate the quality of Adamnan's contribution. To him Columba was a great saint; to us he is that but he is also a compelling personality of the past, and his "Life" becomes through the skill of its composer a stone in the foundation of an invaluable literary form. One can do little else, on the whole, than agree with Montalembert's remark that "The Life of Saint Columba" is *un des monuments les plus vivants, les plus attrayants, et les plus authentiques de l'histoire chretienne,* and read it in that mood of self-forgetfulness without which there can be no understanding of the past.

# 3—Saint Thomas More and King Richard III

*Let us sit upon the ground
And tell sad stories of the death of kings.* — Shakespeare.

IT IS related of St. Thomas More that among the earliest recollections of his childhood was a conversation he had overheard between his father and a friend about a neighbor who exclaimed upon hearing that Edward IV was dead, "By my troth, then will my master, the Duke of Gloucester, be king!" What made the remark startling at this time was Gloucester's remoteness from the throne.

More was five years old, but even at that age he was showing signs of brilliance. Yet to overemphasize the effect upon him of this political discussion and to conclude that therewith was conceived the idea which thirty years later was to come forth as the "History of Richard the Thirde," would be pointless. None the less the boy could hardly have avoided hearing, some four months later (in August, 1483), the stories of the murder of the young princes, Edward and Richard, attributed to the same Duke of Gloucester, and so, through repetition, to have received some vivid impressions.

While these childhood experiences had, doubtless, little or nothing to do with his subsequently choosing to write a "life" of Richard III, yet surely only the hardiest skeptic would deny that the subject once decided upon, the work could not have escaped all trace of the attitude which might thus early have been engendered. For Thomas More's "Life" of Richard III is unique in attitude. No biography of a king before it or since, if one except the propaganda of the latter seventeenth century, has appeared which is so definitely inimical toward its subject. It is permeated with cold hatred toward tyranny in general, of course, as is to be expected of the author of "Utopia," while it implies abhorrence for the life and character of Richard himself.

"It is useless," wrote William Hazlitt, "to comment upon a man about whom the world has already made up its mind" and his statement is more than upheld by the history of Richard III's reputation. From time to time efforts have been made to go behind the "waryle," crooked-backed murderer of More's depiction and bring forth an astute and kingly soul. Sir John Harington implied in his "Metamorphosis of Ajax" that not all the truth had been told; Sir William Cornwallis defended him in his "Essayes"; George Buck in his laudatory "History of the Life and Reign of Richard III" hinted rather broadly at certain effects of Lancastrian propaganda; and much later Horace Walpole in "Historic Doubts on Richard III"; Caroline Halstead, and Sir Clement Markham all tried to remove some of the blemishes, only to be overwhelmed in the tempest of controversy which their attempts stirred up. Time-stressed opinion is too strong to admit of change, as Hazlitt averred. Richard III must remain a monster in spite of later-day efforts to show that he was not; and Thomas More's work was instrumental in establishing the conception.

That is the power of the first impressive biography to appear after its subject is dead — it sets the pattern of opinion to be followed; although it must not be forgotten that Shakespeare's play had enormous effect in popularizing Richard as a royal murderer. More's book, unfinished as it is and printed from what seems to have been a rough draft, had but slight popular effect. In fact, one might say that until it was reissued in 1641 as a political tract under the title "The Pitiful Life and Unfortunate Death of Edward V" few had ever heard of it. However, appearing first in the 1557 edition of his works and subsequently as an appendix to the "Chronicle" of John Harding, it became a part of chronicle history, with the result that authors and scholars made it the basis of much circulated opinion. The most notable example of this is, of course, Shakespeare's "King Richard III" — although in the play the monster of More's characterizing has become a subtly poetic villain. Had the book remained as More left it in 1513, an unfinished manuscript, one which he thought so little of that he neglected even to revise it, who can say what our tradition concerning Richard might have been?

As it is, because of its attitude, an attitude almost unique in early biography, the work is a distinct contribution to the form in that it helps to bridge the gap between the medieval and the modern mode. But its historical interest is by no means the only reason for remembering it. That it fixed Richard in memory as a monster is undeniable, and because it does so one wonders why such a gentle soul as Thomas More chose the subject or why he treated it as he did, for his way much more nearly was ever to love the sinner the while hating the sin.

In order to arrive at some understanding of what aroused his interest in Richard and what inspired his antagonism, one must look back a bit to the circumstances surrounding his youth. The stories that he heard in childhood may or may not have been significant; it would, on the other hand be impossible to disregard the effect of his service in the household of John Morton, Cardinal Archbishop of Canterbury.

Morton, at the time that More became a page in his retinue, was among the most powerful figures in England. After having risen rapidly through the patronage of Bourchier from simple priest in 1441 to Prebendary of Salisbury and Lincoln in 1458, he joined the Lancastrians and was present at the battle of Towton in 1461. Exiled and attainted by the Yorkists, he lost all chance of preferment until, after Tewkesbury, he made peace with Edward IV. Richard III threw him into prison from which he escaped to Flanders, returning to England in 1485 with Henry VII.

During the fifteen years following, under the favor of the king, Morton rose to the lord chancellorship and to the cardinalate. Hence, his political sympathies are not difficult to discover; neither is it difficult to understand how Thomas More, entering the establishment of such a man at the age of thirteen, impressionable and imaginative to a degree far above the average, should have taken on something of the attitudes and opinions of his master, especially since Morton made a favorite of him, talking with him, advising him about his career, in fact going so far once as to point him out to an assemblage of guests at dinner with the remark, "Whosoever liveth to see it, shall see this childe come to an excellent and mervailous proufe."

Not only was it the influence of Morton himself, perhaps, that helped More to take on the opinions and predilections which colored his mind (to speak for the moment more generally concerning him), but also the influence of the character of the group of men gathered in Lambeth Palace — including Henry Medwall, chaplain and writer of comedies. Here were grouped personalities imbued with the spirit of renaissance culture, engrossed in new ideas of conduct and morality, and interested in literature and learning. In short, More, with all his promise, could not have been better placed in order that the faculties with which he was so richly endowed might come to complete fruition, as indeed his study later at Oxford, at New Inn and Lincoln's Inn assured.

It is no doubt directly to Morton himself that both the impulse to write the "Richard" and the attitude to be taken are traceable. Morton's treatment at the hands of the Yorkists had been of a piece with their treatment of all Lancastrians, and the result with him was in keeping with the general result — one of abiding abhorrence for the Yorkist regime. Incidentally, this sentiment became so intense and was so long sustained that even as late as 1640 Charles I considered it politic to commission William Habington and his father to write a "life" of Edward IV in order somewhat to hasten the end of Lancastrian sympathy. As an expression of his feeling Morton is said to have prepared a "life" of Richard in Latin and to have availed himself of More's assistance in the preparation. Report of this work led many to regard More's "life" merely as a translation; but scholars — now that the Early English Text Society has issued the Hitchcock-Chambers edition of Harpsfield's "More" — have concluded that both the Latin and English versions were composed after Morton's death and that doubt of More's direct authorship grew out of nothing more than an idle remark by Queen Elizabeth's godson, the jocund Sir John Harington, that he "had heard" that Morton wrote the "Richard." The choice of subject, as a matter of fact, on More's part was natural.

From the moment of his appearance in the book Richard is shown as the embodiment of evil; in More's own words the emphasis is established. "This Dukes demeanoure," he writes, "ministreth in effecte all the whole matter whereof this booke shall entreate." More stresses Richard's traditional deformity and makes much of his overweening ambition. No opportunity is missed to play up the Lancastrian tales of his cruelty as the outgrowth of abnormality; it had been common gossip since the time of his first coming into prominence, for instance, that he was born "feete forwarde" and also "not untothed." Whatever is said of his policies makes them appear as nothing less than machinations of the devil. It would hardly have occurred to More to mention certain instances which could have been considered favorably by him but would not have reversed his general judgment. Among these might be mentioned Richard's action in having made unlawful the exacting of "benevolences," his having established a protective tariff which, however, permitted the free importation of books, or his efforts by statute to break up huge estates for the wider distribution of land among the middle and lower classes. On the contrary he is accused of having slain Henry VI and of successfully plotting the death of his brother, the Duke of Clarence, besides murdering the princes in the tower. One can say, glibly enough, of course, that these accusations came almost instinctively to a Lancastrian so soon after the event. To smirch the character of one's political opponents is even today the obvious course. Such explanation is easy; only it does not square with our conception of More, in fact with our certain knowledge of him at the particular time when this history was written.

"The History of King Richard the Thirde," indeed, is not Lancastrian propaganda. Though favoring this party, More could none the less draw with complete sympathy the character of Edward IV. On the other hand, when one realizes, for instance, that Richard was born October 2, 1452, and so was not yet nineteen when Henry VI was killed, the conclusion can readily enough be drawn that More's linking him with the affair seems as doubtful as he is obviously mistaken in having Richard present at the battle of St. Albans in 1455.

In reality, the work is a moral treatise. Just as George Cavendish wrote of Wolsey to show the futility of trust in worldly princes, Thomas More wrote of Richard to show the immorality of power derived from force. What he hated was not the human being, but the symbol of royal power usurped — just as later he was to defy Henry VIII as the symbol of spiritual power assumed. For More was not only a humanist; he was likewise a humanitarian. Force, particularly military force, was to him justifiable only as an extreme measure. In fact, More loathed the spirit that fostered mere military glory. He considered aggressive warfare anathema. Hence, as a man of strife, whose ambition was aroused by the result of one battle and whose death came as a result of another and whose motives More condemned, Richard epitomized all that was evil in the ways of government, according to More's developing philosophy. Somewhat in this manner may one reconcile the spirit with which Richard is characterized and the abiding humanity of Saint Thomas More.

There is a further consideration, speculative, to be sure, but none the less enticing: the book was composed in 1513 but was laid aside while yet incomplete. Why? It was written in that period of idleness during which occurred his second marriage — with the Mistress Alice of famous memory. Alice Middleton was a widow with a daughter ten years old, whom he married at the age of thirty-five, only one month after the death of his first wife in order that his young children might be taken care of properly; hence it is difficult to believe that press of affairs caused him to give over the undertaking. Not knowing Thomas More, one might say that after proceeding as far as he did — the work covers a period of only four months — he began to think it a matter of political risk. There is certain plain speaking included concerning the gathering of money as the reason for Englishmen's withdrawing their hearts from a king; and Henry VIII in 1513 was not the ingenuous youth whose accession More had hailed in 1509. However, it is only necessary to recall his subsequent relations with Henry to doubt that fear affected him. What probably caused him to abandon the "Richard" was the idea that later bore fruit as "Utopia," for the "Utopia" was the next undertaking after the "Richard" was abandoned — the famous Book II having been composed early in 1515 during leisure moments while More was on an embassy to Flanders. We have here a much better statement of his philosophy. Tyranny is attacked, force shown to be unnecessary when understanding is created, and the value of wise government extolled. May not More have felt that the "Richard" was alien to his spirit and so sacrificed what he had already done in order to create a work more completely in accord with that spirit?

However that may be, there is no lack of value in the "Richard." Its authenticity as history is doubtful, to be sure; nevertheless it is a distinct contribution to the development of biographic technique — it is the first work to deal unfavorably with its subject, as has been said, and in addition it is the first work of the sort to be written in terms of studied effect.

Before the sixteenth century, biography had been cast in commemorative forms, as in the "lives" of saints, or written as chronicle history when setting forth the character and affairs of kings. In the former, the saint is revealed as the embodiment, naturally, of all virtue; in the latter, the king seldom emerges from the welter of activities in which he has of necessity the chief part. Thomas More, however, was a child of the renaissance. He knew the writings of antiquity; became, in fact, one of the great exponents of the new learning. Tacitus and Suetonius among the historians and Plato among the philosophers are plainly apparent as influences in the "Richard," as is the classical influence apparent in no matter what he wrote. The "Richard," however, becomes the most definitely classical of all when viewed against its background of indigenous chronicle — indeed, it is not easy to withhold from More the credit for influencing the writing of history that usually is given Polydore Vergil, who wrote some twenty years later. It is replete with tragedy, tragedy induced by a sense of fate impending, of men blind to the consequences of evil, "of the vain surety of man's mind in the face of iminent destruction."

The early portion of the book suggests that perhaps More intended to write a history of his own day. There are passages of political exposition, a comment upon the increasing abuse of sanctuary, and the dying oration of Edward IV, all in the traditional manner. Upon the entrance of Richard, however, the spirit of the work assumes a heightened tempo. From that point More concentrates upon the artistic effect of presenting Richard in the toils of destiny. A minimum of digression occurs, Jane Shore is sympathetically characterized, Sir James Tyrell interpreted, and an occasional philosophical aside included; but the unity of the whole is more than adequately preserved, so that a living image is projected — in somber colors but with unmistakable effect.

Chief among the technical devices is the introduction of formal speeches. The oration of Edward IV, for instance; the dramatic discourse between the widowed queen and the Archbishop of York concerning the custody of the young princes; Buckingham's argument to the people, in the effort to persuade them that Richard is their rightful king; Doctor Shaw's sermon; and the speech of John Morton, Bishop of Ely, to the Duke of Buckingham with which the work breaks off — these are designed almost as if for actors in a play. They characterize the speakers and advance the narrative with an artistic integrity worthy the stage of the following generation.

The dramatic presentation of historical episodes also adds to the telling effect. The affair of the strawberries, in which Richard requests that a servant be sent to Holburn for a mess of berries in order for the moment to divert attention from his designs upon Hastings; the description of the crowd as it murmured against Richard's election and then is stampeded into acquiescence by Buckingham's claquers; Lord Stanley's dream; and the analysis of Richard's mental state following the murder of the princes — it would be difficult indeed to discover comparable handling of comparable matter in any other writing of the time.

Moreover, the interpolation of aphoristic comment into the progress of the narrative serves to heighten the sense of reality while developing the work's moral aspect. The common people, More says early in the story, "oftentymes more esteme and take for greatter kindenesse a lyttle courtesye, than a greate benefyte." Again, near the beginning, he comments in a parenthesis upon the gathering of money by tax collectors thus ("which is the onelye thynge that withdraweth the heartes of Englyshmenne fro the Prynce"). "Whoso divineth uppon conjectures," he asserts a page or two farther on, "maye as wel shote to farre as to short." And toward the end he writes, "For a minde that knoweth it self giltye, is in a maner dejected to a servuile flattery." One might continue to pile up such asides; they occur more than frequently and are more than interesting when one remembers that men like Francis Bacon composed mottoes and aphorisms in the century following. But there is another quality of style which is perhaps more nearly significant in the light of subsequent developments.

As has been pointed out, not a little of the form assumed by the work is suggestive of classical models — Tacitus, perhaps, most strongly. In addition, however, there is a further classical color — with something of the homiletic tradition from earlier English — evident in sentence pattern. Sixteenth-century prose is not the flexible instrument that the contemporary verse is; the possibilities were present but development was lacking. Another hundred years were necessary before anything approaching maturity was attained. Hence, to discover concision instead of tumbling awkwardness, balance instead of the haphazard joining of words in loose structures is to understand something more of the effect of his classical studies upon St. Thomas. Some of the sentences in the "Richard," to be sure, are of the old tumbling variety, but others are as sharply focused, almost as artifically constructed, according to Professor R. W. Chambers in his "Continuity of English Prose," as are those of John Lyly written quite three quarters of a century later — they are, as a matter of fact, along with the devices of George Pettie and John Rainolds more than a little prophetic of the "Euphues." In the third paragraph, for instance, occurs this carefully wrought pattern:

> For Richarde the Duke of Gloucester, by nature theyr uncle, by office theire protectoure, to theire father beholden, to them selfe by othe and allegyaunce bownden, al the bandes broken that binden manne and manne together, withoute anye respecte of Godde or the worlde, unnaturallye contrived to bereve them, not onelye their dignitie, but also their lives.

Further on comes a passage commenting upon Edward IV's solicitude for his children's welfare. ". . . whyle," More writes,

> the youth of his children shoulde lacke discrecion of them self and good counsayle of their frendes, of whiche either party

shold counsayle for their owne commodity and rather by pleasaunte aduyse too wynne themselfe favor, then by profitable advertisement to do the children good . . .

In the description of Richard appears, in the choice of words, still another device at once suggestive of classical origin and almost perfectly euphemistic. "Waryle," to be specific, means, literally, "weird-like," that is, "malignant," after the manner of the Saxon "weird" or fate. Here it is used instead of "ugly" in deference to Richard's royal birth. In fact, the whole passage is aptly illustrative:

Richarde the third sonne, of whom we nowe entreate, was in witte and courage egall with either of them, in bodye and prowesse farre under them bothe, little of stature, ill fetured of limmes, croke backed, his left shoulder much higher then his right, hard favoured of visage, and suche as is in the states called waryle, in other em otherwise, he was malicious, wrathful, envious and, from afore his birth, ever forwarde.

Unique, therefore, in conception, a forerunner in both design and style — quite decidedly that last in the opinion of R. W. Chambers — More's "Richard III" is biography of high significance.

# 4—Nicholas Harpsfield
## and "Sir Thomas More"

*Thus readest thou in every book
that teacheth of good living.* — Hilton.

IT IS not so strange as sad that the memory of Thomas More
should have survived in a medley of discordant confusions. His
house at Chelsea was permitted to fall into dilapidation and to
disappear. His tomb remains hidden in shadow. His portrait was
taken out of England unprotested — purchased because of the painter
rather than the subject. And not until the quattro-centennial of his
martyrdom, and until his canonization made mention of him timely,
did anything like adequate modern biographical treatment appear.
It remains even yet for a collection of his letters to be made —
although the work is now under way — and for his works to be
given modern dress.

But it is not only that material relic of him has been lightly
treated: historical opinion has lacked wholeheartedness, and no
clear cut understanding exists in the minds of many of his having
done aught or even of his having been. To Catholics he is a saint
and martyr, and venerable as one who died for the faith. To those
of no faith who in some way are interested, he is either "a foolish
wise man or a wise foolish man." Concerning his position in
literature and government the most recent consensus — as summed
up in a current study — seems to be that

> he was rather fitted to adorn than to extend the domain of
> letters; and as a statesman he took narrow views and mis-
> understood the spirit of his time.

[ 39 ]

And Saintsbury once commented that his "place in the strict history of English literature is very small and not extraordinarily high." Nevertheless Jonathan Swift once said that More was a person "of the greatest virtue this kingdom ever produced," and the solomonic "Cambridge History of English Literature" vouchsafes that his works "deserve more consideration than they usually receive" — to say nothing of Sir William Holdsworth's comment in the "History of English Law": "More's beautiful character would have made him an ideal chancellor at any time."

But there is no need to point up the contentious spirit of the old debates or to show how, in the words of Professor R. W. Chambers, some of his "severest critics have been those liberal-minded people who have abandoned everything of Protestantism except its prejudices." Yet just there the cause of sadness lies, in prejudice, the matrix of confusion. For he was himself all light, such a one as, in the idiom of Nicholas Harpsfield, was of

> sure, constant, stable and grounded judgment, that he was and is the oddest and notablest man of all England . . . one that neither England as I have said, nor, as I suppose, all Christendom had the like,

a characterization that dominates the first full-length biography of More — and the first full-length literary biography in English. Harpsfield wrote it in 1557, and called it "The life and death of Sir Thomas Moore, knight, sometymes Lord high Chancellor of England." At the same time, as has been said, Cavendish was writing the "Wolsey." But Harpsfield's book remained in manuscript until 1935, when, edited by Dr. Elsie V. Hitchcock, with an introduction by Professor Chambers, it was published by the Early English Text Society. It is a distinct contribution to the history of More's reputation and an invaluable addition to the literature of biography. Harpsfield's understanding of his subject and his skill in communicating it result in revealing More as a genius who in accepting martyrdom for the faith, could not possibly have mistaken either the importance of the cause or the risk he encountered in upholding it.

Harpsfield had ample opportunity to learn of More and to become a practical biographer, although, as Lord Acton in his study comments, "he died without having made himself known in literature." He was among those who came under the influence of More as a writer of history distinct from historiography, an influence emanating from the great English chancellor as from one characterized ninety years ago by Sir James Mackintosh as "our earliest prose writer, and the first Englishman who wrote the history of his country in its present language." This influence spread abroad in what Professor Chambers calls "three circles." The first consisted of his household at Chelsea, the atmosphere of which is described by Harpsfield in the passage:

> Surely, if a man had seene and fully knowen, the order, demaine, and trade of his children . . . and of his other famalie, he would have taken great spirituall and ghostly pleasure thereof, and would have thought himselfe to have rather beene in Platoes accademie — nay, what say I, Platoes? Not in Platoes, but in some Christian well ordered accademie and universitie — rather than in any laye mans house. Everybody there so besett himselfe and his time upon such good and fruitfull reading and other vertuous exercises. There should you heare of no strife or debate, of no wanton and unseemely talke, which, with divers other enormities, were cutt away, because ydlenes, the very pestiferous poysoned bane of youth, was quite excluded, and every person well and vertuously set aworke.

The household included more than a dozen persons of whom William Roper and Margaret More — Margaret Roper, that is — were the chief. The second "circle" was composed of those who, although not living in his house, came into personal contact with him: William Rastell (a nephew, who wrote a "life" now unfortunately existing only in tantalizing fragments, and edited the "works" in black-letter), John Heywood, and Thomas Lupset. And the third was made up of men who were affected directly only by his writings, the group in which Harpsfield belonged.

What is known of Harpsfield has survived in Anthony Wood's "Athenae Oxoniensis," augmented by Lord Acton's letter to the "Academy" in 1876, and by Bishop Creighton's sketch in the "Dictionary of National Biography," besides the Chambers' study. The "Catholic Encyclopedia" contains only a one-line reference to him, and no adequate "life" has ever been prepared. There were two Harpsfields, brothers, according to Professor Chambers' study, John, the elder, and Nicholas. They were both archdeacons, and both doctors, the one of divinity, the other of laws. Both became distinguished in the time of Mary and suffered long terms of imprisonment under Elizabeth. John was famous as a scholar and preacher, becoming nicknamed "Dr. Sweetlips," but Nicholas came into notice through his writings and because of his more active life has been more distinctly remembered. Lord Acton says of him:

> At the accession of Elizabeth when the whole Marian clergy made scarcely an effort to avert the ruin which seemed already iretrievable, Harpsfield struggled almost alone to uphold the failing cause.

The family was native to Hertfordshire and is known to have held land under the Abbey of St. Albans from the time of Henry III. Nicholas, however, was born in London in 1519. At the age of ten he was studying at Wincester and in 1535 proceeded to New College, Oxford, where after two years he became a perpetual Fellow. Taking the degree B. C. L. in 1543, he was admitted, says Wood, "Principal of an ancient hostle (mostly for Civilians) called White Hall (on the site of which Jesus College was afterwards partly built)," a position which he held only two years. Concerning the next five years nothing is revealed.

In 1550, because of the religious disturbances under Edward VI, he left England for Louvain, joining in exile Bonvise, the Clements, and the Rastels. He returned to England four years later and was made archdeacon of Canterbury to succeed Edmund Cranmer, brother of the archbishop, who had married. Oxford conferred upon him the D. C. L. in 1554 and he assumed a considerable practice at the Court of Arches. At the same time, moreover, he possessed the living at Saltwood near Hythe, thus reinforcing his ecclesiastical prestige and being enabled to sustain a relationship with Cardinal Pole, the then Archbishop of Canterbury. During the whole of Pole's tenure, in fact, Harpsfield was closely associated with him, supporting him when he was plunged into trouble and weakened by failing health, with the result that Harpsfield himself became so inextricably involved that when Queen Mary died November 17, 1558, and Cardinal Pole followed her twelve hours later, he was among the first to draw the attention of those who had espoused the changing order.

Consequently, on August 11, 1559, when he refused to subscribe to the Act of Uniformity as being against his conscience, his difficulties began — he was fined £200 and deposed as Prebendary of London, an office given as one of the last of Pole's favors. From the day upon which he paid the fine the record is silent until July 28, 1562, when under that date in the "Acts of the Privy Council" occurs the entry:

> This daye the Warden of the Fletes deputye, being called before the Lordes, had commandment geven him to say to his master from their Lordships that he should cause Dr. Scotte, Dr. Cole, the two Harpesfields, Wood, Somerset and Smyth remaining prisoners in his warde, to be kept in closse prisonne, so as they may not have conference with anye nor be suffered to have suche resorte unto them as they have been accustomed.

And in the Fleet the brothers remained for twelve years, to be released on bail August 19, 1574.

From a commonplace book kept by John Harpsfield it seems that upon release both brothers went to Bath to recover their health but had to be present in London in November for the sitting of the Star Chamber Court. The notations include many references to "Starre Chambre dayes" and not a few passages quoted from Nicholas' historical writings. On November 29, 1575, the record states, John appeared alone at the court asking that Nicholas be excused from attendance because of illness, and among the December entries appears:

> *Moritur frater 18 Deceb. 1575,*
> *Dominica 4 ta Adventus.*

A short life and a troubled one, but not unusual at the time. Controversy which led to imprisonment was common enough, and the Harpsfields were active controversialists, John in preaching and

Nicholas in writing. In fact, the whole body of Nicholas' work, whether the "Dialogi Sex," the "Historia Wicliffiana," or the "Life of More," is controversial, the last named, however, being the only work significant today — but hardly because it is controversial.

It was written before April, 1557, a date based upon a passage in Section III,

> His bookes be rare, and the print spent up, and some as well latine as Inglishe never yet put to the print. Howbeit, we trust shortlye to have all his englishe workes, as well those that have beene set forth ere this, as some others, in print, wherin Master Sargeant Rastell doth nowe diligently travell and imployeth his good and careful indevour to the furthering of the saide good purpose;

for "Master Sargeant Rastell" published his black-letter edition of More's writing at the time mentioned. The book conveys the impression of leisure and freedom from the disturbance that characterized most of Harpsfield's life after the death of Pole. For controversial though it is, firm in his adherence to the faith for which More gave his life, Harpsfield uses his subject as much to teach morality in the manner of the hagiographists as to portray a man or to reveal a personality. It is a quiet book, given rather to More's learning, his culture, and his spiritual influence than to the turmoil and strife of the day, although this last is by no means slighted in so far as More was directly affected.

Harpsfield was a disciple of Erasmus and one deeply imbued with the zeal for learning abroad in his world. If for no other reason than that Erasmus admired More, Harpsfield would also have admired him. But Harpsfield had a deeper reason — More's martyrdom to the faith, which was giving evidence of losing its hold upon the people and which it was Harpsfield's dearest wish to restore. Reason enough for a "life" which would at once commemorate an admired character and serve as a weapon in the developing conflict.

In his "Epistle Dedicatoire" to Roper as patron he expresses his use of Roper's "Life," a work which preceded his own by a short time only, one, in fact, which seems to have been composed originally as material for Harpsfield. "Ye shall receave," he wrote,

> I will not say, a pigge of your owne sowe (it were too
> homely and swinish a terme) but rather a comely and goodly
> garlande . . . picked and gathered even out of your owne
> garden.

And what use he made of Roper's "Life" becomes evident from a
comparison of the two books. There can be no doubt whatever that
the greatest biography proceeds from those, to paraphrase Dr.
Johnson's remark, "who have eaten and drunk and lived in social
intercourse" with their subjects: anything less must be but a syn-
thetic substitute. None the less it is possible to make intelligent use
of material produced by the subject himself or find available such
work as in this instance was done by Roper — a concrete record of
his relationship with his father-in-law, which of itself is to be
thought of as biographical writing at its earliest best except that it
is limited to sixty duodecimo pages. If one has evidence of this sort
and is himself capable of discriminate gleaning, as Harpsfield was,
then his efforts should prove only less fruitful than they might have
been had his relationship been direct. In fact, Harpsfield's book,
hagiographical though it is, must be considered not only as the first
full length literary biography in English but also as the first
satisfactory example of scholarly life writing.

The first section treats of More's parentage, his education, his
rise in the world and his consequent difficulties, especially those
with Wolsey and those which arose in connection with the king's
consulting him in the matter of the divorce; and it ends with Henry's
assurance of continued favor. The second section details More's
habits of piety, his hearing Mass before entering upon any matter
of importance, his singing in the choir and serving as parish clerk,
his wearing a hair shirt, his modesty in worldly honors, his charity
to his tenants, his foresight as to the effects of the rising tide of
heresy; and sets forth the three famous wishes:

> "Nowe would to our Lorde, sonne Roper, upon condition
> that three thinges were well stablished in Christendome, I
> were put in a sacke, and here presently cast into the Temmes."
> "What great thinges be those, Sir," quoth Master William
> Roper, "that should move you so to wishe?"

"Wouldst thou knowe what they be, Sonne Roper?" quoth he.

"Yea, mary, with good will, Sir, if it please you," quoth Master William Roper.

"In faith, Sonne, they be these" (saide he). "The first is, That where the most part of Christen Princes be at Mortall warre, they were (all) at an universall peace. The second, that where the Churche of Christe is at this present sore afflicted with many errors and heresies, it were setled in a perfect uniformity of religion. The thirde, that where the kinges matter of his marriage is nowe come in question, that it were to the glory of God and quietness of all partes brought to a good conclusion."

And this section ends with some account of More's family, the learning of Margaret, the temporary heresy of "Sonne Roper," and a comparison of the first and second wives, including the highly characterizing dialogue between More and Mistress Alice, his second wife, in the Tower after the imprisonment:

"What the goodyere, Master More," quoth she, "I mervaile that you (that) have beene alwayes hitherto taken for so wise a man, will nowe so play the fool to lye here in this close, filthy prison, and be content thus to be shutt up among mise and rattes; when you might be abrode at your libertie, with the favor and good will both of the king and his counsaile, if you would but doo as all the Bissopps and best learned of this realm have done.

"And seeing you have at Chelsey a right faire house, your librarie, your bookes, your gallerie, your garden, your orchyarde and all other necessaries so handsome about you, where you might in the company of me, your wife, your children and housholde, be mery. I muse what a God's name you mean here still thus fondlye to trye."

After he had a while quietly heard her, with a cheerefull countenaunce he said unto her:

"I praye thee, good mistress Als, tell me one thing."

"What is that?" quoth she.

"Is not this house," quoth he, "as nigh heaven as mine owne?"

To whom she, after her accustomed homely fashion, not lyking such talke aunswered: "Tille valle, Tille valle."

"Howe saye you, mistress Als?" quoth he, "is it not so?"

"Bone Deus, Bone Deus, man, will this gere never be lefte?" quoth she.

"Well, then, mistress Alice, if it be so," quoth he, "it is very well. For I see no great cause why I shoulde muche joye eyther of my gaye house or of anything belonging thereunto, when, if I should but seven yeres lye buried under the grounde, I should not faile to finde some therein that would bidd me gett me out (of) dores, and tell me it were none of mine. What cause have I then to like suche a house as would so soone forgett his master?"

So her persuasions moved him but a litle.

The third part includes comment upon Rastell's printing of More's writing, his integrity in controversy, his superiority to Erasmus, his disdain of recompense, his confutation of Tindale and of Barnes, his composing with a coal "A Dialogue of Comfort Against Tribulation" and "A Treatise on the Passion" on the walls of his prison; and, most important from the point of view of biography, the statement that More wrote:

> most elegantly and eloquently the life of kinge Richarde the thride. Not onely in englishe, which booke is abroade in printe, but corrupted and vitiated, but in latine also, not yet printed. He did not perfect and finish the same booke, neyther any sithens durst take upon him to sett his hande to the penne to finishe it, (either) in the one or other tonge, all men being deterred and driven from that enterprise by reason of the incomparable excellencie of the saide worke.

Harpsfield's praise of the "Richard" is praise indeed when one remembers that he was of the Yorkist tradition; and the passage becomes the complete answer to those who doubt More's authorship of the book.

The fourth section continues the details of character and personal traits, commenting upon More's reputation as a Latin scholar, his love for Erasmus, the king's dependence upon his company and how Henry infringed upon his time, his relations with Antonio

Bonvise, his courtesy, wit, and economy of time, his personal appearance, his voice, his diet and health, and his interest in animals. The fifth section begins with the surrender of the great seal, and ends with the trial and martyrdom — probably the most interesting part of the book. He relies upon Roper whenever possible; in fact, he seldom even bothers to change Roper's language. But for the account of More's trial (Roper's account was obtained also at second hand) Harpsfield depends upon a "credible report" made by Sir Anthony St. Leger, Richard Heywood, John Webb, and various others, which some twenty years later he rewrote "so far as his poor wit and memory would serve him" — which they seem to have done most admirably. There is set forth the irregularity of the trial (the procedure of which was later made legal by appropriate legislation), and the well-known episodes of the execution, the jest upon the weakness of the scaffold, and the final speech to the headsman:

> Pluck up thy spirites, man, and be not afraide to doo thine office: my necke is very short; take heede therfore thou stryke not awrye, for saving of thine honestie.

And the sixth section is a kind of threnody upon the death of More, dwelling upon his wisdom and virtue, upon the fact of his being the first English lay martyr, and the effect of his martyrdom on some of those tempted to fall away from the faith. The whole concludes with a short account of martyrdom in England.

Two impressions stand out as one closes the book: the somewhat disjointed structure, and the dramatic quality of the story in spite of the structural handicap. Always it is More who dominates the page; no matter what topic is introduced More is never lost sight of. There are asides but they never distract. Books, controversies, friends, abstract questions come in for discussion but always as they affected More or were affected by him. Heightening dramatic reality is much direct discourse, dialogue usually, inserted whenever possible — the device which More himself used with such impressiveness in the "Richard" and which Roper and Cavendish as well as Harpsfield no doubt learned from him. These dramatic qualities together with the full treatment, and Harpsfield's discriminating selection among available materials, constitute the reason for including the "More" among the valuable contributions to the literature of biography. One should place it second only to More's "Richard" itself among Tudor life writings; as in truth it has every right to be, having been written as it was under the influence of More's own work — and profiting accordingly — by one whom Lord Acton describes as

> the most eminent Catholic who, in 1559, neither obeyed the Act of Uniformity nor took shelter from its penalties in flight.

Unquestionably, Nicholas Harpsfield was a brave man and his book is a brave book — both deserving of bright remembrance.

# 5—Cavendish and "The Life and Death of Thomas Wolsey" *

*The great business of life is to be, to do, to do without, and to depart. — Morley.*

AMONG the books that one recalls as having survived in spite of odds against them George Cavendish's "The Life and Death of Thomas Wolsey" is notable in its triumph. Not only did it remain unprinted for almost a hundred years, but even its authorship was wrongfully attributed to William instead of George Cavendish until after 1800.

Cavendish finished the book in June, 1558, only to see Elizabeth on her way to the throne. Swift reprisal would have followed upon publication of a work so slurringly implicative of Henry VIII and Anne Boleyn. The MS. circulated, however, and there were many readers — surreptitious readers, that is — and a number of writers, who, shifting the emphasis to suit their needs, used it as source material: Thomas Churchyard, for example, whose "Tragedy of Cardinal Wolsey" was included by John Higgins in the 1587 edition of "A Mirror for Magistrates"; Shakespeare, who based much of his "King Henry VIII" upon it; and Stowe and Speed, both of whom accepted it as authoritative. In 1641, however, there being some idea abroad that the work might serve as a weapon against Archbishop Laud, a badly twisted and wretchedly printed version appeared. From time to time subsequent editions were made, the best of which — except that it named William Cavendish as author and so

---

* Reprinted with the kind permission of the editor of "The Sign," in the pages of which this chapter first appeared.

gave rise to a confusion which obtained for a century and a half—appeared in 1657. Finally in 1815 S. W. Singer came into possession of the holograph and issued the first authentic edition, including the author's prologue, signed "G. C.," and his address to his book, dated the fourth year of the reign of Mary.

The confusion which grew out of the attribution of authorship to William Cavendish instead of George, notwithstanding Stowe's clear designation to the contrary, and even the confusion which led to such attribution, were natural enough. Both men were sons of Thomas Cavendish, a clerk of the Pipe in the Exchequer, and were born at Glemsford in Suffolk, upon the small family estate. George was the elder, born in 1500. He, however, was content at the age of 26 or 27 (having already married Margery Kemp, niece to Sir Thomas More) to take service as gentleman-in-waiting in Wolsey's household; while William, more ambitious, followed the court and was eventually knighted. He it was who founded the great family of Newcastle, of which William, the old knight's grandson, became the first duke. This last named William it was, too, whose second wife, Margaret, wrote the "Life" and was nominated for immortality by Charles Lamb's "that princely woman, the thrice noble Margaret of Newcastle." Hence, better known than George politically, and also because in 1657 his name was much bruited about in the affairs of the day, William Cavendish, knight to Henry VIII, was thought to have written the "Wolsey." But be that as it may, there is no more question now as to the authorship. In fact before Singer had come across the holograph and so rendered the matter incontrovertible, the Reverend Joseph Hunter, by both internal and external evidence had established it. There is no more question today as to the authorship than there is as to the value of the book.

Of this last there can be small question indeed. Finished as early as it was, it has often been mentioned as the first work of its kind in English. Since the publication in 1935, however, of the Harpsfield "More," one must consider this as contemporary with the "Wolsey," if not its predecessor. No matter—the value of Cavendish's work is not dependent upon priority. It depends, rather, upon a plain man's effort to point up the wondrous mutability of vain honors, the brittle assurance of abundance, the uncertainty of dignities, the flattery of feigned friends, and the fickle trust to worldly princes.

And all this the author accomplished in terms of his day's most glamorous personage — whom he had served first in admiration and finally in pity — with the tragic force of classical drama.

From obscurity to glittering power and on to disgrace and death turns the wheel of Wolsey's fortune; and Cavendish has provided the record. It is a simple record, but real notwithstanding — the kind which helps one to shake off the dust of years and penetrate the recesses of the past. Gold and tinsel, damask and sackcloth, hope and ambition, spirit and flesh, all the pageantry, all the triumph, all the futility of earthly show stand revealed in Wolsey's fabulous career. "Each following day became the next day's master," up to the moment when as he lay dying he said to Master Kingston, "If I had served God as diligently as I have done the king, He would not have given me over in my gray hairs."

In his fruitfully simple style Cavendish brings out weakness as well as strength in Wolsey's character. He might have given more detail; but he was no Boswell accumulating a mountain of facts in the hope of reanimating his subject. He was merely a household attache who some thirty years after the facts looked back and wrote of what he knew with the ridding urge that comes with love, in order, as he says, to offset

> divers and sundry surmises and imagined tales, made of his proceedings and doings, which I myself have perfectly known to be most untrue.

Wolsey's start as an "honest poor man's son" is recorded and his education described. There follows some account of his service as king's chaplain. Then comes the story of his journey from Richmond to Calais and return in less than twenty-four hours, a feat which so astonished Henry, at whose behest the mission had been undertaken, that more and more frequently was he employed upon missions of more and more significance. The sequel was that Wolsey grew in Henry's favor, being entrusted with embassies to the continent until in time his was the final decision in the subtlest of affairs, the king being satisfied with hearing reports after the fact.

The climax of his career is reached when he represents Henry VIII at the court of France and is received and entertained as if he had been royalty himself. In rapid succession following this climax, however, Henry falls in love with Anne Boleyn, whose enmity Wolsey incurs; Queen Katherine is brought to trial and finally put away; Wolsey's power begins to wane because of his refusal to uphold Henry in his demand for a divorce; the king's marriage is celebrated; his withdrawal from Rome takes place; and Wolsey's loss of power, disgrace and death follow inevitably.

As has been said, Cavendish was a gentleman-in-waiting, whose duties were confined to the household. He supervised the great banquets and impressive functions, and arranged the glittering processions in which the Cardinal invariably went through the streets of London. Hence, because of this sort of activity Cavendish is especially interested in details of costume, food, furniture, procedures, bodyguards, horse garniture, and the thousands of specific articles, small customs, and appurtenances involved in the management of the Cardinal's business.

When he went about the city, for instance, in Cavendish's words:

> He rode upon his mule, with his crosses, his pillars, his hat, and the great seal born before him by a nobleman or some worthy gentleman, right solemnly, bareheaded. His gentlemen, being in number very many, clothed in livery coats of crimson velvet of the finest colour that might be invented, with chains of gold about their necks; and all his yeoman and other mean officers were in coats of fine scarlet, guarded with black velvet a hand broad.

When he received suitors:

> After Mass he would return in his privy chamber again, and being advertised of the furniture of his chambers without or with noblemen, gentlemen, and other persons, would issue out into them apparelled all in red, in the habit of a cardinal; which was either of fine scarlet or else of crimson satin, taffeta, damask, or caffa, the best that he could get for money; and upon his head a round pullion, with noble of black velvet set

to the same in the inner side; he had also a tippet of fine sables about his neck, holding in his hand a very fine orange, whereof the meat and substance within had been taken out and filled up again with the part of a sponge wherin was vinegar, and other confections against the pestilent airs.

When he entertained the king:

There wanted no preparations, or goodly furniture, with viands of the finest sort that might be provided for money or friendship. Such pleasures were then devised for the king's comfort and consolation, as might be invented, or by man's wit imagined. The banquets were set forth, with mask and mummeries, in so gorgeous a sort, and costly a manner, that it was a heaven to behold. Then was there all kind of music and harmony set forth, with excellent voices both of men and children.

Upon religious occasions, as upon one Feast of the Assumption:

My lord rose betimes and went to the cathedral church *de notre Dame,* and said his service and Mass; and after Mass, he himself administered the sacrament unto my Lady Regent and to the Queen of Navarre. And that done, the king [of France] resorted unto the church, and was conveyed into a rich travers at the high altar; and directly against him, on the other side of the altar, sat my lord Cardinal in another travers, three gresses higher than the King's.

When faced by adversity he seemed no less humble than formerly he had been arrogant. For instance, Cavendish reports this address to the attendants:

"Most faithful gentlemen and true-hearted yeomen, I do not only lament to see your persons present about me, but I do lament my negligent ingratitude toward you all on my behalf, in whom hath been a great default, that in my prosperity I have not done for you so much as I might have done, either in word or in deed, which was then in my power to do: but then I knew not my jewels and special treasures that I had of you my faithful servants in my house."

And finally, when he came to die, in Cavendish's words, he said:

[ 54 ]

"I can no more, but wish all things to have good success. My time draweth on fast, I may not tarry with you."

Then we began to put him in remembrance of Christ's passion; and sent for the abbot of the place to anneal him, who came with all speed, and ministered unto him all the services of the same belonging; and caused also the guard to stand by, both to hear him talk before his death, and also to witness of the same; and incontinent the clock struck eight, at which time he gave up the ghost.

Interwoven from time to time with the narrative are passages which reveal the author's opinion of Wolsey's progress and his certainty of the Cardinal's impending fate. They seem almost like the speeches of the chorus in Greek tragedy. Cavendish draws a conclusion from Wolsey's revenge, for instance, upon Sir Amyas Pawlet, later to become the jailer of Mary Queen of Scots in Tutbury Castle and Ambassador to France. Pawlet had been unjust to the Cardinal in youth and Cavendish remarked:

Therefore I would wish all men in authority and dignity to know and fear God in all their triumphs and glory; considering in all their doings, that authorities be not permanent, but may slide and vanish, as princes' pleasures do alter and change.

Some pages later appears the same idea in different guise:

Let all men, to whom fortune extendeth her grace, not trust too much to her fickle favor and pleasant promises, under colour whereof she carrieth venomous gall.

And again he comments:

O wavering and new-fangled multitude! Is it not a wonder to consider the inconstant mutability of this uncertain world!

Then, as he draws to a close:

Here is the end and fall of pride and arrogance of such men, exalted by fortune to honours and high dignities; for I assure you, in his time of authority and glory, he was the haughtiest man in all his proceedings that then lived, having more respect to the worldly honour of his person than he had to his spiritual profession; wherein should be all meekness, humility, and charity; the process whereof I leave to them that be learned in divine laws.

In such fashion is the sense of tragic mortality sustained. The narrative action is carried along supported by philosophical comment, until in the final passage the whole is resolved in one crashing chord:

O what inconstant trust and assurance is in rolling fortune!

# 6—Izaac Walton and His "Lives"

*. . . that toucheth gentilesse*
*And eke moralite and holinesse.* — Anon.

TEN centuries are ten centuries in the stream of history, but
they are no more than a day in the early stages of life writing.
It is true that by the time the "Lives" of Walton appeared every
variation which later developments were to render familiar had
been established — as More's "Richard III" and Eadmer's "Anselm"
connote — nevertheless it was the encomiastic that had predominated.
Adamnan and Bede revealed, as ideals to be cherished, their St.
Columba and St. Cuthbert, but with no more enthusiasm than
possessed Walton in showing forth Donne, Wotton, Hooker, Herbert, and Sanderson as patterns of the joy militant as well as the
glory triumphant. And one may with obeisance conclude, that his
desire to preserve in memory the virtues of the men he most admired as representing artists in living as well as in dying, was the
manifestation of his nature in adjustment with the temper of the
age; for the years which served to crystallize his talents, firm in
reliance upon theology, looked to the "lives" of holy men for confirmation of that reliance. Indeed, as much as any other biographer
Walton was the summation of his inheritance as it underwent the
shaping forces of his time. Had there been no hagiographical tradition upon which to draw and no civil strife or ecclesiastical disturbance against which to rebel he might have written *what* he did
because in so doing he found expression for the love and reverence
his subjects had inspired within him, but most surely he could not
have written *as* he did.

To know him best one should rely chiefly upon his own writing; the facts concerning him are few and the records concerning the events of his life are almost negligible. He lived during ninety of England's most stirring years, yet he sustained a tranquillity and a repose of soul almost unique in literary history.

There are, of course, a number of accounts of him, especially that of Sir Harris Nicholas, but as yet no adequate "life" has appeared. Gaps occur in what has been written because the material to supply them has not come to light; and disagreements arise because no definite evidence is available to settle them. The date of his coming up to London from Staffordshire, for instance, is in doubt. Likewise, one cannot be sure about his occupation once he had arrived. Regarding his occupation the only safe thing to say is that he was in London some time before 1614, engaging in some kind of trade in Cornhill, the master of a shop 7½' by 5'. Of the nature of his trade, however, there remains only conjecture. Some writers say that he was a haberdasher, in Fleet Street, near Chancery Lane; Hawkins, in his "Life," said that he was a sempster. From an old deed it may be implied that — at least in 1624 — he was occupying one half of a shop in Fleet Street as a linen draper. The records of the Ironmongers' Company indicate that he was admitted to honorary membership in that body in 1618. And the calendar of the Court of Judicature designates him "gentleman" in connection with a question of certain burned houses. He himself has a comment upon this last condition:

> I would rather prove myself a gentleman by being learned and humble, valiant and inoffensive, virtuous and communicable than by any fond ostentation of riches, or wanting such virtues myself, boast that they were my ancestors.

Strangely enough, too, the name of his mother seems to have been forgotten, and the house in which he was born is not now to be distinguished. All this serves but to confuse; it does, however, suggest two ideas: the lack of detail concerning the man hinders us but little in understanding the author — there exists a sufficiency in the work itself; but it does indicate that an adequate "life" of Walton is long over due.

In spite of the dearth of material, a body of information has accumulated which is all but satisfactory for most purposes. One knows, for instance, that he was born August 9, 1593, in St. Mary's parish, Stafford, that his father was Jervis Walton. One knows also that he was named for Isaac Causabon, the French scholar, who was a friend to both the elder Walton and to Sir Henry Wotton (one of the men treated in the "Lives"), but that Walton himself always wrote his name "Izaac." Further information tells us that he was twice married, first, on December 27, 1626, to Rachel Floud, great granddaughter of Archdeacon Cranmer, brother to the famous archbishop; that by her he had seven children, all of whom died young; that she herself died in 1640. Six years later, he married Ann Ken, half-sister to the Bishop of Bath and Wells, a lady "of much Christian meeknesse," and by her had three children, one, Izaac, who died in infancy; another, Izaac, who became Canon of Salisbury, and a third, Anne, who married William Hawkins, Prebendary of Wincester and one of Walton's earliest biographers.

The outward circumstances of his life even to the last detail would help us to appreciate so unique a personality as that of the man who could compose two such different works as "The Compleat Angler" and the "Lives"; nevertheless an awareness of him becomes more and more sharply focused as we turn the pages of his books. Not only does he comment upon himself directly; but indirectly, too, he provides his reader with the means to know him. For instance, one can piece together certain scattered remarks and say that he was distinguished by "self-reverance, self-knowledge, and self-control"; that he possessed a mind "naturally Christian"; and that he had "sat self-governed in the fiery prime of youth, obedient at the feet of law." Moreover, although but little external evidence exists, one has no difficulty in realizing that somehow he managed to obtain an education sufficient to, if not above, his station. It is clear, for example, that he knew some Latin but not any Greek. Furthermore, one may infer that before he was twenty years old he had already gained the respect of at least one educated person, one S. B., whose poem, "The Loves of Amos and Laura," was dedicated to "My approved and respected friend, Iz. Wa.," in 1613. Most apparent of all, however, is the fact that he learned somehow to write a style among the pleasantest in English prose, a statement easily agreed to by the most casual reader, but amply sustained by the consensus of critics — one of whom, James Russell Lowell, had this to say of it:

> It is enough for us that he contrived somewhere a competent mastery of his mother tongue (far harder because seeming easier than Latin) and a diction of persuasive simplicity and capable of dignity where that was natural and becoming.

Of his education Walton himself said:

> When I look back upon my education and mean abilities, it is not without some little wonder that I am come to be publicly in print.

The only study that one can be certain he followed is that of the Bible; not only does he continually quote from it, but something of its richness is perceptible in all that he wrote. In short, although it is true that "heredity may confer the gift of genius but environment provide the materials," in Walton it would seem rather that "the will of man directs the fate of man."

He was born humbly and he lived humbly; yet it would be difficult to point to a more satisfying life experience — if the evidence available is sufficiently conclusive — for the effects of his own volition are apparent in whatever of his enterprises have become known to us. He went to London to seek his fortune and found it. When he had accumulated a modest competency he retired, remarking that he found it difficult for an honest man to live in London. He, therefore, about 1644, returned to the neighborhood of Stafford and settled into a "wattle and daub" cottage near the river Stowe — a cottage which was unfortunately destroyed by fire, ironically enough, through the carelessness of the caretaker in frying fish.

Here he wrote (having, however, published the "Life of Donne" in 1640, before leaving London) and fished, fishing having been a passion with him always. Here, too, he read curious books like the Prioress of Sopewell's treatise on falconry, heraldry, and angling. Here, too, he received his scores of distinguished friends. Lowell said of his friendships:

> He had a genius for friendship and an amiability of nature

ample for the comfortable housing of many at a time; he had, even, a special genius for bishops and seems to have known the whole episcopal bench in his day. .

Samuel Johnson once remarked about this rare quality of Walton's:

> It was wonderful that Walton, who was of a very low station in life, should have been familiarly known to so many great men, and that at a time when the ranks of society were kept more separate than they are now.

(It was Samuel Johnson, whose opinion of the "Compleat Angler" caused a reprint of the book after it had lain forgotten for fifty years and so gave it an impetus toward the 283 editions that have since appeared, and immortality.)

It may have been these friendships, based as they were upon the firmest conservatism, or it may have been his own predilections, which his associations brought out, that caused him to remain a stanch supporter of the Establishment and a steadfast adherent of the royalist cause throughout the religious and political turbulence of his day. Such, at all events, he was. Among the stories of his loyalty to Charles is one told by Ashmole of his being entrusted with the king's Order of St. George after it was picked up during the battle of Winchester because he was "well beloved of all good men." He carried it to the Tower, although at the risk of his life, and delivered it over to Colonel Blague for safe keeping. Among the expressions of his religious opinion, many of which as may be drawn quite at random from his writings, is:

> I praise God that he prevented me from being of the party which helped to bring this Covenant and those confusions which followed it.

Circumstances and his own inclination, therefore, would seem to have guided him in choosing his subjects as he did; and once having chosen them, he could do no less than the best of which he was capable.

All previous and much contemporary work of the sort had been engrossed, as has been said, with moral purpose. The saint was upheld as an example of virtue; the king was extolled as a model ruler; and permeating "lives" of both was a definite commemorative coloration such that many became not only didactic treatises but "extended epitaphs" as well. However, although it cannot be said that Walton avoided didacticism or shunned commemoration, it can be pointed out that he added something in purpose to both in that, rather than remaining content to teach or to sustain in memory, he recreated the personalities of his subjects for themselves alone. True, he states as his purpose in one of his prefaces:

> Biography is an honor due to the virtuous dead and a lesson in magnanimity to those who shall succeed them;

nevertheless, this statement, connotative of both commemoration and didacticism though it is, is decidedly different in tone from certain contemporary expressions — Richard Baxter's for instance, as found in his preface to the "Life of John Janeway:"

> To teach me better how to live and die, in Faith, Hope, and Love, is that for which I read this narrative; and that thou mayest learn the same is the end of my commending it to thee;

or from that set forth in the last sentence of John Earle's "Character of a Grave Divine":

> His death is the last sermon, where in the pulpit of his bed, he instructs men how to die by his example.

This difference, although insufficient reason for concluding that Walton was without direct moral purpose, is quite sufficient to suggest that such purpose was incidental to a more truly artistic design; and the impression conveyed by the "Lives" themselves bears out the suggestion. His own statement, then, pertinent though it may be and sincere though it unquestionably is, seems somewhat more conventional than definitive, as if while he thought himself writing in the customary fashion he was unwittingly accomplishing something new. In short, one gathers from reading the "Lives" and from thinking over the statement of his purpose that, although he was not averse to teaching by example or to commemoration, his primary aim was to leave behind him images of the men whom he admired almost to the point of reverence — a view which is borne out by Sir Edmund Gosse, who once wrote:

> The five short *lives* which he published, though pale by the side of such work in biography as the end of the eighteenth century produced, are yet notable among the earliest which aim at giving us vivid portraits of men instead of discreet and conventional testimonials.

Some there are, of course, who insist that, no matter how sharp the image, this kind of biography is no more than panegyric and therefore valueless. In fact, an anonymous critic once wrote that Walton's "Lives" were elegaic enough to have served angels as subjects; and Sir Walter Raleigh expressed the opinion that

> Indeed Walton's *Lives* are almost too perfect to serve as models. They are obituary poems; each of them has the unity and the melody of a song or a sonnet; they deal with no problems but sing the praises of obscure beneficence and a mind that seeks its happiness in the shade.

However, whether or not one considers him a panegyrist, it is well to remember that whatever his purpose was, he became an apostle of personality — as must all biographers become. They present their conception of the person in whom they have interested themselves; hence, the image that they transmit is of necessity their image, cast in their brain, colored (or discolored), by their emotional states. If they extol, they probably loved, at least admired; if they attack or disparage, they probably did not even respect. Sincerity, regard for truth, object in writing — these must be considered. Of Walton's character as a biographer the worst that can be said is that he tinted his accounts with the pigments of himself; and Sir Edmund Gosse, again, says just that:

> Without doubt his incorrigible optimism entered into his study of the character of his friends, and it is no part of his inexperience as a portrait painter that he mixes his colors with so much rose water. He saw his distinguished acquaintances in that light; he saw them pure, radiant, and stately beyond mortal guise.

That his work is, because of this quality, valueless as biography, is not to be acknowledged. It shows omissions, bending of fact to suit his theme, and concealment of fault that might deface his portrait. Nevertheless, what he produced was portraiture, just as surely as if he had used a brush. The pictures are selective, interpretative but, notwithstanding, real. Omission, concealment, redaction become vicious if used for the sake of misleading; they are legitimate devices, however, if they contribute to an artist's realization of an ideal. And it was the realization of an ideal that impelled Walton to use whatever devices were available to him. In no circumstances can he be thought of as anything less than sincere; for probably of no other biographer could it be more appropriately said, as he himself said of Dr. Sanderson, using the words of the Psalmist: "Blessed is the man in whose spirit there is no guile."

Guiltless of ulterior motive in writing his "Lives" though he was, undertaking them as if to do so were entirely an act of spontaneous generosity, yet once well started, he became anything but an artless old man whose ruling passion was fishing, and not at all the "God-intoxicated Walton" of at least one commentator. As a matter of fact, he employed every artifice known to the biography of his century. Not only this, but if one compares the various editions of the work which he himself saw through the press, it becomes clear that he revised constantly, adding new material, expanding old, ever changing for the better individual sentences. The sequel was that his became the first biographical writings to strike popular fancy; and they did so with such force that between 1670 and 1675 four editions of the "Lives" thus far composed and issued as one volume were required. The "Sanderson" was added in 1678. Eventually the whole work became the forerunner of a genre in English literature — the most notable example of its influence, of course, is Johnson's "Lives of the Poets." Altogether, therefore, one may say that Izaac Walton's particular aim was to limn forth certain men whom he loved so that posterity might think of them as he did; but that in doing so he became a conscious artist, realizing not a little the potentiality of his medium and exploiting it to the best of his powers.

The first work appeared in 1640, entitled "The Life and Death of Dr. Donne, late dean of St. Paul's, London." It was written in some six weeks, comprised seventeen folio pages, and was intended as an introduction to a volume containing eighty of Donne's sermons. The bookseller, Marriot, had contracted with Sir Henry Wotton to provide the introductory "life," but Wotton died in 1639, before proceeding further than a preliminary gathering of material. As a result, the bookseller planned to bring out the volume of sermons without a biographical introduction. To this, however, Walton, when he learned of the intention, would not listen, as is indicated in the introduction to the Life:

> When I heard the sad news, and likewise that these sermons were to be published without the author's life, . . . indignation or griefe (I know not whether) transported me so far that I reviewed my forsaken collections and resolved the World should see the best picture of the Author that my artlesse pensil (guided by the hand of Truth) could present to it.

He offered to supply it himself, therefore, and the bookseller, knowing of his friendship with Donne — he having been a resident in St. Paul's parish — and learning that Wotton's material had passed into his hands, readily agreed, the more so because he realized that a volume such as he contemplated, without an introduction, would fall short of public expectation.

Thus accidental as was Walton's undertaking to write it, of all the "Lives" the "Donne" is to us nowadays the most interesting. No doubt something of our attitude is due to the subject itself, Donne having been within our generation rediscovered and raised to the front rank among poets; but no small credit must go to Walton because of his artistry in both manner and style. He knew Donne and admired him as among the highest geniuses of the age — but, like the majority of Donne's admirers in the 1630's, Walton admired him because of his pulpit oratory rather than because of his poetry; he did, however, own a copy of the Herringman edition of 1669, the poems in black morocco, blind tooled, containing his own elegy of Donne, in which he made several corrections. Into the "Life" went not only what material he was able to collect — he had no previous accounts to consult — but also the fullness of his personal feeling. The result is a narrative replete with anecdote, with intimate revelations of Donne in some of his most trying situations.

But most interesting of all perhaps—at least to one as much concerned with Walton as with Donne—it is replete with subtle intimations of his relations with the great Anglican dean: a simple layman of the merchant class with one of the most spirited, eccentric, and colorful figures the church of England has ever known. Typical of these references—quite aside from the subject at hand, no biographer worthy of the name has ever succeeded in excluding himself entirely from his work—is this:

> There may be some that may incline to think (such indeed as have not heard him) that my affection for my Friend, hath transported me to an immoderate commendation of his Preaching;

and again:

> And now his life was as a *shining light* among his old friends: now he gave an ocular testimony of the strictness and regularity of it; now he might say as St. *Paul* adviseth his Corinthians Be ye followers of me, as I follow Christ and walk as ye have me for an example; Not the example of a busiebody; but of a contemplative, a harmless, an humble and an holy life and conversation.

Among the striking situations described, one has to do with the apparition which appeared to Donne during an embassy to Paris in company with Sir Robert Drewry:

> Within a few days . . ., the *Embassador*, Sir *Robert*, and Mr. *Donne* left *London*; and were the twelfth day got all safe to Paris. —two days after their arrival there, Mr. *Donne* was left alone, in that room in which Sir *Robert*, and he, and some other friends had dinner together. To this place Sir *Robert* return'd within half an hour; and, as he left, so he found Mr. *Donne* alone; but, in such an Extasie, and so alter'd as to his looks, as amaz'd Sir *Robert* to behold him: inso much that he earnestly desired Mr. *Donne* to declare what had befaln him in the short time of his absence? to which Mr. *Donne* was not able to make a present answer: but after a long and perplext pause, did at last say, *I have seen a dreadful vision since I saw you: I have seen my dear wife pass twice by me through this room, with her hair hanging about her shoulders and a dead*

*child in her arms. . . .* To which Sir *Robert* replied; *Sure Sir, you have slept since I saw you; and, this is the result of some melancholy dream, which I desire you to forget, for you are now awake.* To which Mr. *Donne's* reply was: *I cannot be surer that I now live, then that I have not slept since I saw you: and am as sure, that at her second appearing, she stopt and look'd me in the face, and vanished.* Rest and sleep had not alter'd Mr. *Donne's* opinion the next day. . . . [Sir Robert] immediately sent a servant to Drewry House with a charge to hasten back, and bring him word, whether Mrs. *Donne* were alive? — The twelfth day the Messenger came with the account — That he found and left Mrs. Donne very sad, and sick in her bed: and, that after a long and very dangerous labor she had been deliver'd of a dead child.

The mood seldom strays from the gentle, slightly melancholy spirit of these passages. An analysis of the style would show that both vocabulary and the stately progress of the sentences as well as the choice of incident were contributory in its sustention. It is consciously wrought; anything which for a moment would break the unity Walton had affected, as according to his nature he did of necessity, is consistently ruled out. Somber in feeling, sonorous in phrase — as in the following, for instance:

> Thus *variable*, thus *vertuous* was the Life; thus *excellent*, thus *exemplary* was the Death of this memorable man, —

and harmoniously in keeping with the personality of his friend as he would have posterity remember him, Walton brings the "Donne" to its ordered close in a tone of solemn finality:

> He was earnest and unwearied in the search of knowledge; with which, his vigorous soul is now satisfied, and employed in a continual praise of that God that first breathed into his active body; that body, which was once a Temple of the Holy Ghost, and is now become a small quantity of Christian dust: But I shall see it reanimated.

Of such is "The Life and Death of Dr. Donne." We know that it contains errors, but somehow there emerges the truth that transcends error, or, in George Saintsbury's view:

*The human Donne* whom Walton depicts is so exactly the poetical Donne whom we know, that the effect is uncanny.

Donne's defects were those of a defective humanity; his virtues those of the spirit triumphant. Naturally enough, it is easy to emhasize the former, remembering the Donne who wrote "I can love both faire and browne," but it is not too difficult to think of him as having written also, "Be thine own palace, else the worlde's thy gaol" — and that last is much the better part.

Although the "Donne" is usually considered the most interesting of the "Lives," the "Wotton" is not to be looked upon as much less so. It is more objective, perhaps somewhat remote; nevertheless through it runs a romantic, robust quality almost Elizabethan in flavor, with its atmosphere of intrigue and its interplay of wit. Sir Henry Wotton was a man of extraordinary refinement and natural talent. He was a diplomat, a philosopher, a wit, and, what Walton was not slow to appreciate, a fisherman of parts. His "Life" was undertaken, as was the "Donne," *con amore*, but at the suggestion of Sir Edward Bysshe and Charles Cotton, the elder. Walton explains his interest in it thus:

> Sir *Henry Wotton* was a Branch of such a kindred as left a stock of Reputation to their posterity; such Reputation, as might kindle a generous emulation in strangers, and preserve a noble ambition in those of his Fame and Family, . . .
> *And that* Sir Henry Wotton *did so, might appear more perfectly than my Pen can express it, if of his many surviving friends, some one of higher parts and imployment, had been pleas'd to have commended his to Posterity; But since some years are now past and they have all (I know not why) forborn to do it; my gratitude to the memory of my dead friend, and the renewed request of some that still live solicitous to see this duty performed; these have had a power to perswade me to undertake it; which, truly, I have not done, but with some distrust of mine own abilities, and yet so far from despair, that I am modestly confident my humble language shall be accepted, because I shall present all Readers with a commixture of truth, and Sir Henry Wotton's merits.*

And the tale unfolds in Walton's pleasantly pious manner to show the descendant of a famous house engaged in obtaining secret information abroad, in warning King James of Scotland of a plot to poison him, in receiving knighthood, in drawing, later, the ire of James by warping the phrase *ad mentiendum* so that he could produce the epigram "An Embassador is an honest man, sent to lie abroad for the good of his country," and, finally, in retiring to the "cloysterall life" as Provost at Eton College. Throughout are scattered witty sayings about clerics, opinions drawn from a complex experience of courts, counsels for success among the great, and, not least important in Walton's eyes, arguments in support of the Establishment.

The devices are those already discovered in the "Donne," the anecdote, the dialogue composed to suit the occasion, the letter, the verse tribute, the philosophical aside, and the suspense-creating hint of what is to come; but the atmosphere, naturally, is quite different. The reverence adopted by Walton, the parishioner, toward Donne, the dean of St. Paul's, gives way to a combination of affection for the companion of the angle and respect for the confidant of the king, with sincerity to link the two together.

Having completed the sketch, however, — the "Wotton" is the shortest of the "Lives" by half — he was, seemingly, no more nearly satisfied with it than he had been with the "Donne." As soon as opportunity arose he set about revising, polishing, redacting, and expanding. So dissatisfied was he always with what he wrote, and particularly with his style, that as long as he lived he edited his work. One sentence, for instance, which appears in the "Herbert" passed through three different stages before assuming the concise, yet graceful form in which it now stands. In the "World's Classics" edition the sentence is this:

> Thus he sung on Earth such Himns and Anthems, as the Angels and he, and Mr. *Farrer*, now sing in Heaven.

The first draft, however, was this:

> Twenty eight himns and psalms which was his holy recreation the latter part of his life and is now his employment, where he makes new ditties in praise of that God in three persons to whome be glory.

[ 69 ]

The second this:

> And his better part is now in heaven doing that which was
> most of his employment on earth, magnifying the mercies and
> making himns and singing them, to that God to whome be
> honour and glory.

And the third:

> In heaven where his employment is to sing such himns as
> he made on earth in praise of the God to whom be honour
> and glory.

These revisions indicate, as James Russell Lowell, who found them
on the inside cover of Walton's copy of "Eusebius," points out,
anything but unpremeditated art. However, although his habit was
to refer frequently in subsequent works to persons already treated,
it was Wotton whom he seemed most reluctant to take leave of.
The sketch ends upon the same note of apology with which it
begins:

> And all readers are requested to believe, that he was worthy
> of a more worthy pen, to have preserved his memory, and
> commended his merits to the imitations of Posterity;

but more than this, when, two years later, he published the
"Compleat Angler," as if still doubtful of having done him justice,
he included a further character of his friend:

> My next and last example shall be that undervaluer of
> money, the late Provost of Eton College, Sir Henry Wotton,
> a man with whom I have often fished and conversed, a man
> whose foreign employments in the service of this nation and
> whose experience and learning, wit, and cheerfulness made
> his company to be esteemed one of the delights of mankind.

The "Life of Mr. Richard Hooker" is unique among the "Lives"
in that Hooker was the only man of whom he wrote that he had
never seen, Hooker having died when Walton was seven years old.
It is further unique in serving as a transition between the earlier and
later works. He wrote it when he was sixty-two — at the instigation
of some of his clerical friends, among them Gilbert Sheldon, later

Archbishop of Canterbury, to offset the errors purveyed by John Gaudin's "Life of Hooker," published in 1662 — when the resources of his mind and the rich geniality of his spirit were at their fullest. The work differs from the earlier biographies in that, for one thing, it was written almost at command. It is likewise ampler than the others, perhaps because Hooker, from the point of view of ecclesiastic distinction, was his most important subject, or perhaps because, having gained full command of his instrument, he used it to the utmost. At any rate the "Hooker" and both the "Herbert" and the "Sanderson," which followed it, are of value as much for what they reveal of Walton himself as they are for what they reveal of their subjects.

As he had not known Hooker personally he had to depend upon research to a great degree. He did, however, have among his acquaintances two of Hooker's former students, Edwin Sandys and George Cranmer — who was, incidentally, his first wife's uncle — and from them he obtained intimate detail which aids in rounding out the character as nothing else could have done. For in this "Life" Walton shows his subject against a background of the times, a device which is repeated in his subsequent writings, but which had been unnecessary heretofore. Hooker's best known contribution was the "Ecclesiastical Polity," a work which seeks to show a reconciliation between the Church of England and reason; it admits the authority of precedent but recommends obedience to the Bible, the while insisting that reason must control. In explaining Hooker's contribution, therefore, Walton felt called upon to set forth the circumstances from which the ideas grew; and in doing so he goes somewhat at length into the history of the Establishment, out of which Hooker emerges symbolic of the Elizabethan struggle against Puritanism. Many of the moving characters among Hooker's contemporaries are sketched, Jewel, Jackson, Saville, Reynolds, and particularly Whitgift; and a "character of the Times," going back to the reign of Elizabeth is interpolated. Furthermore, since the "Ecclesiastical Polity" is a work interesting not only as history but also as one of the great examples of English prose, being looked upon as the first work in the language to deal with thought of high abstraction and as accomplishing its purpose in a literary way so well that it brought English prose to be ranked with the prose of antiquity in philosophical discourse, Walton must treat matters concerning its literary quality, particularly the dispute which arose over the validity of the last three books. Hence, the "Hooker" becomes both history and criticism — but most of all it is character delineation.

An air of informality, of affectionate admiration pervades the whole. And it is perhaps the chief distinction of the work that, although so far removed in point of time from Hooker, Walton succeeded so well in communicating the personality of the man. A success which is the result, at least partly, of passages like these:

[Edwin Sandys and George Cranmer once visited Hooker and found him reading Horace while tending a few sheep, as he was accustomed to do when his servant went to eat.]

> But when his servant returned and released him, then his two pupils attended him into the house, where their best entertainment was his quiet company, which was presently denied them: for, *Richard was call'd to rock the cradle;* and the rest of their welcome was so like this, that they staid but til next morning, . . . At their parting from him Mr. *Cranmer* said, *Good Tutor, I am sorry your lot has fal'n in no better ground as to your Parsonage: and more sorry that your Wife proves not a comfortable companion after you have wearied yourself in your restless studies.* To whom the good man replied, *My dear George, If saints have usually a double share in the miseries of this life, I, who am none, ought not to repine at what my wise Creator hath appointed for me.*

[After issuing the "Ecclesiastical Polity" Hooker took up his residence at Borne, where he was sought out by many people. In treating of his new home and Hooker's increasing fame, Walton pauses for a moment to write a résumé of Hooker's character at the time and achieves probably one of the best bits of such writing to be found.]

> . . . But his Books, and the innocency and sanctity of his life became so remarkable, that many turn'd out of the Road, and others (Scholars especially) went purposely to see the man, whose life and learning were so much admired; and, alas,

as Our Savior said of St. *John Baptist, What went they out to see? a man cloathed in purple and fine linnen? No, indeed, but an obscure, harmless man, a man in poor cloathes, his Loyns usually girt in a course Gown, or Canonical Coat; of a mean stature, and stooping, and yet more lowly in the thoughts of his Soul, his Body worn out but not with Age, but study, and Holy Mortifications; his Face full of Heat-pimples, begot by his inactivity and sedentary life.* And to this true character of his person let me add this of his disposition and behavior; God and Nature blest him with so blessed a bashfulness, that in his younger days his Pupils might easily look him out of countenance; so neither then nor in his age, *did he ever willingly look any man in the face; and was of so mild and humble a nature, that his poor Parish clerk and he never did talk but with both their Hats on, or both off at same time:* And to this may be added, that though he was not pur-blind, yet he was short or weak-sighted; and where he fix't his eyes at the beginning of a sermon, there they continued till it was ended.

Whatever the characteristics of the preceding "Lives," the "Herbert" is the most lyrical and seemingly the most spontaneous. It is only less extended than the "Hooker" and so becomes one of the earliest comparatively full biographies of a poet. Walton was seventy-seven when he wrote it. It alone of the five was undertaken without any urge except his own wish, as he explains in his introduction:

*In a late retreat from the business of the World, and those many little cares with which I have too often cumbred myself, I fell into a Contemplation . . . and did look back, and not without some content (at least to myself) that I have endeavor'd to deserve the love and preserve the memory of my two deceased friends, Dr. Donne and Sir Henry Wotton by declaring the several employments and various accidents of their Lives: And though Mr. George Herbert (whose Life I now intend to write) were to me a stranger as to his person, for I have only seen him: yet since he was, and was worthy to be their friend, and very many of his have been mine: I judge it may not be unacceptable to those that knew any of them in their lives, or do now know them by mine, or their own Writings, to see this conjunction of them after their deaths. . . .*

And as it opens, so it proceeds. To Walton, George Herbert was the "Holy Mr. Herbert," whom he admired for his piety and respected for his verse. If his "Life" of him, therefore, approaches the panegyric, it is none the less sincere, because poetic piety was of all qualities the nearest to Walton's heart. It is this predilection that makes the "Herbert" the shining thing it is. In style — notably the manner in which Herbert's verse is made handmaiden to Walton's prose — in the selection of detail, in the delicacy of his touch when commenting upon the Lady Herbert and Jane Danvers (whom Herbert married after a most platonic courtship), in the deftness of the strokes that reveal the character of Herbert himself — in all these is the gentle character of Walton inherent. Probably no other of the "Lives" touched him so nearly, for probably in Herbert he saw what he himself would most have wished to be.

He fails to include any reference to Herbert's early vacillation, to Lady Herbert's strong will, to Donne's opportunism, or to the hesitancy with which Herbert finally took Anglican orders. He does not, however, fail to include particulars that make for reality. Whatever defects were present in Herbert's character, it is impossible to deny him place both as poet, whose verse has edified lovers of religious themes for three centuries, or as a pastor, whose ministrations so affected his parishioners that

> some of the meaner sort of his parish, did so love and reverence Mr. *Herbert,* that they would let their Plow rest when Mr. *Herbert's Saints-Bell* rung to Prayers, that they might also offer their devotions to God with him: and would then return back to their Plow.

And small wonder, if we are to judge from the following:

> In a walk to Salisbury he saw a poor man, with a poorer horse, that had fall'n under his Load; they were both in distress, and needed present help; which Mr. *Herbert* perceiving, put off his Canonical Coat, and help'd the poor man to unload, and after, to load his horse.

Hence, no matter what his difficulties on the way, he found a niche in memory and Walton served to insure his remaining there. The lyric note has seldom been more suitably invoked: author and subject in complete accord; style and theme in harmony conjoined; all united and exemplified in one sentence near the close:

> Thus he liv'd and thus he dy'd like a Saint, unspotted of the World, full of Alms-deeds, full of humility, and all the examples of a virtuous life.

Samuel Johnson once said of Swift, "He could write a Life of a broomstick and it would be interesting," and the "Life of Dr. Robert Sanderson" might suggest a similar remark concerning Walton. For of all the "Lives" this one would seem to have been the least promising in view of its subject. A casuist, and a logician; a man whose reading was so confined that "Aristotle's Rhetoric," "Aquinas's Secunda Secundae," and "Tully" made up the greater part of it; a preacher who could not manage the shortest sermon without a manuscript; and the author of the impossibly dull "Cases of Conscience," Sanderson would have seemed anything but stimulating to the delicate perceptions of the good fisherman. Such, however, was not true. The "Sanderson" provided him an opportunity to express himself fully concerning the abuses arising in ecclesiastical affairs during the Commonwealth and so serves as a second chapter to the "Hooker," to record his satisfaction at the Restoration, and to preserve for posterity the memory of a man whom he had known for forty years and admired for his gentleness of soul, his great learning, and his eminent virtue — if not for his wit.

Walton was eighty-five when he was urged by his friends to collect the scattered memorials of Sanderson and issue them as a section of his then famous "Lives." He was old and tired, but as he wrote in the preface:

> Though my Age might have procur'd me a Writ of Ease, and that secur'd me from all further trouble in this kind; yet I met with such perswasions to begin, and so many willing Informers since, and from them and others, such helps and incouragements to proceed, that when I found myself faint, and weary of the burthen with which I had loaden myself, and ready to lay it down; yet time and new strength hath at last brought it to be what it is now, and presented to the Reader;

[ 75 ]

hence, Dr. Robert Sanderson became rescued from oblivion — and justly so if for no other reason than that he provided the means for Walton to add to his inimitable work.

For although he had lived far beyond the usual span and was to live yet five years longer, one finds no falling off in the quality of his writing. The wonted ease, the ready turn of phrase, the sympathetic understanding, and the recognition of pertinent detail are no less apparent than in his former work; and if in theological digression he is less cogent, or, in the chronicle device of grouping events about a date instead of about an actor, less dramatic, there still emerges the personality of the elusive, timorous scholar about whom he wrote:

> Thus this pattern of *meekness* and primative *innocence* chang'd this for a better life. 'Tis now too late to wish that my life may be like his; for I am in the eighty-fifth year of my age: but I humbly beseech Almighty God, that my death may; and do as earnestly beg of every Reader to say Amen.

In such fashion during forty years a talent flourished. Tranquilly, very slowly it added its gift to the accumulating riches of biography. More brilliant gifts were yet to come, but few were more acceptable. Walton was wise in the choice of his friends, and as wise perhaps in the choice of his art — "as discernible as a natural from an artificial beauty."

# 7—Thomas Fuller

*We do not merely hold a man who
abstains from public affairs as idle; we
hold him useless.* —Pericles.

THAT biography seldom gives us the pleasure of literature, in
addition to a knowledge of fact, is witnessed to by its few
notable works in contrast with the vast array of the undistinguished.
The circumstance itself is not easily explained. Almost all other
literary forms — the lyric, the drama, the essay, the novel — have
had moments of full bloom, in the ages of Elizabeth, of Anne, and
of Victoria, particularly; but biography cannot be said to have predominated in any period during the twelve centuries of its existence
in England. No schools have been established, few traditions have
long endured; from time to time individuals, it is true, have written
a "life" or two and so evolved a canon — which must be thought of
as such only in the loosest sense — but that is all.

Perhaps some explanation lies in the fact that since the lives of
human beings are so infinitely varied, having little except the fact
of existence and their essential humanity in common, no rules or
conventions beyond those implied in simple truth are possible; and
simple truth stands at the very apex of art. Truth in the lyric, the
drama, the essay, and the novel is not unattainable by genius, inherent as it is in depiction of the ideal, where "beauty is truth, truth
beauty." But truth in biography has too often eluded even genius,
for in substance it is restricted to the concrete in the affairs of
human beings, and in treatment, therefore, it avoids the commonplace only at some peril; the least suggestion of idealization, for one

thing, being alien to its spirit. The contrast, therefore, with imaginative writing and the possibilities involved in it, is obvious. Whatever the explanation, however, the condition obtains — among the thousands who have written biographies, the works of fewer than a hundred are worthy consideration as literature.

In any such list one must include Thomas Fuller, in Pepys' phrase, "the great Tom Fuller," by reason of his "The Holy State and the Profane State," published in 1642; and "The History of the Worthies of England," issued posthumously in 1662. The first treats of virtue and vice in the abstract and of the effects of action and accomplishment on the part of the persons delineated, rather than of action and accomplishment in themselves. Although it is usually called a "character book," it is, in the opinion of Professor Walter E. Houghton, Jr., as expressed in his recent and authoritative study, "The Formation of Thomas Fuller's Holy and Profane States," an "estate book." The second is, of course, well known among the earlier biographical dictionaries. Both, however, stand as representatives of their respective categories in giving pleasure as literature and providing knowledge of fact.

On the religious side, it must be noted that Fuller is bitterly antagonistic to the ancient Faith of his fathers and to its teachings. But this attitude, naturally, did not militate against his popularity in the England of his day.

Fuller completed "The Holy and Profane States" in May, 1641 — although his publisher, John Williams, withheld it for a year in order not to disrupt the work of his shop in issuing the highly profitable pamphlets which the turbulent times demanded — hence it was written during a period when the forms and attitudes upon which it draws were becoming well defined. The essay, especially the "character," the biographical sketch, "estate" books, courtesy books, and works of moral economics were being widely read in accordance with the deepening interest in matters of both private and public conduct so characteristic of the changing world of the seventeenth century. The direct emergence of "The States," however, would seem to have been from the "character," and from the biographical sketch.

The first of these two — the "character" — stands forth as among the favorite literary forms of the day. Taking their cue from the Casaubon translation of Theophrastus, their classical prototype — and possibly, as has been suggested, from King James's interest in the form — a school of writers arose. Among them were Joseph Hall, Bishop of Exeter and Norwich, an early satirist, and Fuller's good friend; Sir Thomas Overbury, a courtier, whose purpose, incidentally, was to amuse rather than edify; and John Earle, who succeeded Fuller's uncle, John Davenant, some twenty years after his death as Bishop of Salisbury. These men were pioneers in the form and have remained its most notable exponents. Throughout the century, however, "character" writers flourished. Edition after edition of their works were in such demand that the "character" was in its way almost as important as earlier the sonnet had been or as later the periodical essay was to become.

The "character" was a short prose composition which dealt with some vice or virtue in the guise of a type personality, like a busybody, a hypocrite, a good wife, or an atheist. In time inanimate objects, callings, and institutions came in for treatment, the "character" itself, for instance, being "wit's descant upon any plain song," as Overbury put it. Coffee houses and even the jail were thus featured. By the end of the century, however, it was losing much of its original force through exploitation for political advantage by such men, for instance, as Butler, Clarendon, and Burnet. Moreover, by the beginning of the eighteenth century it was being absorbed by the periodical essay and by the novel, so that finally it ceased to exist save for an occasional adoption by way of echo from the past. Professor Grierson sums up the form by terming it a kind of "prose literature which touches the sermon literature of the seventeenth century on the one hand and its comedy on the other." And Professor Maximilian G. Walten, in the introduction to his edition of "The Holy State and the Profane State," wrote,

> The well-established style in which the authors [of "characters"] generally wrote was naturally enough that combination of euphuistic and theological wit which makes their work so closely analogous to the so-called metaphysical poetry of the period.

Linked loosely with the "character," in the ethical trend that composed the background of Fuller's work, is the biographical sketch. It is rooted in the tradition of hagiography but it partakes also of the nature of chronicle history, and is to be discovered as the form in which some of the "lives" of princes as well as of some of the saints were cast. Concise, dramatic, replete with anecdote and "wise saws," its concern, which at first was with the ways of right living, broadened late in the renaissance to include examples of the mutability of earthly fortune and so took on worldly as well as spiritual significance. Izaac Walton used it to memorialize five men whom he greatly admired and to point up their virtues. Fuller chose it as a means of rendering specifically the qualities which he believed made for virtue or vice. Samuel Johnson adapted it to his purposes in the "Lives of the Poets." And after helping to shape the practices of Southey, Macaulay, and Walter Bagehot, it comes on to us in the writings of Lytton Strachey and of Gamaliel Bradford, purporting to be a penetrating comment upon men as personalities rather than, as in the beginning, a didactic extolling of virtue or a castigation of vice.

The forms at hand, Fuller simply combined them in composing "The States," a book intended as a guide to virtue in both public and private affairs. Among the wittiest and ablest of mid-century Anglican clerics, he reaped popular success in a manner almost unique. Hundreds of books similarly motivated issued from the presses, works shallow and works profound, entertaining and dull, inspiring and depressing, most of which have long since been forgotten. Fuller's work, however, remains as fresh as it was three hundred years ago; and the reason is, as it must always be, the man.

A sentence from his own "Worthies" might stand as a theme for any characterization of him:

> An ounce of mirth, with the same degree of grace, will serve God farther than an ounce of sadness.

Fuller was a Cambridge contemporary of Edmund Waller, Jeremy Taylor, John Milton, and George Herbert; his education was provided by his uncle, John Davenant, master of Queen's College and later Bishop of Salisbury; and he began his career at St. Bennet's in 1630, where, incidentally, he buried Milton's famous carrier, Hobson, dead of the plague. A year later he became prebend at Netherbury-in-Ecclesia, and in 1634 was made rector of Broadwindsor in Dorsetshire. Having retained legal residence in Cambridge, he finally received the B.D. degree in 1634. He obtained the D.D., however, not until twenty-five years later. Settling down at Broadwindsor, he devoted himself to the care of his parish, to antiquarian pursuits, and to writing. By 1638 he began to tire of country life and to look toward London as a more likely field for the exercise of his talents. His marriage to a girl named Ellen, whose surname has been lost; the disturbed state of the nation; but chiefly perhaps the success of his first effort in prose (an earlier attempt in verse came to naught), "The Holy War," published in 1639, provided the urge that made London inevitable.

And so to London he went at the age of thirty — full bodied, with a pretty wit, and a zest to succeed. Of his being a party to the Canterbury Convocation; of his volume of sermons, "Joseph's Parti-Colored Coat," published in 1640; and of his opinion of the Puritans and the Laudian position it is sufficient merely to make mention in passing. For a time he remained secure at the Savoy Chapel, preaching with such success that a contemporary was moved to write:

> He gave such general satisfaction, became so famous, and was thronged with such distant congregations, that those of his own cure were in a manner excommunicated from their own church, unless their timeous diligence kept pace with their devotions. He had in his narrow chapel two audiences, one without the pale, and another within; the windows of that little church and the sextonry were so crowded that it seemed bees had swarmed to his mellifluous discourse.

But events soon took such turns that in 1643 he fled with the Royalists to Oxford. The next few years proved somewhat sterile; he himself had this to say concerning them:

> For the first five years during our actual civil wars, I had little list or leisure to write, fearing to be made an history, and shifting daily for my safety. All that time I could not live to study who did only study to live.

None the less he persevered in his ambition to write, collecting information, anecdotes, epigrams, and figures of speech, and noting down anything that might later be used in the historical and religious works he contemplated. The position of a Royalist clergyman was, of course, precarious. Fuller, however, by force of personality and of his clearly evident loyalty, managed to triumph over his situation. He was made chaplain in Hopton's army and titular chaplain to the infant and ill-fated princess, Henrietta Anne, born at Exeter in 1644, and although compelled to remain away from his home and his own church, he found many ways of making friends, of writing occasionally, and of preaching whenever an opportunity arose. By 1646 he was again in London comfortably installed in lodgings — no doubt provided by the accrued profits of "The Holy War" and "The States."

After 1650 he was well on the way to eminence. His writings, the "Pisgah-Sight of Palestine," his sermons, and especially the "Church History of Britain," in addition to the works previously published were highly successful; these, together with his lectures, were also making him famous. His home at Waltham, where he was pastor to the Earls of Carlisle and of Middlesex, in addition to being court chaplain; and his wife and children — he had married the sister of Viscount Baltinglasse in 1652, his first wife having died in 1641 — all these were making him happy. Such were his gifts and such the use he made of them that, it has been thought, had he not died at the early age of fifty-four, he might have expected the miter. From a literary point of view, however, it was enough for the perpetuation of his name to have written "The Holy State and the Profane State" and "The History of the Worthies of England."

They are what they are because he was what he was. To repeat: it is not always sufficient to say "style is the man" — often a book that approaches the unique in conception defines the man much more nearly. To be sure, his was no spectacular career, even though he lived in a spectacular age. He was a churchman, much in demand, it is true; a scholar of vast learning, of wide taste and endowed with a prodigious memory; and a man of such engaging manners that he was welcome in any company. Possessed of common sense unusual in a student and with powers of observation in extraordinary degree, he was, besides, moderate in his views, sincerely sympathetic in his understanding of people where Catholicism did not enter, and in other ways more tolerant than many of his contemporaries – although like Sir Thomas Browne he did believe in witchcraft. He says somewhere in the "Worthies" that he wrote, among other reasons, chiefly moral, "to entertain the reader with delight, and to make some honest profit to myself." Nevertheless in all his works his stress is ethical – at no cost to entertainment.

A glance at the contents of "The States" is immediately revelatory. "Characters" from that of "The Good Child," through "Of Anger," "The True Gentleman," "Of Books," and a whole gamut of traits and qualities, on to "lives," including "Monica," "Haman," "Paracelsus," and "Lord Burleigh" – to select a number at random which serve as illustrations of the traits and qualities defined – comprise the work. Only slight threads bind the matter together, although the "estates" of the family, the commons, and rulers are all apparent. Book I characterizes home life and family relationships and includes "lives" of Abraham, Paula, Eliezer, and Hildegardis as well as of Monica. Book II comments upon professional and occupational activity and points to Dr. Whitaker, Julius Scaliger, Francis Drake, and Mr. Cambden, among others, as examples. Book III is concerned wholly with attitudes; Book IV with officialdom; and Book V with things of the spirit. In all there are seventy-two "characters" and thirty sketches, with two historical pieces of little biographical interest, arranged according to no apparent pattern, sometimes as many as five "characters" appearing in sequence and as many as three biographical sketches one after another; Book III alone is made up entirely of "characters."

One speaks of these pieces as "characters" although they are not properly so called. The genre as practiced by Theophrastus and carried on in England by Hall, Overbury, and Earle, and their followers emphasized human nature as addicted to vice or confirmed in virtue by means of characterizing speech, act, and thought for the simple purpose of pointing out and defining vicious or virtuous traits as such, with the hope, no doubt, of uprooting the one and upholding the other. Hence, their influence was exerted chiefly in spiritual matters. Fuller, however, was more nearly occupied with temporal affairs. The "character" inclined toward the indicative;

Fuller's work bore toward the admonitory. This difference a comparison between his "The Good Child" and Earle's "A Child," for instance, makes clear. It is this difference in purpose that causes one to think Fuller's work less philosophical in being more political, and, hence, as an "estate" rather than a "character" book. At all events, such is Professor Houghton's category for it; and his opinion is amply evidenced.

In the beginning "estate" books sprang from a requirement of feudalism (although one can go back to the maxims of the Egyptian Ptahhotep, 2000 B.C., for comment upon conduct right and wrong), their office being that of safeguarding the social hierarchy; helping, that is, to sustain the nobility, the clergy, and the commons in the spheres of their respective privileges and responsibilities. This type, which includes also courtesy books and various kinds of writings in treatment of conduct and government, germinated in Aristotle's "Magnanimous Man," was engrafted with Senecan Stoicism, and finally enriched by Christian ethics to assume the proportions of a philosophy bordering upon the ritualistic. Besides works in prose, much early poetry commented upon the habits, personal and official, of noble and cleric, magistrate and merchant, ploughman, mechanic, and clerk in order to isolate evil and so lessen its effect upon the body politic. As the transition to the sixteenth century and its disruptions progressed, "estate" books multiplied to such extent that from 1500 to 1600 more were printed than had appeared during the previous two hundred years — with disruption the need to combat forces inimical to the *status quo* had increased in startling degree. Naturally, therefore, when in his own day Fuller saw the threat to the society which he knew and wished maintained, he turned to the medium best suited to his gifts for the purpose of upholding the cause of order socially, functionally, and ethically — as tallied with his point of view. If he and those of his contemporaries who were like minded failed to stem the tide of disillusionment, he at least wrote a book which succeeding centuries have preserved, largely because it is the record of a personality and the relic of an entertaining man.

For no matter how admonitory or how didactic his purpose, Fuller never lost sight of the fact that he must temper philosophy with wit. Possessed of profound knowledge of human nature and vividly aware of the predilections of his day, he chose such traits as he knew could be effectively brought home to his readers and such lives as he knew would be best illustrative. Setting these forth in a way that suggests high pleasure on his own part, he seldom fails to transmit it to us. It mattered little to him that in adapting a "life" to a trait defined he at times bends fact to art, or in following his gleam as a clergyman he could "speak no evil of the good and no good of the evil" without seeming to contradict "the decision of the Almighty." Moreover, it mattered no more to him that although he made use of documents and cited sources, his text and the originals did not always agree; or that he could seldom resist the impulse to spin out a sentence for the sake of a jest. Yet, as was to be expected, the world was entertained by him, of whom Charles Lamb could say:

> Such was [Fuller's] natural bias to conceits, that I doubt not upon most occasions it would have been going out of his way to have expressed himself out of them. But his wit is not always a *lumen siccum,* a dry faculty of surprising; on the contrary, his conceits are oftentimes deeply steeped in human feeling and passion;

and of whom Coleridge, in somewhat headlong fashion, to be sure, remarked:

> I am not certain whether Thomas Fuller, beyond all other writers (except Shakespeare) does not excite in me the sense and emotion of the marvelous.

When at last he came to make final preparation of his "Worthies" for the press — some parts of it had previously been printed — he was too late; he died before the task was completed. Completion was left for his son John, at the time a young clergyman at Cambridge. The book was published in 1662, and Samuel Pepys records on February 10 of that year that he examined it in a book shop at Paul's Churchyard,

> being much troubled that (though he had some discourse with me about my family and arms) he says nothing at all, nor

mentions us either in Cambridgeshire or Norfolk. But I believe, indeed, our family were never considerable, —

a comment which no doubt echoed the thoughts of many persons
who, like Pepys, may have hoped for inclusion in this first "Who's
Who."

The "Worthies," however, is something more than a biographical
dictionary. The matter is not confined to details about the lives of
persons: the design is more complex than that which subsequent
similar works have followed; and, of course, the colorful style is
quite at variance with the dry effectiveness of biographical lexicographers in general. A glance at John Fuller's dedication to the
king satisfies one as to material and purpose. He wrote:

> The matter of this work, for the most part, is the description
> of such natural and peculiar commodities as the several coun-
> ties of your kingdom afford, with a revival of the memories of
> such persons which have in each county been eminent for
> parts or learning. If this age abound with the like, it is their
> glory; if not, the perusal may perhaps beget in them a noble
> emulation of their ancestors.

The work is, as described, divided according to the counties of
England and Wales. Each section sets forth the chief products and
natural resources of the counties considered and then includes
sketches of "Worthies," arranged according to rank and profession,
native to or residing in the respective districts. Each section includes
also a table of the gentry concerned from the time of Henry VI,
and ends with a list of sheriffs, to the time of James I or Charles I,
together with their arms and a notation of their homes. To the
whole is prefixed an introduction which defines the plan, the
material, the order, and the style. Even in his introduction, however,
Fuller characterized himself, bearing out the idea that some commentator has expressed, "One cannot read a single page of Fuller
without a smile, or three pages running without laughter." He went
to some lengths to show how methodical he had been, answered
criticism before it could be offered, and apologized for errors of
which he was certain he had been guilty. A quotation or two will
illustrate:

*Exception* 1. — You usurp the style of princes, speaking often in the plural: "come we now;" "pass we now;" "proceed we now;" which is false grammar from a *single*, ill ethics from a *private*, person.

*Answer* First, I appeal to any exercised in reading books, whether the same be not used in other authors. Secondly, *we* in such cases includeth the writer and reader; it being presumed that the eye of the one goeth along with the pen of the other.

Thirdly, it also compriseth all other writers out of whom anything is transcribed, and their names quoted in the margin.

Let me add, to God's glory, my friends' credit, and my own comfort, that *we* is comprehensive of all my worthy friends, who, by their pains or purses, have been contributive to my weak endeavors.

*Exception* 4. — You only report the virtues, but conceal the faults of many persons within our own memories.

*Answer.* — I consider myself to do so, by the rules of charity. When an orator was to praise a person deceased, generally and justly hated for his viciousness, it was suspected that he would for a fee force his conscience by flattery to commend him, whose expectations he thus defeated. "This dead person," saith he, "must in one respect be spoken well of by all, because God made him; and in another respect should not be spoken ill of by any, because he is dead; *et de mortuis nil nisi bonum.*" How much more, when men have many good virtues, with some faults, ought the latter to be buried in their graves with forgetfulness!

And the same qualities pervade the text. Although Fuller's concern was with highly distinguished persons, he did not cavil over his word "Worthies." Sergeants-of-the-law appear; bishops, and archbishops, generals, lord mayors, masters of colleges, writers, and statesmen are given adequate space. Whenever possible, stories of poor boys who became famous are highly stressed. Likewise physical endowment is not neglected; unusual fertility is made much of, and great physical strength is paid due respect. Throughout one finds, in addition to fact, details and references which sometimes approach the fantastic and yet sometimes reveal profoundest insight.

His saying, for instance, that in one place strawberries grew in such profusion that riders could pick them from the saddle lies in one direction; his quoting a palpable lie with the aside that "no doubt the first founder of so damnable an untruth hath long since received his reward" lies in quite another. Legends appear and doubtful stories about the great: Raleigh and his cloak, even King Arthur and the Round Table, for instance, although an accompanying caution reveals his attitude toward this last — "the tale whereof hath trundled smoothly along for many ages; it never met with much belief among the judicious." In short, "The History of the Worthies of England: Endeavored by Thomas Fuller, D.D.," is as nearly an example of biographical writing which gives knowledge of fact together with the pleasure of literature as one can very well find. Fuller was a wit, but he was likewise a man of sense —

> While airy sounds soon lose their empty name,
> Surviving record is substantial fame.

# 8—Margaret Newcastle and Her "Life" of the Duke

> *Love is a great Thing; yea, a great and thorough Good; by Itself It makes everything that is heavy light; and it bears evenly all that is uneven.* — Baxter.

ALTHOUGH the subject of a biography almost always overshadows the author in point of interest, it does not invariably do so. At times the author is the only reason for the book's continued existence. For instance, Boswell, Trevelyan, and Lockhart, distinguished though we hold them, are obscurities in the presence of Johnson, Macaulay, and Scott. On the contrary, Richard Savage and John Sterling would long since have been forgotten had not Johnson and Carlyle insured them against oblivion by virtue of their own great fame.

But neither of these categories is quite suited to include a third species, examples of which, in fact, are so variable that each requires, one is tempted to say, a category of its own. There are not many, not more than a score perhaps in comparative biography, and they have appeared at widely differing times. Their only point in common is that each is its own excuse for being; their subjects, in comparison with the undying great, are of little fame, and their authors are not writers of particular distinction. Some extraordinary combination of time, personality, and circumstance occurred and a biography resulted without which the form would have been by much the poorer.

Among the earliest of these and perhaps the best known is "The

Life of the Thrice Noble, High, and Puissant Prince, William Cavendish, Duke, Marquis, and Earl of Newcastle; Written by the Thrice Noble, Illustrious, and Excellent Princess, Margaret, Duchess of Newcastle, His 2nd Wife." The book was published in London in 1667, during the lifetime of both subject and author.

Margaret Newcastle's book was reprinted in both English and Latin during her own life. And it has since been the subject of scholarly attention by men like Sir Charles Firth and Dr. Henry Ten Eyck Perry, is a matter of frequent reference by critics and students of literature, and has been the theme of lively essays by both Charles Whibley and Virginia Woolf. Finally, the work itself is a not unpopular item in the Everyman Series. Not many commentators, however, have attempted to account for its survival; for the most part they are content to wonder at it. No less an enthusiast than Charles Lamb, none the less, saw fit to remark upon it in this fashion in his "Detached Thoughts on Books and Reading":

> But where a book is at once both good and rare — where the individual is almost the species, and when that perishes;
>
> We know not where is that Promethean touch
> That can its light relumine —
>
> such a book, for instance, as the "Life of the Duke of Newcastle" by his Duchess — no casket is rich enough, no casing sufficiently durable to honour and keep safe such a jewel.

It does not lend itself easily to analysis. It is not authentic as history. It is not particularly valuable as social comment. It is, however, a fascinating book because it is an attempt on the part of one of the most astonishing women of her century to insure posterity's appreciation of her husband — and so perhaps obtain some part of that appreciation for herself. From one point of view it is a "life" of one of England's most unsuccessful soldiers — Newcastle commanded the Royalist forces against Cromwell in the North, went into exile after the defeat at Marston Moor. And it is written by one of England's least known writers, for though the Duchess published sixteen books in fifteen years, only "The Life of the Duke of Newcastle" is significant. In that it is the realization of a character and the revelation of a personality, it deserves high place in memory.

It fits into none of the usual categories; its uniqueness is its chief characteristic. The structure is unlike that of any comparable work. The purpose and the point of view although both are obvious and frequently appear (an adoring soul burning the incense of commemoration is all too common among biographers), are in this instance entirely uncommon.

The volume opens conventionally enough with a dedication to the king; but quite unconventionally it carries a second dedication — *to the subject himself.* Next appears a preface, which sets forth what the author thinks biography should be. Follows an epistle by John Rollestone, secretary to the duke, concerning his opinion of his master, with some remarks upon his affairs. At this point, "The First Book" begins. It is devoted almost entirely to an account of Newcastle's military career. "The Second Book" describes the long exile. Opening "The Third Book" the duchess wrote, "I shall now conclude with some particular heads concerning . . . his own person . . . humour, disposition, qualities, virtues, his pedigree, habit, diet, exercises, etc." None the less she goes on to include "The Fourth Book," which contains "several essays and discources gathered from the mouth of my Noble Lord and husband, with some few notes of mine own." At first thought the arrangement of the material seems a hodge-podge, and yet upon review one sees the order that controls the whole. The subject is introduced more or less abruptly as engaged upon the great enterprise of his life. Gradually the incidents and details draw closer to the personality of the man. And in the end appears a record of his mind at work. The whole is a not illogical process, from the effect of the man upon his surroundings and of his surroundings upon him, to the causes which shaped these effects, and as such it is different from almost every other example in the form.

Scores of biographers have written commemorative works, but not one of them seems to have had quite the point of view or the purpose of the Duchess of Newcastle. It is not unusual for a relative of a distinguished person to turn biographer. But almost never has the subject been a blood relative when the work itself attained distinction — Trevelyan is the exception outstanding and Hallam Tennyson and Dr. Christopher Wordsworth are the most pointed demonstrations. Seldom, however, has even a spouse been so completely convinced of a subject's perfection. Lucy Hutchinson, for instance, George Herbert Palmer, and Mrs. Kingsley, intimately revealing though their writings are, were restrained to a degree which the duchess could not have understood. There is scarcely a sentence that does not exhibit her feeling that Newcastle was a paragon. And there can be small doubt of her sincerity.

She married him during the period of exile, having accompanied Henrietta Maria to France. Shy in manner, and entirely alien in spirit to the court at St. Germain — having never before been separated from her mother and her lively brothers and sisters, or been accustomed to any but the company of intimates — she provoked both the sneers and the laughter of courtiers because of her thoughtful, retiring ways; hence they were all amazed when her betrothal to so glittering a personage as Newcastle was announced. She herself, it seems, was hesitant, writing much later:

> He did approve of my bashful fears which many condemned, . . . and though I did dread marriage and shunned men's company as much as I could, yet I . . . had not the power to refuse him.

The Duke who possessed an estate valued in excess of two million pounds and who ranked among the English princes — although his title was new (he being grandnephew to George Cavendish) — was content to wed the obscure Margaret Lucas in a private chapel in Paris, which belonged to his friend Sir Richard Brown, Charles I's ambassador to France.

If, however, the point of view is unique only in degree, the purpose is unique in point of fact. It would be difficult to find any other work which shows so clearly the author's bid for fame. Boswell was convinced, as his preface indicates, that his name would live as long as Johnson was remembered; but Margaret Newcastle set about deliberately to share her husband's renown, acknowledging, in fact, in her Memoir, "All I desire is fame." That she loved him this side idolatry every sentence of her book bears witness. Only, she loved herself in almost equal measure. She wrote to enshrine her subject in the memory of posterity — but she was well aware that if she succeeded her name would share the fame with his. The sequel, however, is beyond anything she may have hoped; we remember the Duke of Newcastle after three hundred years, it is true, but we do so because his wife wrote his "life." In an effort to achieve fame she wrote of a man whose memory, she thought, would live forever; but in doing so she has come to be remembered for herself.

Her book by indirection is almost as clearly revealing of herself as by direction it discloses her conception of the duke; but then all biographic writing is more or less autobiographical. A pattern of conventional conduct, one of the best ceremonialists England ever bred, is presented as a master of men by one whom Charles Lamb characterizes in "Mackery End" as "The thrice noble, chaste and virtuous — but again somewhat fantastical and original-brained, generous Margaret Newcastle." But we need not go to Lamb for an impression. She herself provides all the necessary materials, for no matter what she wrote she achieved autobiography. Poetry, drama, letters, philosophy, history — it is all self-revealing. And not content with "indirection that finds direction out" she wrote a "Memoir" of herself, in which the following passage occurs:

> I think it no crime to wish myself the exactest of nature's works, my thread of life the longest, my chain of destiny the strongest, my mind the peaceablest; my life the pleasantest, my death the easiest, and myself the greatest saint in heaven. Also to my endeavor, so far as honour and honesty doth allow of, to be the highest on Fortune's wheel, and to hold the wheel from turning if I can; and if it be commendable to wish another's good, it were a sin not to wish my own; for as envie is a vice, so emulation is a virtue, but emulation is in the way to ambition, or indeed it is a noble ambition. But I fear my ambition inclines to vain-glory, for I am very ambitious; yet 'tis neither for beauty, wit, titles, wealth, or power, but as they are steps to raise me to fame's tower, which is to live by remembrance in after-ages.

But for her to have entertained wishes such as these is not to be wondered at. The seventeenth century was rich in "original-brained" women: Margaret Baxter, Katherine Fowler, Lady Letice Morrison,

Lucy Hutchison, Lady Mary Warwick, Anne Halket, Maragaret Godolphin, Aphra Behn, Lady Anne Fanshawe, to point out a few at random; but it is doubtful if any woman of the period was more brilliantly endowed — and at the same time more splendidly spoiled — than Margaret Newcastle, *nee* Lucas.

She was born, it is conjectured, in 1623, at St. John's near Colchester, the daughter of Sir Thomas Lucas, gentleman, "which title," she wrote, "is granted by merit, not by princes." Her mother she describes in a characteristic passage:

> She was of a grave behavior, and had such a majestic grandure, as it were, continually hung about her, that it would strike a kind of awe to the beholders, and command respect from the rudest; . . . also her beauty was beyond the ruin of time, for she had a well-favoured loveliness in her face, a pleasing sweetness in her countenance, and a well-tempered complexion, . . . even to her dying hour, although in years, and by her dying, one might think death was enamoured with her, for he embraced her in a sleep, and so gently, as if he were afraid to hurt her.

And about her three brothers and four sisters she has equally flattering things to say.

Of her rearing, again her comments show the same trend. She was bred "virtuously, modestly, civilly, and on honest principles." "As for plenty," she wrote, "we had not only for necessity, convenience, and decency, but for delight and pleasure to a superfluity." She was indulged in finery from the beginning. "As for garments," a passage records, "my mother did not only delight to see us neat and cleanly, fine and gay, but rich and costly"; and "I always took delight in singularity, even in accoutrements of habits." Serving men were never permitted to enter the nursery, "lest in their rude love-making they might do unseemly actions, or speak unhandsome words in the presence of the children." The education of the children was haphazard, it seems or at least not taken seriously, for concerning it she wrote:

> As for tutors, although we had all sorts of vertues, as singing, dancing, playing on musick, reading, writing, working,

and the like, yet we were not kept strictly thereto; they were rather for formality than benefit.

In a later passage, however, she particularizes somewhat her own study:

> As for my study of books it was very little, yet I chose rather to read than to employ my time in any other work, or practice, and when I read what I understood not, I would ask my brother, the Lord Lucas, he being learned, the sense or meaning thereof; but my serious study could not be much, by reason I took great delight in attiring, fine dressing, and fashions.

Her comments are always in the same vein, whether she speaks of herself or her relatives. Everything that touched her life, in her own eyes, was elegant, costly, graceful, comely; and every one she knew was heroic, learned, beautiful, and good.

And her "Life" of the duke is of a piece with her Memoir. Throughout there is reiterated insistence upon the truth of what she says and a disdain for the opinions of society concerning herself or her affairs. In the beginning, for instance, embedded in the dedication to the king, the insistence commences:

> I have . . . taken the boldness . . . to dedicate to your Majesty this short history (which is as full of truths, as words) of the actions and sufferings of . . . My Lord and husband.

And the preface repeats the claim:

> When I first intended to write this History, knowing myself to be no scholar, . . . I desired My Lord, that he would be pleased to let me have some elegant and learned historian to assist me; which request his Grace would not grant me. . . . I humbly answered, that without a learned assistant, the History would be defective: But he replied, that truth could not be defective. I said again, that rhetorick did adorn truth: and he answered that rhetorick was better for falsehoods than for truths.

"The First Book" contributes further:

> Since my chief intent in this present work, is to describe the life and actions of My Noble Lord and Husband . . . I shall

do it with as much brevity, perspicuity, and truth, as is required of an impartial historian.

And again she insists. Commenting upon the critics of historians who say "that those who write histories of themselves and their actions, or of their own part . . . are partial," she says:

> It is very improbable, worthy persons, who having done great, noble, and heroic exploits, deserving to be recorded, should be so vain, as to write false histories. But if they do, it proves their folly; for truth can never be concealed. . . . I fear not any such blemishes in this present History, for I am not conscious of any crime or partiality or falsehood, but write it whilest my Noble Lord is yet alive, and at such a time when truth may be declared and falsehood contradicted; and I challenge anyone (although I be a woman) to contradict anything that I have set down, or prove it to be otherwise than the truth; for be there never so many contradictions, truth will conquer all at last.

However, although she thus maintains the truth of her history, she would have us think her careless of adverse opinion. "Indeed," she writes in the dedication to the duke:

> I matter not the censures of the age, but am rather proud of them; for it shows that my actions are more than ordinary; and according to the old proverb, *It is better to be envied, than pitied*: for I know well, that it is merely out of spite and malice, whereof this present age is so full, that none can escape them, and they'll make no doubt to stain even your Lordship's loyal, noble, and heroic actions, as well as they do mine, though yours have been of war and fighting, mine of contemplating and writing.

Her confidence in herself and in the worth of what she is undertaking established, she proceeds to portray Newcastle as a Paladin, an Adonis, and a Jove; or in her own words, she says that he had "the valour of a Caesar, the fancy and wit of Ovid, and the tragical, especially the comical art of Shakespeare." That history remembers him otherwise detracts not at all from her effect. Newcastle was, unquestionably, a personality; only, the duchess was too eager to attribute to him perfection. A great soldier, a loyal subject, an ideal lover, and a great poet — all these he seemed to her.

For instance, he was so skillful in the training of horses, that a group of Spanish visitors, upon seeing some of his mounts put through their curvets and voltoes during a display, blessed themselves and shouted, "Miraculo." He put the results of his experience in training horses into a huge folio called "New Method to Dress Horses," which contained almost a hundred portraits, and had it published at Antwerp at a cost of thirteen hundred pounds. Furthermore, he presented Charles with a treatise upon government, which had engaged much of his leisure. Dryden based "Sir Martin Mar-all" upon his translation of Moliere's "L'Etourdi"; Shadwell used his "The Triumphant Widow or a Medley of Humours" as the basis for "Bury Fair"; although some critics have thought that the playwright was merely reclaiming his own; and his play "The County Captain," which was acted with applause in 1649, survived, despite Pepys' sneer, until 1661 but perhaps not a little of its virtue was due to the pen of James Shirley. Hence, he is not undeserving of respect in literary affairs. However, he was not "the best lyric and dramatic poet of his age," as the duchess would have us believe; and it is doubtful if one can relish the little poem she wrote about his gifts, except as a token of her affection:

> A poet I am neither born nor bred,
> But to a witty poet marrièd,
> Whose brain is fresh and pleasant as the Spring.
> Where fancies grow, and where the Muses Sing:
> There oft I lean my head, and listening hark,
> T'observe his words, and all his fancies mark;
> And from that garden flowers of fancy take,
> Whereof a posy up in verse I make:
> Thus I that have no garden of my own
> There gather flowers that are newly blown.

Her descriptions of military matters are no less enthusiastic. Concerning the final encounter, at Marston Moor, she writes:

> My Lord . . . hastening to see in what posture his own regiment was, met with a troop of gentlemen-voluntiers, who formerly had chosen him their captain, notwithstanding he

was general of an army; to whom My Lord spake: "Gentlemen, You have done me the honour to chuse me your captain, and now is the fittest time that I may do you service; whereof if you'll follow me, I shall lead you on the best I can, and shew you the way to your own honour." They being glad of my Lord's proffer, as My Lord was of their readiness, went on with the greatest courage; and passing through two bodies of foot, engaged with each other not at forty yards distance, received not the least hurt, although they fired quick upon each other; but marched towards a Scots regiment of foot, which they charged and routed; in which encounter My Lord himself killed three with his page's half-leaded sword, for he had no other left him; and though all the gentlemen in particular offered him their swords, yet My Lord refused to take a sword of any of them. At last, after they had passed through this regiment of foot, a pike man made a stand to the whole troop and though My Lord charged him twice or thrice, yet he could not enter him; but the troop dispatched him soon.

In all these encounters My Lord got not the least hurt, though several were slain about him; and here I cannot but mention by the way, that it is remarkable, that in all the actions and undertakings where My Lord was in person himself, he was always victorious, and prospered in the execution of his designs; but whatsoever was lost or succeeded ill, happened in his absence, and was caused either by treachery, or negligence and carelessness of his officers.

The fact that Newcastle gave up a career of pleasure to devote his services and resources to the king's cause testifies to his character — but his willingness to serve was not all he needed. One wonders if the Cavaliers could not have chosen a more suitable commander for their northern campaign. He was a fine gentleman, accomplished in all the arts of the court, and vastly rich; but he had no genius in things military. Clarendon defends him somewhat ironically against the charge of deserting the cause as soon as it seemed lost and escaping to Holland. He says:

All that can be said for the Marquis is that he was utterly tired with a condition and employment so contrary to his humour, nature, and education. He was a very fine gentleman, active and full of courage, and most accomplished in those qualities of horsemanship, dancing, and fencing, which accompany good breeding — in which his delight was. Besides that he was amorous in poetry and music, to which he indulged the greatest part of his time.

Farther on Clarendon comments upon him more particularly as a soldier:

> He liked the pomp and absolute authority of a general well, and preserved the dignity of it to the full; and for the discharge of the outward state of it and the circumstance of it, in acts of courtesy, affability, bounty, and generosity he abounded; which in the infancy of the war became him, and made him for some time very acceptable to men of all conditions. But the substantial part of it, and fatigue of a general, he did not in any degree understand (being utterly unacquainted with war), nor could submit to.

He is not to be defended as a military leader, of course; but there is no denying his loyalty. He was among the first to offer his services to Charles and he made good his offer by huge contributions of money and men, raising a force of eight thousand troops which he equipped himself. And if ultimate defeat cost him his fortune and a long period of exile, the Restoration recompensed him very little. Charles II, in acknowledgment of what he had done, made him chief justice in Eyre Trent-North, raised his rank — upon solicitation — from that of marquis to that of duke and created him Earl of Ogle after having made him Knight of the Garter during his exile. Notwithstanding, his position at court never became equal to his not unjust expectations.

It may have been that the "fickle favor of earthly princes" was in expression, or it may have been that Charles did not like Newcastle personally, and personal liking went a long way at the Restoration court. He had been Charles's governor in the old days, and kings seldom forgive those once in authority over them, especially those who, as Newcastle once did to Charles, caution them against "becoming seared with majesty"; besides the king was deeply in debt to him. But then Charles did not like the duchess either. Or it may all have come about because of the rapidity with which the social face of England was changing, and the Duke and Duchess of Newcastle were simply outmoded. From another point of view, likewise, it would be hard to imagine them happy in a society dominated by La Belle Stewart and Lady Castlemaine, the duchess especially, when one remembers her saying, "I am chaste both by nature and education, in so much as I abhor an unchaste thought"; then, too, the duke was probably not comfortable at a court which would be slow to forget that much of its former ill fortune was attributable to his military ineptitude. Furthermore, he was unable to carry on financially in the manner of one who had once spent twenty thousand pounds for the king's entertainment, for Cromwell had not included Newcastle in his general pardon and so his property had been entirely sequestered — not to be restored until Charles arranged for its return in 1660. Exception can be made only for an occasional item which his brother, Sir Charles Cavendish, by hazardous residence — and the duchess herself by hazardous visit — in England had managed to save for him. In short, tired, deprived for the most part of the king's favor, and far reduced in circumstances, Newcastle and the ever faithful duchess retired to Welbeck, a favorite estate which he had moved heaven and earth to recover — the one which with Bolsover had been the scene of his sumptuous entertainments for Charles I, at two of which Ben Jonson had presented his masques, "Love's Welcome at Welbeck" in 1633, and again "Love's Welcome at Bolsover" in 1634. It was there he sought to find refuge from a world with which they were no longer in step. There, then, the duchess continued to compose her various books, and especially to write the curious letters about which Charles Lamb in "The Two Races of Men" burst forth:

> But what moved thee, wayward, spiteful K. to be so importunate to carry off with thee, in spite of tears and adjurations to thee to forbear, the letters of that princely woman, the thrice noble Margaret Newcastle? — knowing at the time . . . thou most assuredly would'st never turn over one leaf of the illustrious folio.

And the duke busied himself in restoring Welbeck to its former productivity, for during his absence a series of Cromwellian tenants had all but ruined it. He seems, however, not to have been depressed by his changed estate, if his wit — upon which the duchess dwells, not always perspicaciously — as displayed in the following be indicative:

> After my Lord's return . . . it chanced that the widow of Charles Lord Mansfield, My Lord's eldest Son . . . to whom he had left a jointure of two thousand pounds a year, died; . . . for whose death, though My Lord was heartily sorry, and would willingly have lost the said money, had it been able to save her life; yet discoursing one time merrily with his friends, was pleased to say, that though his earthly king and master seemed to have forgotten him, yet the King of Heaven had remembered him, for He had given him two thousand pounds a year.

But Welbeck did not occupy them during all the year. There were frequent trips to London. And while there the duchess devoted herself to dress, gaiety — and to philosophical enterprise. Some idea of what she wrote under the guise of philosophy may be drawn from one of her own comments upon her ways of thought:

> I have lived in the great world a great while, and have thought of what has been brought to me by the sense more than was put into me by learned discourse; for I do not love to be led by the nose, by authority and old authors; *ipse dixit* will not serve my turn.

But to come upon addresses made to her by Vice-Chancellors and Public Orators of the Universities about her wisdom is to be astounded — until one remembers the not infrequent rewards of flattery. This exclamation, for instance, on the part of Bishop Pearson may have benefited somebody:

> What shall we think of your Excellency, who are both a Minerva and an Athens in yourself, the Muses as well as an Helicon, Aristotle as well as his Lycaeum!

And this, from the Vice-Chancellor of Cambridge:

> Most excellent Princess, you have unspeakably obliged us all; but not in one respect alone, for wheresoever we find

ourselves nonplussed in our studies, we repair to you as our oracle; if we be to speak, you dictate to us; if we knock at Apollo's door, you alone open to us; if we compose a history, you are the remembrancer; if we be confused and puzzled among the philosophers, you disentangle us and assoil our difficulties.

But most curious, aside from certain items in the collection of adulatory comment which Newcastle made after her death, is the official acceptance of her gift of the "Life" to the University, a letter which includes the promise

to cease not to bestow ten thousand embraces upon every page of the book which hath so noble and immortal a subject as his grace the Duke of Newcastle.

Hobbes, long in the service of the Cavendish family as tutor, dedicated his "Treatise on Optics" to the duke and contributed a eulogy to one of the volumes presented to the duchess by her admirers in which he said that her writings had given him "more and truer ideas of virtue and honor than any book of morality he had ever read" — although he could never be persuaded to dine with his patrons. And no less a body than the Royal Society entertained her at Arundel House. She saw air weighed and two cold liquids made hot by being poured together.

Not everybody, however, accorded her such homage. There were those who thought little enough of her. Among them was the king, as has been said. Upon one occasion the Chevalier de Gramont, in explaining that certain misadventurers had caused him to be late in attendance, said:

To increase my ill-humor, I was stopped, as I was getting out of my chair, by the devil of a phantom in masquerade. However, I must tell that it was worth while to see her dress; for she must have had at least sixty ells of gauze and silver tissue about her, not to mention a sort of pyramid upon her head, adorned with a hundred thousand baubles.

"I bet," said the king, "that it was the Duchess of Newcastle."
Edmund Waller once said that he would give all his poems to have written her lines on a stag; but he added, in his usual caustic

vein, that he would willingly make any sacrifice to save the reputation of a lady who wrote so ill. At another time he wrote upon the flyleaf of his copy of her "Philosophical and Physical Opinions":

> New castles in the air this lady builds,
> While nonsense with philosophy she gilds.

Likewise, Mistress Evelyn could find nothing about her to admire, in spite of the relationship existing between Newcastle and the Evelyn family, Mistress Evelyn having been the daughter of the Sir Richard Brown whose private chapel in Paris had been the scene of the Newcastle wedding. At least one of her letters contains a passage disparaging enough:

> I was surprised to find so much extravagance and vanity in one person not confined within four walls. Her particular fantastical dress, not unbecoming a good shape, which she may truly boast of. Her face discovers the facility of her sex, in being yet persuaded it deserves the esteem years forbid, by the infinite care she takes to place her curls and patches. Her mien surpasses the imagination of the poets, or the descriptions of a romance heroines greatness; her gracious bows, seasonable nods, courteous stretching out of her hands, twinkling of her eyes, and various gestures of approbation, show what may be expected of her discourse, which is as airy, empty, whimsical, and rambling as her books, aiming at science, difficulties, high notions, terminating commonly in nonsense, oaths and obscenity.

And Sir Egerton Brydges, author of "Censura Literaria," bears out this last idea in a comment which characterizes her speech as filled with "expressions and images of extraordinary coarseness, flowing from a female of high rank brought up at court," comments which seem at variance with her reputation for chaste living in a corrupt age. Dorothy Osborne in one of her letters to Temple reveals her opinion thus:

> First let me ask you if you have seen a book of poems newly come out, made by my Lady Newcastle? For God's sake if you meet with it send it to me; they say it is ten times more extravagant than her dress. Sure, the poor woman is a little dis-

tracted, she could never be so ridiculous else as to venture at writing books and in verse too.

Somewhat later, moreover, she continued in similar vein:

> You need not send me my Lady Newcastle's book at all, for I have seen it, and am satisfied that there are many soberer people in Bedlam. I'll swear her friends are much to blame to let her go abroad.

It is left for Samuel Pepys, however, to sum up the adverse opinion of herself and the "Life" of her husband in an oft-quoted passage:

> "I have now read the ridiculous history of My Lord New-castle, wrote by his wife; which shows her to be a mad, conceited, ridiculous woman, and he an ass to suffer her to write what she writes to him and of him."

"Fantastical" no doubt she was; almost every one who mentions her uses the word sooner or later; and perhaps a little ridiculous, as Pepys insisted. There is no doubt that she lacked entirely any sense of humor, else she could never have written as she did. And there is likewise no doubt that the position in which she found herself, the daughter of a simple English gentleman raised to the rank of duchess and married to one of the most glittering personalities of the day — there is no doubt that her position softened the defects of the world about her, making her see everything as through a rose tinted veil. Nevertheless, she and her book have lived three hundred years.

# 9—Dryden and Plutarch

*Every intellectual product must be judged from
the point of view of the age and the people in
which it was produced.* — Pater.

*Now the writers of biographies are most suited
to my purpose, since they dwell on intentions
more than on incidents, more on that which proceeds from within than on that which happens
without. That is why, in all kinds, Plutarch is the
man for me.* — Montaigue.

THE Church, which was once the mother of poets no less
than of Saints," in Francis Thompson's phrase, could with
equal truth be called the mother of biographers, for, as has been
said, within the shadow of her altars were written the earliest "lives."
But something besides the chronicling of sanctity was necessary
before the form assumed the qualities which later characterized it.
In the "lives" of saints lies the germ, and in the "lives" of rulers is
to be found not a little of the sustaining force; contemplative
morality thus became animated by narrative action, and both commemoration and didacticism were adapted to things temporal as
well as to things spiritual. It was left to the preoccupation of the
sixteenth century with questions of conduct and government, however, to bring about the fusion. How best to avoid the pains of
hell and yet enjoy the pleasures of power attained the proportions
of an ideal, and biography emerged, together with the maxim, the
emblem, the apothegm, and treatises upon courtesy, policy, and
"estates" as something of a guide in such accomplishment. For

throughout the period of the Tudors men were concerned with problems of ordered life whether moral or political. Individual conduct in its guidance was referred to as *sapientia;* public action, as *prudentia,* and an ever-increasing body of writing attested the preoccupation with both — as has been pointed out in connection with Thomas Fuller. Not any of it would have come to be, however, without an accompanying interest in the affairs of antiquity. At first educated men relied upon the records as they found them in Greek and Latin, reading Plato, Aristotle, Cicero, Seneca, and Plutarch in the original. In time translations began to appear, not only of the more obvious philosophical and historical works but also of the more obscure, so that by the end of the sixteenth century a large body of classical writing was available in English. Heroditus, Thucydides, Livy, and Sallust had all appeared, along with Golding's "Caesar," Holland's "Suetonius," and Savile's "Agricola." Not all are equally well done, naturally, especially as some were not translated directly but at secondhand through the French.

Noteworthy among these last was Thomas North's rendering of "Plutarch" in 1579, based upon the French version by Jacques Amyot, Bishop of Auxerre, issued in 1565. Amyot, in turn, had been preceded by Ulrich Hahn in 1470, by Alexander Jaconello of Riete whose translation had appeared in 1482, and by Alfonso de Pallencis who completed his version in 1491. But neither the Latin, the Italian, nor the Spanish work attained the widespread influence of the French; Amyot had caught the spirit of the Greek original, but in addition he possessed a style (and that at the time when French was beginning to assume its dominant position as a world language) such that his genius became the means by which Plutarch's "Lives" was ultimately added to world literature. It was not free from errors, however, and North perpetuated these besides making not a few of his own. None the less his English rendering was widely read and became widely influential upon subsequent biographers, scarcely a man among them neglecting to profit by it, thus absorbing into English biography something of the art which Plutarch had bequeathed.

Influential though his work was and influential though North's translation was, no adequate version of Plutarch appeared until during the years 1683 to 1686 a composite translation was issued under the supervision of John Dryden — who himself provided a biographical introduction. The title was *"Plutarch's Lives,* Translated from the Greek by Several Hands. To which is Prefixed the *Life of Plutarch."* Among the "Several Hands" were Richard Duke and Knightly Chetwood, Fellows of Trinity College, Cambridge; Thomas Creech, Wadham College, Oxford; Edward Brown, M.D.; Dr. Adam Littelton, author of the Latin dictionary; John Caryl, one of Pope's friends; Joseph Arrowsmith; Thomas Rymer; Dr. William Oldys; John Evelyn; Lord Somers; and twenty-nine others. Jacob Tonson was the bookseller, and of course, Dryden was the moving spirit.

It was characteristic of Dryden that although he never failed to illuminate whatever he chose as a theme, he was, strangely enough, unable to create themes for himself, and, was required, because of this seeming blind spot, to rely upon the works of others. For instance, his greatest play was built upon Shakespeare's "Antony and Cleopatra"; and some of the finest writing he did is to be found in the "Fables," a collection of adaptations from Chaucer, Boccaccio, and Ovid. However, aware though the reader is of Dryden's indebtedness, he is no less aware of his consummate artistry. And what is true of the poetical works is true likewise of the translations, no doubt partly because of his ability to adapt; in fact, Dryden seems to have found in translation a most congenial medium, having in the progress of his career made some of the best in the language. It was almost inevitable, therefore, that when Tonson thought to issue "Plutarch's Lives" he should commission Dryden to oversee the work; and it was likewise almost inevitable that Dryden, accepting the commission, should write the biographical introduction; and in so doing he developed, in fewer than one hundred pages, a work vital to the advance of biography — although here, again, he was the adapter.

It is not to be thought that Dryden's "Life of Plutarch" is definitive as a "life" of the great biographer and moralist. He wrote it hurriedly after a rapid survey of the existing material, for the most part relying upon the memorial by Suidas, and upon the data and references accumulated by Rualdus in 1624. The work, as a result, is inaccurate and incomplete. It gives the impression, for instance, that Plutarch spent almost half his life in Rome — which is wholly wrong. It is insecure in the matter of dates and even in the number and names of his children, details which modern scholarship has now corrected. In representing the character and personality of its subject, however, it is as authentic as reasonable expectancy requires; and in setting forth Plutarch's philosophy, particularly his *daemonic* belief, it is the basis for most subsequent comment. And, after all, his philosophy is the key to an understanding of Plutarch, for he was primarily a moralist, not an historian. Personal character, action, and the motivation of action were to him far more important than battles, politics, or the fate of empires. In fact scattered throughout the "Lives" but particularly in the "Alexander" are to be found passages which reveal this emphasis unmistakably. "It must be borne in mind," he said on the first page of the "Alexander," for instance:

> that my design is not to write histories but *lives*. And the most glorious exploits do not always furnish us with the clearest discoveries of virtue or vice in men; sometimes a matter of less moment, an expression, or a jest, informs us better of their characters and inclinations, than the most famous sieges, the greatest armaments, or the bloodiest battles whatsoever. Therefore, as portrait painters are more exact in the lines and features of the face, in which the character is seen than in the other parts of the body, so I must be allowed to give my more particular attention to the marks and indications of the souls of men, and while I endeavor by these to portray their lives, I may be free to leave more weighty matters and great battles to be treated by others.

And as with Plutarch, so with Dryden, for he, too, was interested in the *being* rather than the *doing* as the basis of biographical treatment. The "Life" under his hand, therefore, although he undertakes to reveal Plutarch in three dimensions — and succeeds in proportion as his materials permit — becomes a vehicle for the communication of a theory of biography. And it is for his theory that he is to be remembered among the exponents of the form.

He begins by detailing the facts that were available to him, and in his clear, luminous style, guided as always by an impeccable taste, marshals his scant material into a surprisingly realistic character. There follows a comment upon the kinship between biography and history. And the work ends with a critique of Plutarch's writings. The whole is one of the earliest examples of critical biography — and one among the best.

As always, none the less, Dryden is the adapter. Bacon and Margaret Newcastle had both realized that intimate detail far outweighs public act as revelation of character, and there are not a few expressions of a similar point of view by lesser persons. Dryden, however, in his comment crystallizes the whole developing attitude and sets it forth with such clarity and authority that all future biographers profited to greater or less degree. His conception may be drawn from the following passage:

> Biographia, or the history of particular men's lives comes next to be considered; which in dignity is inferior to the other two, as being more confined in action, and treating of wars and counsels, and all other public affairs of nations, only as they relate to him whose life is written, or as his fortunes have a particular dependence on them, or connection to them. All things are here circumscribed, and driven to a point, so as to terminate in one; consequently, if the action or counsel were managed by colleagues, some part of it must be either lame or wanting, except it be supplied by the excursion of the writer. . . .
>
> Yet though we allow, for the reasons above alleged, that this kind of writing is inferior in dignity to History and Annals, in pleasure and instruction it equals, or even excels, both of them. It is not only commended by ancient practice to celebrate the memory of great and worthy men, as the best thanks posterity can pay them, but also the examples of virtue are of more vigor, when they are thus contracted into individuals. . . .
>
> Biographia, or the history of particular men's lives, though circumscribed in the subject, is yet more extensive in style than History or Moral Philosophy; for it not only comprehends them both, but has somewhat superadded, which neither of them have. The style of it varies, according to the occasion. There are proper places in it for the plainness and nakedness

of narration, which is ascribed to annals; there is also room reserved for the loftiness and gravity of general history, when the actions related shall require that manner of expression. But there is withal a descent into minute circumstances, and trivial passages of life, which are natural to this way of writing, and which the dignity of the other two will not admit. There you are conducted into the rooms of state, here you are led into the private lodgings of the hero; you see him in his undress, and are made familiar with his most private actions and conversation. You may behold a Scipio and a Laelius gathering cockleshells on the shore, Augustus playing at bounding stones with boys, and Agesilaus riding on a hobbyhorse among his children. The pageantry of life is taken away; you see the poor reasonable animal as naked as ever nature made him; are made acquainted with his passions and his follies, and find the demigod, a man. Plutarch himself has more than once defended this kind of revealing little passage; for, in the Life of Alexander, he says this: "In writing the lives of illustrious men, I am not tied to the laws of history; nor does it follow, that, because an action is great, it therefore manifests the greatness and virtue of him who did it; but, on the other side, sometimes a word, or a casual jest, betrays a man more to our knowledge of him, than a battle fought wherein ten thousand men were slain, or sacking of cities, or a course of victories."

In another place, he quotes Xenophon on the like occasion: "The sayings of great men in their familiar discourses, and amidst their wine, have somewhat in them which is worthy to be transmitted to posterity." An author therefore needs no excuse, but rather deserves a commendation, when he relates, as pleasant, some sayings of his heroes, which appear (I must confess it) very cold and insipid to us. For it is not his meaning to commend the jest, but to paint the man; besides, we may have lost somewhat of the idiotism of that language in which it was spoken; and where the conceit is couched in a single word, if all the significations of it are not critically understood, the grace and pleasantry are lost.

It is clear, consequently, that Dryden, taking over points of view from his predecessors and adding to them the attitudes of Plutarch himself, has reworked his material in his own inimitable fashion;

and the result is the first distinguished contribution to what is even yet insufficient — biographic criticism. Biographers themselves, in their comments upon their purpose and methods, have been, for the most part, the chief critics and historians of the form. Of late, it is true, a number of commentators have made valuable additions to our slowly increasing knowledge, notably Dr. W. H. Dunn, Dr. D. A. Stauffer, Dr. Mark Longaker, and Mr. Edgar Johnson in his "One Mighty Torrent," but the amount of such contribution is still slight in comparison with critical comment upon other forms. Bacon, Margaret Newcastle, and Dryden established a tradition which has been allowed to lag far behind. Centuries, for instance, lie between the iconistic portrayals of the middle ages and the denigratory portraits of today; but Dryden's "private lodgings of the hero" is hardly one remove from Gamaliel Bradford's psychographical devices, or from William Hazlitt's

> The great charm of biography consists in the individuality of details, the familiar tone of the incidents, the bringing us acquainted with the persons of men whom we have formerly known only by their works or names.

# 10—Roger North and His Brothers

*Who knows only his own generation remains always a child.* — George Norlin.

*The habit of preferring oneself and the present to whatever is ancient degrades the nature of man and leaves the genius without development and without enthusiasm.* — Laurentie.

*There is no cutting off and dividing into separate departments the scenes and acts of human life, which can only be enjoyed fully when viewed as parts of the whole.* — Digby.

LYTTON STRACHEY in his "Portraits in Miniature" commented upon Roger North's "Life" of his brother John in this way:

> Only by sheer accident, when some particular drop from the ocean of empty water is slipped under the microscope — only when some Roger North happens to write a foolish memoir which happens to survive, and which we happen to open — do we perceive for an amazed moment or two the universe of serried and violent sensations that lie concealed so perfectly in the transparency of oblivion;

and in his customary disparaging fashion considers the Norths disposed of. But did he really do anything more than exploit the moment? We all read Strachey partly because we love disparagement — "death loves a shining mark" not half so well as mediocrity detests distinction. Only, not the least of our errors lies in thinking our point of view modern and a virtue, when, as a matter of record, Pericles, twenty-five hundred years ago, pointed out and accounted for the same attitude. "Men are always ready," he said in one of his speeches,

> to listen to the praise of others as long as each man supposes that he could perform what he hears; but whatever is recorded exceeding that point they regard as an object of envy and reject as incredible.

The irritations of history tempt us, it seems, into ignoring the past, imagining with Virginia Woolf that "about December, 1910, human character changed." In the welter of what (with apologies because there seems to be no term for it) may be called our "contemporatism," we forget that to disregard the accumulated stupidities and successes of the past is only less absurd than to take unction to ourselves for the noses, the ears, or the innate tendencies we possess; or, as Carlyle sneered, "Whoso belongs only to his own age, and reverences only its gilt Popinjays or soot-smeared Mumbojumbos, must needs die with it."

Roger North is not among the great biographers, and not anything said here is meant to imply that "The lives of Baron Guildford, Lord Keeper of the Great Seal under Charles II and James II; of Sir Dudley North, Commissioner of the Customs, and afterward of the Treasury to King Charles II; and of the Honorable and Reverend Doctor John North, Master of Trinity College, Cambridge, and Clerk of the Closet to King Charles II"—not any of this is meant to imply that either the author or his work is deserving of first place in our remembrance. It is rather to make a claim for the virtue of knowing what has been, in order the better to comprehend what is, if not what is to be. Roger North's contribution to history is of value, and, while not vital, his gift to biography is welcomed; even though neither is indispensable.

"Free your minds of cant," said Dr. Johnson, and such freedom is necessary for any appreciation, especially necessary perhaps for an appreciation of a more or less obscure Restoration lawyer who wrote about his brothers because he loved them and cherished their memory. He lived a long and comparatively uneventful life, and had he not occupied himself in his retirement with writing the "Lives" probably neither he nor his brothers would have triumphed over oblivion. As it is we have the likeness of a man eminent in the law, of one influential in commerce, and of one distinguished in learning, all communicated by their younger brother, a man not one whit less worth knowing than they themselves.

Roger North was born in 1653 and lived to be eighty-one. The youngest of six sons, he was nevertheless carefully educated, at first by the redoubtable Ezakial Catchpole, next at Thetford School, but prepared for the University by his father, Dudley, fourth Baron North. Entering Jesus College, Cambridge, he studied under the tutelage of his brother John, eight years his senior and later the Master of Trinity. In 1669, however, he took up residence in the Middle Temple, having found Cambridge little to his liking after two years. He was called to the bar in 1675 and came at once into the patronage of his brother Francis, with whom, incidentally, he shared quarters in Elm Court. Through him he received much practice — so much, in fact, that although his fees seldom exceeded £20 he eventually acquired an income of £4000 a year, and was noted for having had to keep three "fee bowls" on his table. Upon the accession of William of Orange, however, becoming a nonjuror, he retired to Rougham in Norfolk, where he settled down to develop the estate, study music, mathematics, and architecture, breed horses, collect books, and write. Yet during his lifetime he published nothing except his "Discourse of Fish and Fish Ponds," which appeared in 1683. His son Montagu brought out the "Examen," a criticism of White Kennett's volume of the "Compleat History of England," and the germ of the "Lives," in 1740; and finally the "Lives" themselves in 1742–1744. His "Autobiography" — naturally, he did not call it so; the word did not come into existence until after Southey used it in 1820 — did not appear until in 1887, although it was probably written before 1696. It remained incomplete even for an autobiography, but was edited by Jessopp and published with a selection of the letters. Indeed, these last reveal him more effectively than does the "Autobiography," which elaborates his ideas concerning music and architecture and sets forth the difficulties he experienced in connection with Sir Peter Lely's will, but communicates little of himself and his everyday affairs. Possibly he would have agreed with the late Samuel McCord Crothers that "every man is his own myth-maker," and so erred through leaning backward. The following letter to his son at Cambridge, for instance, is more intimately characterizing than are any of his opinions about the moral effects of singing or the proprieties of horse garniture:

Roughan, 16th November, 1730

Dear Montagu,

I observe that you are settled in a chamber, I cannot say too good, but much too big for you, for it held Dr. North and myself. My study was up a little stair by the bedside and his by the chimney. The greatest inconvenience is the sun's heat in summer afternoons, and then we retired into the bed chamber. In short, if you get to be a Fellow, you need not change your chamber, which is not the ordinary lot of a Pensioner. But I have a confidence that what is preternecessary will not turn to your inconvenience, that is, pretending to entertain idle company. I mean *vino fugi* of the *fumosum genus*, for I would be loathe you should confirm the scandal charged upon the universities of learning chiefly to smoke and to drink. You are shipped upon a voyage of adventure of the good or evil of your whole life, and precious NOW lost will never be regained. You must be very observant of your tutor, who will faithfully direct you in all concerns as well of study as course of life, and in the end be (as I am fully persuaded) a very good friend. And you have to gather not only learning but a good character, both in your college and university. These are the elements of good fortune in the world.

I am your most loving Father.

My service to Mr. Bradshaw.

Quiet, modest, a man who says of himself that he was timid and given neither to ready speech nor quick thought, one who described himself as "though not the prime of my rank, yet not contemptible," Roger North has come to be remembered by reason of the candor, sympathy, and insight with which he wrote of brothers who far outstripped him in life and yet who, even by any unconsciously revealing phrase, seem never to have moved him to envy. The family "were a numerous flock, and not one scabby sheep in it," he wrote, and sustained the theme throughout.

His "Lives," however, are not panegyrics. He wrote them at a time of developing realism, and admire his subjects though he did, he omitted few of their defects. He sometimes, it is true, turns faults humorously aside; nevertheless there they are — he probably knew as well as we that "transgressions are easily pardoned if they provoke a smile." In thinking of the effect of his work, moreover, he may or may not have concurred with Plutarch's idea as set down in the "Timoleon":

> It was for the sake of others that I first commenced writing biographies; but I find myself proceeding and attaching myself to it for my own; the virtues of these great men serving me as a sort of looking-glass, in which I may see how to adjust and adorn my own life. Indeed, it can be compared to nothing but daily living and associating together; we receive, as it were, in our inquiry, and entertain each successive guest; view their stature and their qualities and select from their actions all that is noblest and worthiest to know.
>
> Ah, and what greater pleasure could one have, or what more effective means to one's moral improvement?

And he may or may not have thought that "to read biography is, in a measure at least, to learn how to live." At all events he disclaims direct aim at anything more than preservation in memory, for, "I may be here told," he wrote in the "Life" of John North,

> that if I think by these descriptions, to exhibit the portrait of a great man, I am out of the way . . . I answer that I am not giving the portrait of a perfect man; and whoever pretends to do so is a foul flatterer.

He did, however, hint, as may be drawn from a passage in Jessopp's introduction to the "Lives," that "coming to know is coming to love":

> With regard to the character of Lord Guildford himself, although the biographer has evidently delineated it under the influence of feelings which rendered it impossible for him to be truly impartial, he has yet stated all his facts so candidly

and ingeniously that we have little difficulty in forming a just estimate of the Lord Keeper's real character —

a statement, which with the following from his own introduction, generalizes his attitude,

> Nay, scars and blemishes, as well as beauties, ought to be expressed; otherwise it is but an outline filled up with lillies and roses.

Roger North did more than evolve an attitude and sustain it through all his "Lives"; he aided in establishing a way of looking at men and their accomplishments more nearly objectively. If even then he is less objective than one might wish, it must be remembered that blood-ties are strong and that where one loves, self-interest impels one to praise. And it was a point of view which for more than a century was to hold in check the traditional belief that the dead must be regarded as impeccable and that any suggestion to the contrary was not only bad morality but bad biographic practice. Roger North knew that his brothers were men, with faults now and virtues then; and it was as men, not paragons, that he wished to portray them — hence his methods and his style.

As was pointed out a page or two earlier, the "Life of Baron Guildford" grew out of the youngest North's "Examen," a critique of the ideas of White Kennett as expressed in the "Compleat History of England." His avowed purpose in that work was "to vindicate the Honour of Charles II and His Happy Reign," and he succeeds admirably in explaining the career of Shaftesbury in connection with the Popist Plot and the Sham Plots from the partisan standpoint of the Stuart cause, but he is at his best perhaps when dealing with the latter years of Charles's reign and the part played by the Lord Keeper. It was Kennett's disparaging comment, therefore, that urged the writing of the "Examen," and it was a natural sequence that the author should undertake to write in full the "Life" of, as he called him, "my best brother" for the purpose of offsetting what he feared would be posterity's misapprehension. Having completed the first "Life," and having found that recalling events, circumstances, and affairs which they two had experienced together was a great pleasure, he determined to prolong the task and so wrote of

Sir Dudley North, the Turkey merchant and Commissioner of Customs, and finally of Dr. John North, the Master of Trinity.

The first is at once the most interesting of the three but the poorest in construction. The interest lies in the personality of the subject as revealed by his official acts, by his idiosyncrasies, and by the author's statements of his affectionate dependence upon him. As an official — besides being Lord Keeper of the Seal he was also the acknowledged head of the Church of England party — he maintained a high order of integrity in situations of tense political conflict. His views tended toward upholding the royal prerogative but at the same time were not a little biased in favor of constitutional government. As a practising lawyer and later as a judge, he was, his brother insists, only second to Solon. But even after discounting brotherly affection, one realizes that Francis North conducted his affairs in a manner more than honorable in contrast with what was expected in his day — in support of which may be advanced his attempts to correct the abuses of the courts and to simplify and order more closely the administration of the law and the body of its content. All in all, if he did not rise above the prejudices and feelings of his age, he did not, like many of his colleagues, sink without shame into the mire of corruption. Admitted to the Middle Temple in 1655, he began to practice in Elm Court. Upon being appointed as Reader he spent so much upon his "Feast" — £1,000 — that although such feasts were traditionally extravagant, his lavishness led to the abolition of the custom. He became in turn Solicitor and then Attorney General, Chief Justice of the Common Pleas, and finally in 1682, Lord Keeper of the Seal. This last appointment he received from Charles himself, who said, "Here, take it, my Lord; you will find it heavy," a prophecy the truth of which he later acknowledged by saying that he had not enjoyed one easy or contented moment after having come into the office. He lived to enjoy the favor of both Charles and James, although, to be sure, he died before James commenced his more unconstitutional measures.

Francis North was not a man of extraordinarily strong personal feelings perhaps. The account of his efforts to acquire a wife — desiring one whose fortune would serve to augment his own slender resources and being so dominated in the six attempts he made before becoming successful — is definitely revealing and highly entertaining. His kindness to his friends, however, and his affectionate concern for his brothers, as constantly noted and illustrated, are unusual in human relationships during the Restoration. In personal traits he seems to have been innately orderly, although on more than one occasion he is shown as breaking over into some mild debauch. The story of his falling asleep on horseback and being carried into a pond, for example, and the accounts of adventures during his many journeys contribute both concretely and by implication to the reality of the Lord Keeper as a human being.

The structure of the narrative serves to detract from the vitality of the portrait. The account is rather sharply divided into two parts, the one dealing with public affairs, the other with private matters, as if the two were so unrelated as to have no reference to each other. Such device sometimes appears in historiography, one of the clearest examples being the Habington "Edward IV," but it is seldom effective. For the student of history it may be convenient to have, as in this narrative, references to Shaftesbury, Chief Justice Hales, the Mildenhall affair, and comparable material isolated; but for the reader interested in the development and expression of personality, straight continuity and indicated causal relationships are very much more satisfying.

The second "Life," that of Sir Dudley North, is, both in attitude and structure, quite different from the first. The author had not had the opportunity to know him as well as he knew Francis. Dudley left England early and for years resided in the Levant, a highly successful merchant. For the section covering those years, therefore, the "Life" depends upon letters and comments made by the subject himself, which contribute toward an impression of the geographic and political as well as the commercial conditions in which Dudley North found himself, but the man seldom emerges in his own three dimensions, for he was none too articulate on paper. One finds much to inform him in the affairs of the Vizier Azem, in the account of the Misteria Privilege in Turkey, and in what passed between Sir John French and the Grand Signor; but it is only after Dudley North's return to London that one begins to know the man. At that point the author treats of familiar things; how the returned wanderer continued at times to wear his Turkish garb, although he did shave his mustachios; how he was surprised to find coffee houses all over the city, for in Constantinople whence the coffee came there were no such resorts; how he became one of the sheriffs of London; how he married Lady Gunning in spite of such letters as the following, which passed before the settlement with the lady's father:

Sir:
My answer to your first letter is an answer to your second.

Your humble servant
R. C. (Sir Robert Cann)

Sir:
I perceive you like neither me nor my business.

Your humble servant
D. N. (Dudley North);

how he was called to serve in the commission of the customs; how he refused to aid a brother-in-law in evading responsibility; how he returned to private life and became finally one of the best economists of his time; and how he fell ill and died — matters like these bring the subject clearly into focus and show him an actor in the scenes in which he played a part. On the whole, perhaps neither Lady Castlemaine nor the Duchess of Newcastle would have found him worth a second glance, and no doubt William Wycherley would have thought him dull company had they two met at Will's. Nevertheless the king was guided by his opinion, members of the treasury consulted him, and shareholders in the Turkey and African companies admired and trusted him. On the other hand, the House of Commons investigated him, and he was somewhat addicted to irascibility. Yet he was among the first to advocate a policy of free trade and there can be small question that he aided considerably in establishing England's world wide commercial relations. And finally, he was the first merchant to be accorded a full-length biography.

To open the "Life of the Hon. and Rev. Dr. John North," the "least brother" sets forth his aim in a passage of significance to biographic technique:

My design in these papers is to frame a short history of the life of an honourable person, some time since deceased, and to represent his character as near to truth as my stock of materials will enable me. Works of this kind may be useful to such as had rather profit by the example of others, than apply any invention, or industry, of their own, towards a moral improvement; or, it may be, to wear away some heavy hours in reading. As for the importance of the present subject, I shall hang out no bush, but submit to the peruser the determination, whether there was need of such a proverbial signal, or not. Some have affected to write the lives of persons long since dead and gone, and their names preserved only by some formal remains, and (even) dubious traditions. So painters copy from obscure draughts half obliterated, whereof no member, much less the entire resemblance is to be found. But fiction, supported upon seeming probability, must fill up the blanks, and supply all defects. In this manner some lives have become *redivial,* but with partial views, tending either to panegyric, the advance of some favorite opinions, or factious intrigues; which are fiercely pursued, while the lifescraps come out very thin and meagre. And, after great length of time, how should it come off better? My choice is of what the present undertaking aims at, the life of a person known to some yet living, and done by a close acquaintance and frequent companion, who hath neither inclination nor temptation to court the public, or flatter the private.

And in a sentence closely following he says, "The moral intent here is to do justice to the person, and service to his family; both which may result from the present endeavor to retrieve his character." "To retrieve his character" becomes, therefore, the prime motive.

As a matter of fact, there was no reason why a "life" of John North should ever have been written. He was more obscure than the average Master of Trinity, and decidedly more unpleasant. His health was feeble and his resulting manner shy and difficult. He tried to learn to play the organ but failed. He could not be happy in the common room and so retired to private society, diverting "himself with feeding spiders in great glasses." He preached before the king, made his father's chaplain recant a "vile Heresey," became professor of Greek, was made Clerk of the Closet to the king, and eventually quarreled with most of his colleagues. Of florid countenance but weak constitution he was afflicted with "rheums and a swollen uvula," the remedy for which was "to take amber, as tobacco, in pipes, and to have certain astringent powders blown through quills into his mouth." The result was that he became completely ill, and finally, while admonishing two scholars, he dropped in an apoplexy. Passing into a stupor, he lay for some days until his mother arrived to care for him. Her remedy was noise, in order that he might be kept awake. Hence, "there was a concert of tongs, firegrate, wainscot drum, and dancing of curtains and curtain rings, such as would have made a sound man mad." He lived to recover his faculties after a fashion, however, but his malady soon passed into palsy and then into hemiplegia; and so the end came, in the words of his brother, to this "bright example of orthodox religion, learning, justice, and good will."

The character is "retrieved" from the author's memory almost entirely, because Dr. North "took express care that nothing real should remain, whereby, in after-times, he might be remembered." Nevertheless the "Life" as presented is the best in structure of the three. There is about it a continuity and a wholeness that the others lack. One feels, to be sure, that the relationship between author and subject was not of the closest, but the feeling rather lends the impression that the biographer is being fair. Virtues are presented, but they are accounted for as having developed; and faults appear as the result of natural causes. Detail follows detail and situation situation inevitably. So well rounded a pattern is far to seek at so early a time.

One "hangs out no bush" for the Norths or for their "Lives." There have been better men and far better books. But to read the "Lives" is not only to know the men; it is also to perceive, in a degree how men may leave alms for oblivion.

# 11–Samuel Johnson and
## "The Lives of the Poets"

*There are some men whose lives are their greatest work.* — Bradford.

*Oblivion is not to be hired.* — Browne.

DR. SAMUEL JOHNSON'S place among biographers is by right above the salt, but because of precept rather than performance. Boswell, it is true, praised his performance extravagantly. "To write," says he at the beginning of his great book,

> the Life of him who excelled all mankind in writing the lives of others, and who, whether we consider his extraordinary endowments, or his various works, has been equalled by few in any age, is an arduous and may be reckoned in me a presumptuous task.

Nevertheless at almost the same time he was writing to Temple that his own work would be "without exception, the most entertaining" Temple had ever read. Furthermore, in the description of his method he included this sentence:

> As it is, I will venture to say that he [Johnson] will be seen in this work more completely than any man who has ever yet lived.

Hence it would seem that even though he considered Johnson among the greatest biographers, he was not unwilling to be numbered among them himself — and with the amplest justification.

[ 123 ]

However, he would never have become so if the subject himself had not directly and indirectly prepared him for the task — and, incidentally, Goldsmith and most subsequent biographers for theirs as well. For Johnson taught them all what biographical writing is, what its material comprises, what its purposes and range are, and what spirit should pervade it. And no one else had ever been better equipped for such teaching, not only by education and experience but also by predilection. As a matter of fact, his enjoyment of biography as he once suggested to a group at the Mitre — and in different fashion on later occasions — amounted almost to self-indulgence. "Bayle's Dictionary," he said,

> is a very useful work for those to consult who love the biographical part of literature, which is what I love most.

He loved it, without doubt, but he loved human nature more, the last probably accounting for the first. That his love for mankind was deep and abiding is apparent in all his writing and his resulting sympathy for individuals is manifest in his private acts — as Boswell, Arthur Murphy, Mrs. Piozzi, Madame D'Arbley, Dr. Robert Anderson, and Sir John Hawkins all testify. The blind, the weak and suffering, the Robert Leverets, the Ann Williamses, even the Bet Flints looked to him not only for refuge but sometimes for rehabilitation as well. It was human nature he loved; hence his emphasis upon biography, the record of individual humanity.

Pope had written that "the proper study of mankind is man," and Johnson's bent was in complete accord, as the quotation was a favorite with him, and as, when he came to reveal the results of his observation and experience, his writings and conversation show — although, to be sure, he would have maintained that the proper study of each man is himself. In the course of time, as his practice proceeded, his philosophy grew until, in the end, as has been pointed out, his precept outstripped his performance. For his genius was essentially didactic; hence his value. By implication at least, morality must ever underwrite the art that defies oblivion.

Johnson's earliest biographical undertakings were no doubt thrust upon him; he wanted above all else to write and so followed the obvious course: solicited employment with a bookseller, the phlegmatic Cave, "who had no great relish for mirth, but could bear it," editor of the "Gentleman's Magazine," with whom for many years he worked in harmony and whose "life" he ultimately wrote. However, in 1736, when he resolved to try his fortune in London, "commencing author," if one were patronless, was excessively difficult. To realize how difficult, one has but to remember DeQuincey's story of Kit Smart's leasing himself to a bookseller for ninety-nine years; or to read Macaulay's comment:

> At the time when Johnson commenced his literary career, a writer had little hope from the patronage of powerful individuals. The patronage of the public did not yet furnish the means of comfortable subsistence. The prices paid by booksellers to authors were so low that a man of considerable talents and unremitting industry could do little more than provide for the day which was passing over him. The lean kine had eaten up the fat kine. The thin and withered ears had devoured the good ears. The season of rich harvest was over, and the period of famine had begun. All that is squalid and miserable might now be summed up in the word Poet.

Nevertheless after weary days and many discouragements — significant of which were Wilcox's advice to him to get "a porter's knot," and the letter to Cave ending, "I am, Sir, yours, *impransus*" — Johnson began the career in which he was to gain the heights and so live on.

His first effort in biography was the "Life of Father Paul Sarpi," a matter of assignment by Cave for the "Magazine" in 1738. It was significant of little that was to come, being no more than a two-page puff for a proposed translation of the "History of the Council of Trent." His interest lay in the direction such writing must take, however; he accomplished Cave's purpose and was ready for the next task. And tasks came fast enough. Among regular assignments he was soon ready to include special commissions. At yearly intervals, therefore, appeared "lives" of Dr. Herman Boerhaave, Admiral Blake, and John Phillip Barretier, that extravagant youth who had mastered five languages at the age of nine. In 1741 he completed a somewhat extended "Life of Sir Francis Drake"; and a year later a "life" of Peter Burman as well as a sketch of Thomas Sydenham to introduce the Swan edition of Sydenham's works. His account of Francis Cheyney appeared in "The Student" in 1751; and after the death of Cave he composed a brief memoir which the "Gentleman's Magazine" carried in 1754. During 1756 he wrote a "life" of Sir Thomas Browne to be prefixed to an edition of that author's "Christian Morals"; and in 1761, a "life" of Roger Ascham to introduce the Bennet edition of the great schoolmaster's works. In all he wrote thirteen such sketches, a nondescript collection of Dutch, Italian, and English sailors and philosophers treated with varying biographical success, not any item becoming memorable and not any showing more than a spark of the genius that was later to pervade "The Lives of the Poets." The whole group is to be found buried in Volume Two of Arthur Murphy's third American edition. Johnson's reputation as a biographer rests not upon this sort of work, which he undertook in the ordinary routine of hack writing, but upon one slim volume which he issued in 1744, the "Life of Savage"; and upon the great work of his career, "The Lives of the Poets," the first volumes of which appeared in 1779 and the last two years later. In order to get some perspective upon the "Savage," however, it may be well to look first at "The Lives of the Poets, of which ultimately it became a part.

Whatever opinion may now be current, in its day Johnson's "The Lives of the Poets" marked the climax of a career to which every circumstance seems to have contributed something: his life of hardship while gaining a foothold in literary London; his contacts with the dregs of society during that time; his habit of omniverous reading, begun in his father's bookshop in Lichfield and becoming inveterate at Oxford; the variety of his contributions to the "Gentleman's Magazine," the "Adventurer," the "Universal Visitor," and the "Literary Magazine"; besides such independent undertakings as the "Rambler" and "Idler" papers, the "Dictionary," the "London," "The Vanity of Human Wishes," and "Rasselas." All these resulted in the recognition which took tangible form in the pension which, upon application by Wedderburne to Lord Bute, the Crown granted him; and in the prestige which had so far developed that by 1764 he could establish — upon a proposal by Sir Joshua Reynolds — the Literary Club and include as members some of the most powerful men in

England. The events of such a career could hardly fail to point toward "The Lives of the Poets" as the culmination of the tendencies that combined to produce one of the great reputations in English letters. Hence, when the committee composed of Davies, Strahan, and Cadell, as representatives of forty London booksellers, waited upon Johnson that Easter Eve of 1777, he was the one man best suited in all England to carry out their plans. The Martins, booksellers of Edinburgh, had issued a collection of the poets pirated from the London copyright holders. As a result the men who held the copyrights banded together to issue such a work on their own account. Toward that end they sought to interest Johnson in serving as editor and critic-biographer — although certain members of the group had held out for Percy Stockdale. Johnson, however, was finally chosen and accepted the commission, the choice being based upon the significance of his name, as Boswell shrewdly concluded in a letter written from Glasgow, April 24, 1777:

> Pray tell me about this edition of *The English Poets,* with a Preface, biographical and critical, to each Author by Samuel Johnson, LL.D. which I see advertised. I am delighted with the prospect of it. Indeed I am happy to feel that I am capable of being so much delighted with literature. But is not the charm of this publication chiefly owing to the *magnum nomen* in the front of it?

But aside from all other considerations, it was his philosophy of life writing which made him the ideal choice.

This philosophy — not a little of which, as a matter of fact, was derived from Plutarch, an edition of whose works he once thought of preparing, and from Dryden — is set forth in his writings and his conversation but most clearly perhaps in the sixtieth "Rambler" paper and in the eighty-fourth "Idler." In "Rambler" No. 60 for instance, which appeared October 13, 1750, he had this to say:

> All the joy or sorrow for the happiness or calamities of others is produced by an act of the imagination that realizes the event however fictitious, or approximates it however remote, by placing us for a time, in the condition of him whose fortune we contemplate; so that we feel, while the deception lasts, whatever emotions would be excited by the same good

or evil happening to ourselves. . . . It is not easy for the most artful writer to give us an interest in happiness or misery, which we feel ourselves never likely to feel. . . . Histories of the downfalls of kingdoms, and revolutions of empires, are read with great tranquillity. . . . Those parallel circumstances and kindred images, to which we readily conform our minds, are, above all other writings, to be found in narratives of the lives of particular persons; and therefore no species of writing seems more worthy of cultivation than biography, since none can be more delightful or more useful, none can more certainly enchain the heart by irresistible interest, or more widely diffuse instruction to every diversity of condition. . . . I have often thought that there has rarely passed a life of which a judicious and faithful narrative would not be useful; for there is such a uniformity in the state of man. . . . that there is scarce any possibility of good or ill, but is common to human kind. . . . We are all prompted by the same motives, all deceived by the same fallacies. . . . It is frequently objected to relations of particular lives, that they are not distinguished by any striking or wonderful vicissitudes. The scholar who passed his life among his books, the merchant who conducted only his own affairs, the priest whose sphere of action was not extended beyond that of his duty, are considered as no proper objects of public regard. . . . But these notions arise from false measures of excellence and dignity. . . . It is, indeed, not improper to take honest advantages of prejudice, and gain attention by a celebrated name; but the business of a biographer is often to pass over slightly those performances and incidents, which produce vulgar greatness, to lead the thoughts into domestic privacies, and display the minute details of daily life, where exterior appendages are cast aside, and men excel each other only by prudence and by virtue. . . . If the biographer writes from personal knowledge, and makes haste to gratify the public curiosity, there is danger lest his interest . . . tempt him to conceal, if not to invent. . . . If we owe regard to the memory of the dead, there is yet more respect to be paid to knowledge, to virtue, and to truth.

And nine years later, in No. 84 of the "Idler," published November 24, 1759, he had these further ideas to contribute:

Biography is, of the various kinds of narrative writing, that which is most eagerly read, and most easily applied to the purposes of life. . . . In romances, when the field of possibility lies open to invention, the incidents may easily be made more numerous, the vicissitudes more sudden, and the events more wonderful, . . . the most artful tale may be sometimes read as a model of . . . style, or those who are weary of themselves, may have recourse to it as a pleasing dream. . . . The examples and events of history press, indeed, upon the mind with the weight of truth; that when they are reposited in memory, they are oftener employed for show than for use, and rather diversify conversation than regulate life. . . . The mischievous consequences of vice and folly, of irregular desires and predominant passions, are best discovered by those relations which are leveled with the general surface of life, which tell not how any man became great, but how he was made happy; not how he lost the favor of his prince, but how he became discontented with himself.

To summarize, biography is useful, because, more than any other literary form, it is influential toward just and ordered living. Johnson stresses this idea not only in these excerpts but in many places in other writings and in conversation with his friends. For instance, he once remarked to Lord Monboddo, "I esteem biography as giving us what comes near to ourselves, what we can turn to use." In addition to utility he would have it productive of pleasure, as in apologizing for the length of "The Lives of the Poets" he wrote, "I have been led beyond my intention, I hope, by the honest desire of giving useful pleasure."

With this point of view, therefore, and a literary experience of vast proportions, when at the age of sixty-eight he was asked to compose biographical-critical sketches of the English poets from Cowley through those of his own day, to accompany selections from their works, he entered upon the task as upon one of his own choosing. Earlier in his career, in fact, he had entertained the idea of writing an account of English literary history, stressing particularly the lives of the authors; and then one day in February, 1767, at the invitation of the librarian, Sir Frederick Barnard, he visited the library at Buckingham House and suddenly found himself face to face with the king, George III. After a brief conversation chiefly about the affairs of the day, in Boswell's words,

His Majesty expressed a desire to have the literary biography of this country ably executed, and proposed to Dr. Johnson to undertake it. Johnson signified his readiness to comply with his Majesty's wishes.

Nevertheless, it was not until ten years later, and after a second but entirely incidental meeting with the king — which seems to have escaped Boswell — that he did so; and even then it was only after the matter had been presented to him in detail, including mention of his fee. This last was left to his decision and he fixed upon two hundred guineas, a sum quite out of proportion, as Malone, in a note to the "Life," says:

Had he asked one thousand or even fifteen hundred guineas, the booksellers, who knew the value of his name, would have readily given it. They have probably got five thousand guineas by this work in the course of twenty-five years.

The booksellers did, however, pay him subsequently two hundred guineas more in further acknowledgment of his worth to them — even so, Cadell later paid Mrs. Piozzi £ 500 for her Johnson letters.

Having made the agreement, he set immediately to work. He had been given full powers to include what poets he would and to say what he pleased about them. Most of the selections were made on the basis of comparative reputations, but certain men were chosen arbitrarily: Thomson, Blackmore, Pomfret, Yalden, and Watts, for instance. Goldsmith, whose "The Traveller" he had pronounced the best poem since the day of Pope, was omitted — because Thomas Carnan, the son-in-law of Newberry, the elder, possessed the copyrights and would release nothing for the proposed edition. While Johnson was engaged in making the selections Boswell once asked him, "Would you write about any dunce if they [the booksellers] asked you?" "Yes, Sir," he answered, "and say that he was a dunce."

He had not made much progress before he realized that what he was attempting was to become far more important and serious an undertaking than he had at first conceived. In the beginning he had spoken of the sketches as "little lives," but he was not long in revising his opinion. There were some "little lives," to be sure; the "Stepney," for instance, requires but two pages in the Everyman's Library edition, the "William Walsh" two, the "Halifax" four, and a number of others vary up to ten or twelve. The "Cowley," on the other hand, extends to forty-seven, The "Milton" to sixty, the "Dryden" to eighty-four, and the "Pope" to one hundred and two. In fact, he discovered that a lifetime of reading had so enriched his mind that nothing short of self-imposed limits would permit him to do justice both to his employers and to the task itself.

So formidable did the quota of fifty-two "Lives" become that two years elapsed before anything was ready for publication. Hence, it was March, 1779, that the first volumes came out. The full title was "The Works of the Most Eminent English Poets with Prefaces, Biographical and Critical." The "Cowley" was the first of the individual "lives." It had been sent to press in December, 1777, some eight months after the project had been agreed upon. The "Waller," the "Denham," and the "Butler" followed. The "Milton" was among the last of the first group to be finished, having been started in January, 1779, and completed in six weeks. In the original edition the first volume contained the "Cowley" and the "Waller"; the "Milton" and the "Butler" made up the second; the third was devoted wholly to the "Dryden"; and the fourth was given over to the shorter accounts of Denham, Sprat, Roscommon, Yalden, Otway, Duke, Dorset, Halifax, Stepney, Walsh, Garth, King, J. Philips, Pomfret, and Hughes. Two years later, during the summer of 1781, six more volumes were issued, making ten in all. The whole work required a few months more than four years to complete. The Prefaces themselves were subsequently issued as "The Lives of the Poets."

The undertaking occupied Johnson from his sixty-eighth to his seventy-second year. He was an old man when he began, old and ill. That he was the literary dictator of his age hindered rather than helped. If he could omit special consideration of John Donne and damn the whole group, including Cowley, with the pejorative "metaphysical" in accordance with neoclassical tradition, berate Milton for his politics, misunderstand Gray, and make many categorical statements which later opinion has discredited, it was a matter of defective performance, not in the least the effect of defective theory. Likewise, in spite of his protestations, when he begins a sketch with an apology as sometimes he does: "Of Thomas Otway, one of the first names in English drama, little is known," for instance; "Of Mr. Richard Duke I can find few memorials"; or "The brevity with which I am to write the account of Elijah Fenton is not the effect of indifference or negligence. I have sought intelligence among his relations in his native country but have not obtained it" — when he begins thus with excuses, it was merely that he was too weary to persevere in the search for material. He knew exactly what to do and how; but he had grown old and sick and weary, besides becoming arrogant beyond brooking advice, George Steevens being one among only two or three to whom he would willingly listen.

However, to intimate that the work falls short except in minor respects or to damn it because it occasionally falls into the *argumentum ad hominem* is to do it far less than justice. It became immediately — if one except certain critical carping, notably that of Cowper, of Bishop Newton, and of several Whiggish reviewers concerning the "Gray" and the "Lyttelton" especially — the accepted neoclassical standard and a pioneer in the genre of critical biography. It is of no importance that now and then a sketch remained incomplete through lack of industry, as is readily apparent in many places. Such lack was a subject of indifference to Johnson. Mrs. Piozzi records that upon one occasion she overheard Boswell advise him that Lord Marchmont be consulted concerning Pope, and Johnson reply that he did not care to be troubled. "But, Sir," she broke in, "Mr. Boswell thought that since you are to write Pope's life you would wish to know about him." "Wish!" Johnson retorted. "Why, yes. If it rained knowledge, I'd go hold out my hand; but I would not go in quest of it." Such detail bears small weight in the balance against the influence of the work upon the history of literary criticism. Thomas Warton was satisfied to rely upon it; William Roscoe followed it; Peter Cunningham considered it sound; and twentieth-century criticism looks back upon it as the repository of much that is now available in no other form.

Authoritative though it was at the time and has since remained, its value lies, aside from detail concerning the affairs of the more obscure, in the comparative simplicity of the style — the "Palladian architecture" manner of the earlier work having disappeared — and in the justness and vigor of its critical opinions. As biography, on the other hand — compare Johnson's "Dryden" with Malone's, for instance — it fails in many respects to follow the precepts its author so emphatically set down. The "Pope," the "Cowley," the "Addison," and the "Thomson" are notable exceptions, of course; but the best of all the "lives," from the point of view of biography as such, is the "Savage."

Here again is a work which illustrates the effect of emotional engagement. Savage was a friend in adversity, particularly from 1737 to 1739. Together they had wandered the streets, eaten when and if they could, hobnobbed with the dwellers in mews, and slept in the warmth of pottery kilns, the while they thought great thoughts and dreamed of fame to come — or as Johnson once told his old schoolfellow and subsequent biographer, Sir John Hawkins:

> Whole nights had been spent by him and Savage in conversation . . . not under the hospitable roof of a tavern, where warmth might have invigorated their spirits, and wine dispelled their care; but in a perambulation round the squares of Westminster, St. James in particular, when all the money they both could raise was less than sufficient to purchase for them the shelter and sordid comforts of a night cellar.

Hence, because Savage was condemned to death for killing a gentleman in a tavern brawl but was later pardoned, only to die in 1743 amid the most wretched poverty, Johnson, in order to reclaim his friend from scandal mongers and gloating sensation seekers, decided to write an account of his life.

He spent six months in gathering material: ransacking his memory; consulting mutual friends; ferreting out the verse which Savage had contributed to the "Gentleman's Magazine"; studying his drama, "Sir Thomas Overbury"; becoming absorbed in "The Wanderer," a moral and descriptive poem of Savage's which Johnson praised as "a heap of shining material thrown together by accident"; studying another poem, "The Bastard," a censure upon Savage's supposed mother, the Duchess of Macclesfield; and analyzing the reports of the crime, the trial, the pardon, and the affairs of the last unhappy years.

In August, 1743, he published in the "Gentleman's Magazine" a letter by way of preliminary announcement of his forthcoming work:

> Mr. Urban, — As your collections shew how often you have owed the ornaments of your poetical pages to the correspondence of the unfortunate and ingenious Mr. Savage, I doubt not but you have such regard for his memory as to encourage any design that may have a tendency to the preservation of it from insults and calumnies; and therefore . . . intreat you to inform the publick, that his life will speedily be published by a person who was favored with his confidence, and received from him an account of most of the transactions which he proposes to mention. . . .
>
> (No signature)

The book appeared in February, 1744, after Johnson had, in his eagerness as he said, "written forty-eight printed octavo pages . . . at a sitting," and it proved to be, according to Boswell, one of the most "interesting narratives in the English language." The incidents are related in a highly vigorous manner, and the whole is permeated with the purpose "to guard men of warm passions from a too free indulgence of them." No sooner did the volume make its appearance than James Ralph, then proprietor of "The Champion," printed the following review in his columns:

> This pamphlet is, without flattery to its author as just and as well written a piece as I ever saw. . . . As to the history of the unfortunate person whose memoirs compose this work, it is certainly penned with equal accuracy and spirit, of which I am so much the better judge, as I know many of the facts mentioned to be strictly true and very fairly related. . . . The author's observations are short, significant, and just, as his narrative is remarkably smooth, and well disposed. His reflections open to all the recesses of the human heart; and, in a word, a more just or pleasant, a more engaging or a more improving treatise, on all the excellencies and defects of human

nature, is scarce to be found in our own, or, perhaps, in any other language.

This is high praise, especially for the work of one as little known to fame as Johnson was in 1744, for it was in connection with the "Life of Savage" and a highly complimentary opinion of it expressed by a Mr. Harte that Cave related the famous story of Johnson's dining behind a screen because he was too shabby for company. But equally high praise is implied in the story of Sir Joshua Reynolds' reading the "Savage" while leaning against a chimney piece and becoming so deeply absorbed that, being unable to stop before the end, found his arm benumbed almost to the point of disablement.

The "Savage" is among Johnson's best pieces of prose. And so far as biographical technique is exemplified, only one fault is to be found, and that arose because Johnson's precept was far better than his ability to follow it. The "Savage" is "useful" in inculcating morality; it places us "for a time in the condition of him whose fortune we contemplate"; it provides those "parallel circumstances and kindred images, to which we readily conform our minds"; it leads "the thoughts into domestic privacies" and "displays details of daily life." Nevertheless, "if the biographer writes from personal experience, and makes haste to gratify public curiosity, there is danger lest his interest" perhaps not "tempt him to conceal" or "to invent," as in this instance was not true, but to write without "full possession of the facts," for there was much about Savage that Johnson either did not know or refused to admit. Savage was, according to Boswell, a person "marked by profligacy, insolence, and ingratitude," yet, according to Hawkins, of captivating address "to a marked degree"; but Johnson characterized him as of "a grave and manly deportment, a solemn dignity of mien; but which upon a nearer acquaintance, softened into an engaging easiness of manners" — which last, not to labor the point, always had a fascination for Johnson. Quite aside from his personality, however, Savage won the championship of Johnson through having shared with him the sordid pressures of Grub Street as much as by their common intellectual sympathy, and through his vivid, if undisciplined, imagination. And such was Johnson's charity that not for a moment could he allow the memory of his friend to suffer, especially a friend whose "days were fewer than his sorrows" — even though he could write:

> He willingly turned his eyes from the light of reason, when it would have shewn him . . . what he never wished to see, his real self.

Hence the "Life" as it appears. Does it matter that Savage was very probably not the son of the Duchess of Macclesfield, but of quite humble origin? And what if neither "The Wanderer" nor "The Bastard" has secured for him "the eminence of rank in the classes of learning" that Johnson promised would be his? Such quibblings all disappear when one reads the "Savage" and sees the tragic figure come to life as few have been reanimated.

# 12—William Mason and
Thomas Gray

*Few speak the truth. Nobody expects them to.* — Millay.

BIOGRAPHY may or may not be the record of race admiration.
There can be small doubt, however, of its place among the
records of affection; even a casual survey reveals example after example of affinity as the impelling force behind authentic accomplishment: Asser and Alfred; Walton and Donne, Wotton, and Sanderson; Johnson and Savage; Stanley and Arnold; Carlyle and Sterling;
Traubel and Whitman; and of late Vera Brittain's "Testament of
Friendship" to Winifred Holtby — the roll might be looked upon as
a list of famous friendships as well as of notable biographies. In
fact, one is tempted to conclude that until historical methodology
developed sufficient effectiveness to render the use of it authoritative
and so added the "informative" to biographic types — as instanced
by Malone's "Dryden" and works similar in purpose which followed
— friendship played no minor part in life writing.

One of the most memorable works to be thus rooted in friendship
is the "Memoirs of the Life and Writings of Thomas Gray," which
William Mason prepared and published privately in 1775. The book
is at once a memorial to the relationship which existed between the
poet and his biographer, and a signal advance in the developing
literary form.

Many particulars and details bear witness to the intimacy in
which the two men were joined. They were friends for almost
twenty-five years. In 1747 one of Gray's acquaintances prevailed
upon him to revise Mason's manuscript poem, "Musaeus, a Monody

to the Memory of Mr. Pope," a somewhat ambitious imitation of Milton's "Lycidas." So much impressed was Gray by the younger man's work — Gray was eight years the elder — that he sought him out and began the friendship that terminated only with his death in 1771.

To have been able to sustain an unbroken friendship with Thomas Gray during so long a period was something of a tribute to Mason — one remembers how slight a difference disturbed the Gray-Walpole intimacy, and how difficult Warton sometimes found him. Indeed, Mason alone of Gray's intimates seems never to have quarreled with him. It is true, Gray in keeping with his chumminess and his fondness for Fescennine writing"; was often teasingly vexing in his treatment of Mason, nicknaming him "Scroodles," among other flippancies. It must be remembered, however, that he referred to himself as a "shrimp of an author." And once in a letter to Dr. Warton he seems to have been quite unpleasant, writing that Mason's "wants do not make him move a foot the faster, nor has he properly speaking, anything one can call a passion about him, except a little malice and revenge." Then, too, he was at times a bit severe with his friend's writing, as in a letter dated December 19, 1757, about Mason's poem "Elegy in the Garden of a Friend" — evidently Mason had complained about his tone — he wrote,

> My advices are always at your service to take or to refuse, therefore you should not call them severe. You know I do not love, much less pique myself on criticism; and think even a bad verse as good a thing or better than the best observations ever made upon it.

If Gray's criticism was sometimes a bit disturbing, however, one remembers that posterity's has been harsh, Saintsbury, for instance, saying "his couplets are tinsel" — and this concerning a man highly respected in his own day as a poet, a dramatist, a critic of art and music, and an authority on gardening. So high was Mason's reputation, in fact, that Hartley Coleridge in his "Northern Worthies" says of him that he was "the most considerable poet that Yorkshire had produced since Marvel," adding that "for many years he was

England's greatest living poet," and Macaulay comments that "a few of his strophies are among the masterpieces of an age of consumate excellence." Not only this, but upon the death of Colley Cibber and the proffer of the laureateship to Gray, the Ministry apologized to Mason for not offering it to him on the ground that he was in orders. In spite of such opinion, however, we today remember only his "Memoir."

Abounding proof of Gray's sincere regard for Mason exists. When in 1756, for instance, the poet was planning a slow wandering journey through Switzerland, it was Mason to whom he turned for company — in spite of the unpleasant result of his previous experience when traveling with a companion; while quite early in their friendship Gray composed the following sketch of Mason's character:

> He was one of much fancy, little judgment, and a good deal of modesty; a good, well-meaning creature, but in simplicity a perfect child; he reads little or nothing, writes abundance, and that with a design to make a fortune at it; a little vain, but in so harmless a way it does not offend; a little ambitious, but withal so ignorant of the world and its ways, that this does not hurt him in one's opinion; so sincere and undisguised, that no one with a spark of generosity would ever think of hurting him he lies so open to injury; but so indolent, that if he cannot overcome this habit, all his good qualities will signify nothing at all.

Furthermore, he once suggested that he and Mason find a house and lodge together. And his letters, as Dr. John Draper points out in his study, "William Mason," are closely sprinkled with phrases like these: "Adieu, my best Mason; I am pleased to think how much I am obliged to you, and, that, while I live, I must be ever yours"; and "Adieu, dear Mason, believe me most truly yours." Sometimes, however, the expressions are more specific. For illustration, "I am sensible I cannot return to you so much of this assistance as I have received from you"; and "Adieu, dear Mason, and remember me; and remember too that I have neither company, nor pleasure, nor spirits here, and that a letter from you stands in place of all these. Adieu." But it is not only in correspondence with

Mason himself that sentiments such as these occur; Gray expressed a similar attitude toward him in letters to both Walpole and Warton, which last, incidentally, was no admirer of Mason. Referring to him once when writing to the latter, for example, he spoke of "our best Mason"; and again, in a note of condolence to Warton upon the death of his son, Gray excused himself for not paying a visit because Mason was about to come to him and he was "unwilling to miss him." As a marked indication of Gray's attitude, however, one need only recall the frequent visits he paid to Mason's rectory at Ashton, not shrinking from the journey even in winter, although he suffered intensely from the cold — always wearing a muff in freezing weather — and, besides, he was timorous about flooded rivers, yet several had to be crossed on his way.

Naturally so close a friendship found expression in practical affairs. For instance, Gray instantly accepted Mason's suggestion that "Elegy" be substituted for "Stanzas" in the title of his best known poem; and among similar requests at various times, he eagerly sought his advice on the revision of "The Bard," as shown by a letter dated May, 1757:

> You will observe, in the beginning of this thing, some alterations of a few words, partly for improvement, and partly to avoid repetitions of like words and rhymes; yet I have not got rid of them all; the six last lines of the fifth stanza are new, tell me whether they will do. I am well aware of many weakly things towards the conclusion, but I hope the end will do; give me your full and true opinion, and that not upon deliberation but forthwith.

As a matter of fact, their literary sympathies extended so far that they once thought of collaborating upon a history of English poetry — an undertaking which unfortunately never proceeded beyond discussion. But it was not only in literary matters — with them the most natural — that their regard for each other took practical form. Mason was in a position to be generous. He was the son of a comparatively wealthy clergyman, and had himself taken orders and been provided with the comfortable living at Ashton and a residentiary canonry at York besides the chaplaincy to George III.

His income in all was around £1500 a year. He frequently made Gray valuable gifts. One was a subscription to Stuart's "Book of Attic," probably the most distinguished work of the time in Greek scholarship — and one of the most expensive — and once, Gray at the time being unable to do so, Mason carried the insurance upon his house for him. However, Gray left a final proof of his regard in the bequest to Mason of £500 and "all books, manuscripts, coins, music printed or written, and papers of all kinds, to preserve or destroy at his own discretion." And Mason's final tribute — not to dwell upon his paying for the poet's tomb in Westminster Abbey or his establishing a fund in his honor for the rebuilding of Pembroke College — was, of course, the "Memoir" itself.

And seldom has a biographer approached his task with more complete equipment. He was provided with the private documents which came to him as literary executor, possessed of scores of letters which in the course of their friendship Gray had written to him, and supplied with those written to Walpole, Warton, Nichols, Stonehewer, Beattie, and a number of others — Robinson, however, and Bonestetten were unwilling to permit the use of theirs. In addition, his literary experience was more than adequate to the undertaking. A number of persons objected to his becoming Gray's biographer, Robinson among them, and the expressed reason for his refusal to permit the use of his letters was that he "did not consider Mr. Mason equal to the task." There were just as many, however, who favored him; Beattie commented, for instance, thus: "The admirers of Mr. Gray will be happy to think that he has made choice of such an able executor as Mr. Mason." But the best of all his equipment was his intimate knowledge of Gray's personality gained during a quarter century of association, this together with the sympathetic understanding which had aided in sustaining without a break so long and so close an intimacy.

On the face of it, therefore, few biographies have ever been attempted under more promising circumstances. In both training and temperament, besides his wealth of material, Mason appears to have had everything in his favor. And, as if this were not enough, biography itself had reached a stage approaching ultimate achievement — in fact sixteen years later Boswell's "Life of Johnson" came

[ 141 ]

forth and the ultimate was achieved. For the tendency toward realism initiated by the seventeenth century had become crystallized in the theory set forth by Dryden and in the practice attempted by Roger North; hence the tradition of ethical intention, concerned almost exclusively with the inner sanctities, was giving way before the realization that biography should be neither an ancillary device in the teaching of morality, nor, as Samuel Johnson once sarcastically termed it, "funeral oratory." It should be the concrete revelation of personality toward the end that a man might be remembered for what he was rather than, as the elder age had sometimes insisted, for what all too frequently he was not. Hence Mason's way was clear and he followed it in such fashion that critics hailed his work as a "new species of biography." And so it was — at least in method.

He states at the outset clearly enough what he intends to do. "The lives of men of letters," he begins,

> seldom abound with incidents; and perhaps no life ever afforded fewer than that which I have undertaken to write. But I am far from mentioning this by way of previous apology, as is the trite custom of biographers. The respect which I owe to my deceased friend, to the public, and (let me add) to myself, prompts me to waive so impertinent a ceremonial. A reader of sense and taste never expects to find in the memoirs of a philosopher, or a poet, the same species of entertainment, or information, which he would receive from those of a statesman or general: he expects, however, to be either informed or entertained; nor would he be disappointed, did the writer take care to dwell principally on such topics as characterize the man, and distinguish that peculiar part which he acted in the varied drama of society. But this rule, self-evidently right as it may seem, is seldom observed. It was said, with almost as much truth as wit, of one of these writers [David Mallet], that when he composed the Life of Lord Verulam, he forgot he was a philosopher; and therefore, it was to be feared, should he finish that of the Duke of Marlborough, he would forget that he was a general. I shall avoid a like fault. I will promise my reader that he shall, in the following pages, seldom behold Mr. Gray in any other light than that of a scholar and a poet: and

though I am more solicitous to show that he was a virtuous, a friendly and an amiable man, than either; yet this solicitude becomes unnecessary from the very pages he has bequeathed me, and which I here arrange for the purpose: since in these the qualities of his head and heart so constantly appear together, and the fertility of his fancy so intimately unites with the sympathetic tenderness of his soul, that were it my intention, I should find it impossible to disjoin them.

And the book as a whole is composed in the manner described: Gray's letters are arranged in five sections with comment interspersed to sustain the continuity, so that there might never be related "a single circumstance of Mr. Gray's life in my own words, when I could employ *his* for the purpose."

It is clear, therefore, what the reviewers meant by calling the work "a new species of biography." For new it was, in the sense that it — as had previously been done only in obscure instances — utilized material written by the subject himself as the principal means of character revelation. From the point of view of emphasis, therefore, Mason was the first to use the "autobiographical method."

However, although Mason's emphasis upon it was new, autobiographical material had been used from time to time almost from the beginning. Not a few "lives" composed during the Middle Ages had included letters — all formalized after the fashion said to have been established by Stona, the mother of Xerxes, and brought to perfection by Cicero. As a matter of fact, one of them, Eadmer's "Anselm," as has been pointed out, had made use of recorded conversation. Eddius had used letters, as had Walton, Gilbert Burnet in his "Life of Bedell," Hacket in the "Scrinia Reserata," Richard Parr in the "Life of Usher," and finally Conyers Middleton in the "Life of Cicero." The latter work, regarded as a classic in Mason's day, is one which is not to be overlooked as a possible influence upon him. In addition to biographies which contained letters one must remember also that books containing nothing but letters had been increasing in demand for more than a century. Margaret Newcastle published her collection in 1664. A translation of the "Portuguese Letters" became popular several years later, as did the letters of Abelard and Eloise. At almost the same time James

Howell's "Epistolae Ho-Elianae" appeared, and after the turn of the century the letters of Lady Mary Montagu enjoyed a very great vogue indeed. With the eighteenth century, too, had come an interest in the letter as a device in fiction, as in Richard Wellington's "The Adventures of Lindamira," for instance, and later in the novels of Richardson, and of Robert Bage. Hence Mason's use of Gray's letters in the "Memoir" was not without precedent. It may be that he got hints from Middleton's "Cicero," and that, as John Mitford, the distinguished editor of Gray, points out, he also learned something from Quirini's "Epistolae Reginaldi Poli," or it may be that his work was the natural culmination of a natural trend — however all this may be, Mason himself explains his use of the letters thus:

> I am well aware that I am here going to do a thing which the cautious and courtly Dr. Sprat (were he now alive) would highly censure. He had, it seems, a large collection of his friend Mr. Cowley's letters, a way of writing in which he particularly excelled, as in these he always expressed the native tenderness and innocent gayety of his heart: yet the Doctor was of the opinion that nothing of this nature should be published and that the letters that pass between particular friends (if they were written as they ought to be) can scarce ever be fit to see the light. What! not when they express the native tenderness and innocent gayety of a heart like Mr. Cowley's? No, by no means, for in such letters the souls of men appear undressed, and in that negligent habit they may be fit to be seen by one or two in a chamber but not to go abroad in the street. Such readers as believe it incumbent on every well-bred soul never to appear but in full dress will think that Dr. Sprat has reason on his side; but I believe that the generality will, notwithstanding, wish he had been less scrupulously delicate and lament that . . . the letters in question are not now extant. . . . In a word, Mr. Gray will become his own biographer, both in this first section and in the rest of the sections into which I divide the work. By which means, and by the assistance of a few notes which I will occasionally add, it may be hoped that nothing will be omitted which may tend to give a regular and clear delineation of his life and character.

[ 144 ]

That Mason intended to reveal Gray as he had known him, there can be no question; his statements to that effect are obvious. But that he failed to do so is equally evident — there is ample reason to believe that in handling his material he was only less "scrupulously delicate" than Dr. Sprat, whose practice he so definitely deplores. One feels throughout the work that the same friendship which impelled him to write the memoir restrained him from full revelation. Of course, his day was very different from ours — when "curiosity would seem to be monarch of all that should not be surveyed"; reticence was welcomed, was even expected in biography. Something in addition to the spirit of the age, however, was behind Mason's treatment. The late Henry Van Dyke might exclaim, "But, thank God! we have not to estimate a true man by his worst but by his best"; none the less one cannot help thinking that unless we know the worst we have no proper perspective for a view of the best and so must often miss the substance in grasping the shadow. Mason's memoir defines Gray as a poet and a philosopher, but later scholarship has shown "the demi-god a man."

A comparison between Mason's version of the letters and the Toynbee-Whibley edition shows something of the liberties Mason took with his material. It becomes clear that Mason changed punctuation, grammar, and spelling; suppressed the ampersand; took liberty with dates; and deleted the ribaldy so that frequently amusing, informal material becomes stuffy and artificial. None the less, Mason's ideal of Gray as a poet, a philosopher, and the most learned man in Europe, as he unquestionably was, is well sustained — an ideal that could survive even Johnson's scorn as expressed to Boswell:

> Sir, he was dull in his company, dull in his closet, dull everywhere. He was dull in a new way and that made people think him great.

Granted that Mason did use Gray's letters as if they had been "raw material" for his book (as Austin Dobson once suggested) and so cooled, corrected, and made less natural their warm, defective, and altogether human qualities — does it matter? We today say that his was not a proper editorial practice; his own day considered that it was. In fact there was some remark among critics at the time that he had revealed too much, not too little of Gray's character and convictions; just as many of Johnson's friends objected to his publishing "Prayers and Mediations" on the score of its being too personal an expression. However, it is worth noting that Samuel Johnson read Mason's book because it was "a common topick of conversation," but found it "mighty dull," and "as to style, it was fit for the second table." Nevertheless Boswell sets forth in his introductory comments that he resolved "to adopt and enlarge upon the excellent plan of Mr. Mason in his Memoirs of Gray." The truth is (to return to the general attitude as far as it was unapproving, and one may suspect even if he cannot demonstrate) that the times did not understand men like Gray. The "Monthly Review," for instance was of the opinion, concurred in by the "London Review," that he was "a man of singularities too violent for the commerce of society." And Mason was well aware of such points of view. Hence, "though the pencil of friendship," in the phrase of a contemporary review, "has thrown much into the shade," it would seem that it was wielded more sparingly than posterity realizes. Mason wished to perpetuate the memory of the man whom he loved. He understood him — most people did not. He fell inevitably between two stools — and the long debate as to what the biographer may reveal and what he should suppress continues; every age decides anew for itself. Whatever one may think of Mason's use of fact, there can be no gainsaying the effectiveness of the form he adopted. To him must go the credit for bringing into focus the advantages of the autobiographical method and so establishing it in the service of the genre, preparing thus the way for Boswellian perfection. Gray has had other and better biographers, but their work could not have been done except for Mason's contribution.

# 13—Goldsmith and His "Lives"

*Fate holds the strings, and men like children move
But as they're led: success is from above.* — Granville.

THE aptness of an epitaph is not infrequently an intimation of a man's just claim to celebrity. The very great, "the mighty benefactors of mankind," as Wordsworth calls them in his "Essay Upon Epitaphs," require nothing beyond the mention of their names and "an intuition, communicated in adequate words, of the sublimity of their power,

> What needs my Shakespeare for his honored bones
> The labour of an age in piled Stones;"

and the obscure may be commemorated in "some thought or feeling belonging to the mortal or immortal part of our general nature touchingly expressed." In the opinion of Samuel Johnson, in his "Dissertation on Pope's Epitaphs," few men are worthy of human praise, or, in his own words "the greater part of mankind have no character at all." Between the two, however, come those who although not among the "mighty benefactors," nevertheless richly deserve "the praises poets well repeat." These, because of some definite trait or some specific excellence, lend themselves to characterization in phrases as deathless as their own fame, and sometimes just that occurs — the apparency of their worth is revealed in the aptness of the inscriptions they inspire.

Unfortunately the occurrence is not invariable, Mason's lines upon the tomb of Gray are neither just nor beautiful. And Wordsworth's monody over the death of Charles Lamb would have served rather to weight that spirit than to preserve it had the long poem been used. None the less, there are scores of instances to support the contrary, the most striking perhaps being Johnson's words carved upon the tomb of Oliver Goldsmith: *Nullum quod tetigit non ornavit,* for in a very literal sense Goldsmith "touched nothing he did not adorn." Poet, dramatist, novelist, essayist — all these he was to distinction. But in addition, although as yet the critics and historians of literature have been slow to recognize him as such, he was a biographer of taste and discernment and the first great stylist to adopt the form.

He has come slowly to recognition as a biographer no doubt for two reasons; the circumstances under which his "lives" were written, and the fact that he had not "eaten and drunk and lived in social intercourse with" his subjects; hence, what seems at first sight inadequate accomplishment resulted. A close reading, however, discloses values more than sufficient for admitting him into the canon.

One reads early biography to little purpose if he does not soon discover that the most splendid examples spring form some intimate relationship between author and subject. They are written against a background of emotional engagement, so to speak, and seldom, if ever, at the arbitrary request of a publisher and never directly for purposes of financial gain. Goldsmith, therefore, was handicapped from the start — although it is well to remember that allusion to biographical writing like that of Colly Cibber, David Malet, Dryden, Spence, Sprat, and Middleton, for instance, is frequent enough both in his own writing and in his recorded conversation to mark a more than casual interest in the form.

That he succeeded even in minor fashion, points up his work as unique; for all his "lives," with the possible exception of the "Parnell," were ordered of him by booksellers and all were written — if partly because Goldsmith had to write or perish spiritually and one form was as good as another to him — almost wholly to make money, circumstances for which he cannot possibly be blamed, if, indeed, they may not be looked upon as providing foils against which his achievement gleams the brighter.

The first "life," that of Voltaire, if one overlooks his translations, "The Memoirs of a Protestant" and "My Lady B.," was written for

Griffiths to accompany a translation of the "Henriade." And a more ill-fated project has seldom been launched. At the time, 1758, Goldsmith was doing hack work for the "Monthly Review," edited by Ralph Griffiths and his wife, but so small were his earnings that sometimes he was not sufficiently clad to leave his lodgings during the day — a far cry from the plum-colored coat, the blue silk and the new velvet (one remembers his appearing in scarlet breeches for examination in theology, not to mention the black velvet costume of his days as medical practitioner) and the extravagant chambers later on. The price agreed upon was £20, to be applied toward refurnishing Goldsmith's wardrobe. The tailor was paid, but the project was never completed as planned. The translation was to have been supplied by Edward Purdon, a fellow hack with Goldsmith and an old companion of his Dublin days, whom he later characterized in the famous epigram:

> Here lies poor Ned Purdon, from misery freed,
>  Who long was a bookseller's hack;
> He led such a damnable life in this world,
>  I don't think he'll wish to come back.

But Purdon, in his customary discouraged way, failed to complete the translation on time. He did eventually finish it, however; for the "Public Advertiser" of February 7, 1759, carried a notice announcing that the *Life of Monsieur Voltaire* was "speedily to be published." Nothing appeared, however, at that time; in fact Goldsmith's share of the work, although printed, did not come out at all until portions of it were reprinted in "The Lady's Magazine" during 1761. It was first added to his collected works in 1837. The upshot as far as Goldsmith was concerned was that the £20 went for badly needed clothing and was beyond recovery, and Griffiths was incensed — the beginning of the end of the unfortunate Griffith-Goldsmith personal relationship, as Goldsmith left the "Monthly Review" some months later to be pursued by an accumulation of Griffith's maledictions even after death.

That Goldsmith thought little of the "Voltaire" is suggested by a letter written to his brother, a portion of which follows:

> I know not whether I should tell you — yet why should I

conceal these trifles, or indeed anything from you? There is a book of mine will be published in a few days, the life of a very extraordinary man — no less than the great Voltaire. You know already from the title that it is no more than a catch-penny. However, I spent but four weeks on the whole performance, for which I received twenty pounds.

Historically considered, the work contains almost all the available information concerning Voltaire's exile in England, and is written in the author's graceful and simple style, but Goldsmith, with his spirit of adulation for Voltaire, was little competent to gauge the harmful influence exercised upon mankind by the refined scoffer at religion.

Scholarship of late in connection with Goldsmith, particularly that of Professor Ronald S. Crane of Chicago and Professor J. E. Brown of Princeton, has shown his extraordinary indebtedness to the French, the "Lettres chinoises" of D'Argens, especially, with the writings of Marivaux. Besides, as Professor Brown has pointed out, the essay "Of Eloquence," published in "The Bee," November 17, 1759, is almost a direct translation of Voltaire's article on eloquence, supplemented by passages from D'Alembert's article on the same subject, as both appear in Diderot's "Encyclopedie." Furthermore, it is thought that the idea for the "Citizen of the World" perhaps grew out of a sentence which Voltaire included in his essay, "Contradictions": *Un Asiatique qui voyagerait en Europe pourrait bien nous prendre pour des païens.*

In keeping with this leaning, and in view of the sympathetic attitude shown toward Voltaire in the "Memoirs," both indications of admiration, perhaps his self-styled "catch-penny" was not undertaken entirely at request, but was an expression of emotional engagement rather sadly misplaced. He was caught in the lure that fatally influenced so many others.

Whether or not there was emotional engagement involved in the "Voltaire," nothing but hack drudgery for low pay is evidenced by the biographical writings with which — except for the "Life of Richard Nash" in 1762 — he was occupied during the next several years. For instance, the younger Dodsley contracted with him for "A Chronological History of the Lives of Eminent Persons of Great

Britain and Ireland," to appear in two volumes, and agreed that "Oliver Goldsmith shall print his name to said work." This last was significant of his growing reputation; but not a line was ever written. Newberry employed him in composing a "Compendium of Biography," an ambitious enterprise which was to include many volumes but was discontinued with the seventh, completely eclipsed by Dilly's "British Plutarch." "The Lives of the Fathers," for which Newberry paid him ten guineas, could not have absorbed him as in it he included little more than was readily obtainable from William Cave's "Apostolica" and "Ecclesiastici." Neither could he have been much engrossed with "The Life of Christ," published first in the "Christian Magazine" and later as a shilling pamphlet — a work which Professor R. W. Scitz suggests was adapted from the Reading "Christ." There is nothing in any of these writings indicative of much beyond the fact that a demand for biography existed and that booksellers were exploiting it.

Of such, however, the "Life of Richard Nash" most decidedly was not. It is by wide margins his best work in the genre, and it was, unquestionably, the one that most nearly captured his interest: Newberry had paid him 14 guineas for it; none the less Goldsmith added new material and improved the old when a second edition was demanded, *and he did so without any recompense whatever in connection with a book published without his name.* (Incidentally, at the Spoor sale in 1939 a first edition brought $230.) To explain fully his interest in the "Nash" one would very probably require the training of a psychiatrist. It must suffice to say that the world of fashion was to Goldsmith extraordinarily alluring. He loved finery, the ebb and flow of affairs at such places as Bath and Tunbridge, and people who frequented the clubs, resorts, ballrooms, and smart assemblies. Hence he admired Beau Nash as the apotheosis of social sophistication. But beneath this surface lay a more fundamental source of attraction — between author and subject there existed a moral similarity such that when Goldsmith points up Nash's virtues and cries down his faults he seems unconsciously to be characterizing himself, an idea which Forster in his "Life" stresses by saying that the "Nash" is a curious, and . . . probably an unconscious, revelation of [Goldsmith's] character. No one was more poignantly aware of defect in himself than was Goldsmith and no one knew better than he what he should do to improve — that he did nothing is another matter. And so it was but natural that he should find similar flaws in others and suggest the proper remedies. For instance, he has much to say about imprudence as the greatest cause of disaster — he, who was never prudent in his life. He speaks of charitable giving, insisting that open-handed generosity always tempts to imposition — and yet he himself when asked for money went about borrowing if he had none in his pocket. And "Nothing debases human nature so much as pride," he writes; but whose pride was greater — if one remember the "Mistake of a Night" underlying "She Stoops to Conquer"? He deplores gambling, showing it to have been Nash's dominant passion, but who more than Goldsmith was addicted to the excitement of Rolly-Polly, Marlborough's Battles, Loo, Primero, or In-and-In? One may run the gamut of Nash's vices and match each item with one of Goldsmith's own. In their virtues they were also akin: charity to all who applied, chivalry almost to absurdity, and an abiding human sympathy — as Nash's hospital at Bath and Goldsmith's "The Vicar of Wakefield" testify. In short, the author had a variety of reasons for being drawn to the subject; and "The Life of Nash" is full evidence that he was, although there was much in the career of Nash with which Goldsmith was not at all in sympathy.

Another cause of his interest in the undertaking, hack work though it was, lies inherent in the state at the time of biography itself. Newberry and Goldsmith both knew as well as anybody in London what the reading public wanted and were as anxious as anybody else to supply it. They could not have been unaware, therefore, that since before the turn of the century the trend in popular demand had been toward the "lives" of rascals, criminals, underworld characters in general, adventurers, and the more sensational among persons of quality — this besides the normal demand for "lives" of the justly famous. They knew about Esquemeling's "Die Americaenische Zee-Roomers," surely, and had no doubt seen the notorious "Petticoat-Pensioners," which came out in 1749. Likewise, they could not have failed to be familiar with the extraordinary success of Edmund Curll and his "Lives of the Most

Eminent Persons Who Died in the Years 1711, 1712, 1713, 1714," or with the "Works" of Captain Alexander Smith who between 1714 and 1730 delighted sensation seekers with accounts of highwaymen, famous beauties — "from fair Rosamund down to the Present Time" — bailiffs, jailers, and executioners, not to stress persons involved in secret scandals among the nobility. Then, too, there was Theophilus Lucas' "Memoirs of Lives, Intrigues, and Comical Adventures of the Most Famous Gamesters," mention of which Goldsmith includes. The "Life of Richard Nash" is in the trend with these, and yet because of Goldsmith's impeccable taste and his sympathetic insight, it is far from being a sop to the prurient.

In structure it, like all his "lives," is chronological. Nash's forebears are named, his education described, his enthronement as "King of Bath" accounted for, the details of his adventures set forth, his character delineated, and his death and funeral projected in full color. The opening paragraphs, moreover, reveal Goldsmith's philosophy of biography to be decidedly in advance of hack writing practice, influenced, as Professor Brown holds, by Johnson's ideas as defined in the "Rambler," the "Idler," and the "Sir Thomas Browne." The work as a whole implies a grasp of its subject's significance in an evolving society, a grasp immensely superior to most current effort. "Thus no one can properly be said to write history," the second paragraph begins,

> but he who understands the human heart, and its whole train of affections and follies. Those affections and follies are properly the materials he has to work upon. The relation of great events may surprise, indeed; they may be calculated to instruct those very few who govern the millions beneath; but the generality of mankind find the most real improvement from relations which are levelled to the general surface of life, which tell — not how man lived to conquer, but how they endeavored to live — not how they gained the shout of the admiring crowd, but how they acquired the esteem of their friends and acquaintances.

> Every man's own life would perhaps furnish the most pleasing materials for history, if he only had candor enough to be sincere, and skill enough to select such parts as, once making

him more prudent, might serve to render his readers more cautious. There are few who do not prefer a page of Montaigue or Colley Cibber, who candidly tell us what they thought of the world and the world thought of them, to more stately memoirs and transactions of Europe, where we see kings pretending to immortality that are now almost forgotten, and statesmen planning frivolous negotiations, that scarcely outlive the signing.

It is candor, therefore, and simple truth that Goldsmith seeks — in fact, as Sidney Lee remarks, "Candor . . . is a cardinal principle of right biographic method; panegyric and the superficial show of life contribute nothing"; and he submits that the darker reaches of the soul require to be plumbed if the brighter are to be understood. The psychology of the beau was, of course, influenced by his surroundings and agreed with his own temperament, though it is destructive of the human will to endeavor to make of it the inevitable result of the forces that played upon him. Note the character of society when Nash began his reign:

> General society among people of rank or fortune was by no means established. The nobility still preserved a tincture of Gothic haughtiness, and refused to keep company with the gentry at any of the public entertainments of Bath. Smoking in the rooms was permitted; gentlemen and ladies appeared in a disrespectful manner . . . in aprons and boots;

as he began to assume power:

> We are to see him directing pleasures which none had better learned to share; placed over rebellious and refractory subjects, that were to be ruled only by the force of his address, and governing such as had long been accustomed to govern others.

This shows to a large degree the dominance of his own will over the society about him. Changes became almost immediately apparent:

> The amusements of the place wore a very different aspect from what they formerly did. Regularity repressed pride, and that lessened, people of fortune became fit for society. Let the morose and grave censure an attention to forms and ceremonies,

and rail at those whose only business was to regulate them. . . . The natural gradation of breeding begins in savage disgust, proceeds to indifference, improves into attention, by degrees refines into ceremonious observance and the trouble of being ceremonious at length produces politeness, elegance, and ease.

Finally, there is a passage which draws us closer to Nash and at once serves to characterize him, to throw some light upon his age, and to further illustrate Goldsmith's manner:

> As Nestor was a man of three ages, so Nash sometimes humorously called himself a beau of three generations. He had seen flaxon bobs succeeded by majors, which in their turn gave way to negligents, which at last were totally routed by bags and Ramilies. The manner in which gentlemen managed their amours, in these different ages of fashion, were not more different than their periwigs. The lover in the reign of King Charles was solemn, majestic, and formal. He visited his mistress in state, languished for the favour, kneeled when he toasted his goddess, walked with solemnity, performed the most trifling things with decorum, and even took snuff with a flourish. The beau of the latter part of Queen Anne's reign was disgusted with so much formality; he was pert, smart, and lively; his billet-doux were written in a quite different style from that of his antiquated predecessor; he was ever laughing at his own ridiculous situation; till at last he persuaded the lady to become as ridiculous as himself. The beau of the third age, in which Mr. Nash died, was still more extraordinary than either; his whole secret in intrigue consisted in perfect indifference. The only way to make love now, I have heard Mr. Nash say, was to take no manner of notice of the lady; which method was found the surest way to secure her affections.

There is no denying the beauty of Goldsmith's style, the quality of which may be realized partly from his own comment upon contemporary blemishes: "Let us try to write naturally; not hunt after lofty expressions to deliver mean ideas, nor be forever gaping when we mean to whisper"; and partly from a remark by Percy in the "Memoir": "His elegant and enchanting style in prose flowed from him with such facility that in whole quires he had seldom occasion to correct or alter a single word." But most satisfactorily the quality will be realized from reading his work. No matter what he wrote, a review of Murphy's "Orphan of China" or the "Vicar of Wakefield," a hurried essay for the "Bee" or the "Deserted Village," the "Life of Richard Nash" or the "Good-Natured Man," his purity and native grace permeated it. It is a singular fact that as soon as he took up his pen, whether at the time he was among "the beggers of Axe Lane" or "with Lord Clare in the country," whatever may have inclined him toward either the sordid or the ostentatious became ineffectual and his style ran clear, fluent, and chaste. Truly it may be said of him that he wrote scarcely a line for which he himself need ever have blushed and none at all for which need any one else. Indeed he wrote, in Francis Thompson's phrase, so that

> every sentence was deftly shaped, as easy as the song of the bird; the phrasing unobstrusively perfect as we have lost the art of perfecting it in our selfconscious age;

or in William Godwin's

> with such easy copiousness, and grace that his prose resembles the song of the Sirens.

Naturally, therefore, when one turns to the "Parnell" he expects distinction of style; and he is not disappointed, for the book contains some passages of his best. Besides this quality its greatest claim to distinction is that it was abstracted by Johnson in his "Lives of the Poets." "The Life of Dr. Parnell," Johnson begins,

> is a task which I should very willingly decline, since it has lately been written by Goldsmith, a man of such variety of powers, and such felicity of performance, that he always seemed to do best that which he was doing; a man who had the art of being minute without tediousness, and general without confusion; whose language was copious without exuberance, exact without restraint, and easy without weakness.
> What such an author has told, who would tell again?

Goldsmith wrote the "Parnell" in 1769, during odd moments, it must have been, snatched from more important matters, for at the time the "English History" was his chief concern, although the

"History of Animated Nature" was under way also, and "The Deserted Village" was being advertised as soon to be published. He had a particular interest in Parnell, however, as is intimated by his remark that his material was what he remembered having heard in boyhood "from my father and uncle, who knew him"; and, besides, the poet was his own countryman. The book is scarcely more than an essay — in fact it was composed as an introduction to an edition of its subject's poems. It was reissued as a separate volume almost at once, although it occupies not more than twenty pages in the Cunningham edition. None the less, it is more than adequate, abounding in comment both apt and informing. This, for instance, is Goldsmith's remark concerning the difficulties involved in obtaining biographical details of famous men before they have come to fame:

> A poet, while living, is seldom an object sufficiently great to attract much attention; his real merits are known to but a few, and these are generally sparing in their praises. When his fame is increased by time, it is then too late to investigate the peculiarities of his disposition; the dews of the morning are past, and we vainly try to continue the chase by the meridian splendor.

Included are opinions on the merits of Parnell's translations; hints of Pope's probable indebtedness to him; letters from Pope, Gay, and Arbuthnot; criticisms of ornate poetry. Through it all — in spite of certain animadversions concerning Gray and Collins — welding it together in harmony, there is the sustaining force of Goldsmith's inimitable manner.

The work was issued during the summer of 1770 and so gratifying was the result to Tom Davies, whose project it was, that he immediately engaged the author to write a memoir of Bolingbroke to introduce a new edition of the "Dissertation on Parties." To us this is the least interesting of Goldsmith's biographical writing — probably because he seems to have done little more than paraphrase the account in the "Biographia Brittanica." Style obtains, but even the style is something below Goldsmith's usual excellence. Not the worst result of this memoir was his laying himself open to stinging criticism. Some of the reviews more than hinted — absurd though the charge was — that Johnson's influence was apparent throughout; and that not a few sentences were ambiguous, which last is all too true, unfortunately. Davies' purpose, of course, was to exploit the moment, one of intense party strife; but Goldsmith was never one to write political pamphlets. The only approach to distinction is to be found in the character of Bolingbroke with which the sketch closes, but even that is insufficient to save the book from sinking to the lowest rank among Goldsmith's biographical works.

Naturally, therefore, the critical success of the "Parnell" was not repeated in the "Bolingbroke," further editions of the former having been required in close succession, and the only surviving dissent being Johnson's comment to Boswell upon the book's first appearance — a criticism which has become almost a maxim with students of biography:

> Goldsmith's Life of Parnell is poor; not that it is poorly written, but that he had poor materials; for nobody can write the life of a man but those who have eat and drunk and lived in social intercourse with him.

In fact so imperfect was the "Bolingbroke" that the "Monthly Review," of which Ralph Griffiths was still editor, fairly gloated over what it considered an opportunity at fair game, beginning a bitter attack thus:

> We have long had a desire at heart to expose that false, futile, and slovenly style, which to the utter neglect of grammatical percision and purity, disgraces . . . and no author ever gave a fairer opportunity of discharging it than the author of this Life of Bolingbroke.

Notwithstanding its lack of worth, the interest at the time in political affairs created something of a demand for the work. Published first in connection with Bolingbroke's once celebrated "Dissertation," it was reissued as a separate work during the same year, and in 1774, was prefixed to a complete edition of Bolingbroke's works. However, its contribution to Goldsmith's fame was negligible, and to biography as an evolving literary form nothing at all, although as a collector's item the 1771 edition has risen above the "Nash" in value, having been bought at a recent auction for $310.

Goldsmith's reputation, to be sure, rests upon a much more solid base than the "Voltaire," the "Nash," and the "Parnell." What is to be said in their favor is that they have style, a quality which is far to seek in life writing. Sir Thomas More had it, and Walton, Conyers Middleton, and Dryden; but in general biographers are not stylists — why, it is not easy to decide. It may be that until here of late, practised writers have not been drawn to the form; hundreds of biographers have been men of one book, and so lack the experience of novelists who have written a shelf full. Or it may be that the limits imposed by range and purpose are too narrow to allow the full expression of personality so essential to a distinguished style. However that may be, Goldsmith was one of the first truly great authors to become interested in life writing. With the advent of the nineteenth century, as everyone knows, and the appearance of men like Southey, Carlyle, and Trevelyan, style became the accustomed thing; nevertheless even today a comparison with other forms would probably show that, prose for prose, biography more often than not falls below excellence.

As it is, Goldsmith's style, unquestionably, is involved in Johnson's *Nullum quod tetigit ornavit*; it is his bequest to biography.

# 14—Boswell and the "Johnson"

*The soul shall have society of its own rank.* — Emerson.

IT SEEMS a paradox that biographers should themselves seldom be made the subject of biography. More, Johnson, Goldsmith, and Carlyle have been superbly treated, to be sure, but hardly because they wrote "lives." On the other hand, what of Walton, Boswell, Lockhart, Trevelyan, Forster, and the others, many of whom rank higher in the canon? These last have received certain attention, it is true — Boswell and Lockhart have been treated in no slight manner, for instance, the former by Dr. Rogers and Professor Chauncey Tinker and the latter by Andrew Lang — only, nothing in keeping with their own work has yet appeared. Perhaps the tardiness with which biography has come to recognition as literature is the reason why its exponents have been but grudgingly accepted on equality with poets, novelists, dramatists, and essayists; or perhaps it is because the form is so difficult and comparatively so unremunerative that but few writers have cared to adopt it, more promising material having engaged their interest. But whatever the reason, the fact remains and the paradox stands.

That James Boswell, of all men, should, a century and a half after his death, still lack proper biographical treatment is a double paradox; not only has no one come forth with a distinguished "life," but most of those who have written of him viewed him more or less as a literary sport. Saintsbury, of course, could remark:

> The inspired-zany and the devout-hero-worshipper-with-a-few-personal-flaws theory shall rest. One thing is clear, that Boswell was a great artist, for he set himself to do a most difficult thing and he did it consumately.

And Carlyle could say:

Boswell was a person whose mean or bad qualities lay open to the general eye, visible, palpable to the dullest. . . . That he was a wine-bibber and good liver, gluttonously fond of whatever would yield him a little solacement, were it only of a stomachic character, it is undeniable enough. That he was vain, heedless, a babbler, had much of the sycophant, alternating with the braggadocio, curiously spiced, too, with an all pervading dash of the coxcomb; that he gloried much when the tailor by a court suit had made a new man of him, . . . and, in short, if you will, lived no day of his life without saying and doing more than one pretentious ineptitude, all this unhappily is evident as the sun at noon. . . . On the other hand, what great and genuine good lay in him was no-wise so self-evident.

None the less Macaulay had it that

We are not sure that there is in the whole history of the human intellect so strange a phenomenon as this book. Many of the greatest men that ever lived have written biography. Boswell was one of the smallest men that ever lived, and he has beaten them all. He was, if we are to give any credit to his own account or to the united testimony of all who knew him, a man of the meanest and feeblest intellect.

Lytton Strachey submitted that

It would be difficult to find a more shattering refutation to the lessons of cheap morality than the life of James Boswell. One of the most extraordinary successes in the history of civilization was achieved by an idler, a drunkard, a lecher, and a snob. . . . Boswell triumphed by dint of abandoning himself, through fifty years, to his instincts.

Robert Lynd sneered that Johnson was the invention of a Scottish humorist named Boswell; Washington Irving called him an "incarnation of toadyism"; Peter Pindar scoffed that he was "the pilot of our literary whale"; and finally John Forster commented in his "Goldsmith":

By one of the most moderately wise men that ever lived the

masterpiece of English biography was written. What would we now give to have had a Boswell for every Johnson! to have had in attendance on all our immortals, as much self-complacent folly with as much shrewd clear insight; the same lively talent to do justice to their sayings, the same reverence to devote it to that humble service, and the same conceit full-proof against every degradation it involved. We have but to turn to the biography of any other man of letters, to comprehend our debt of gratitude to Boswell.

"It is an uncontrolled truth," wrote Jonathon Swift, "that no man ever made an ill figure who understood his own talents, nor a good one who mistook them," and Boswell is an apt illustration. He devoted not quite half his fifty-five years to preparing his "Life of Johnson," but not until all his other plans had come to nothing did he consider it all important, as in his Journal are frequent repinings at his lack of success in professional undertakings and just as frequent expressions of hope that in the end his writings would compensate for failure to provide for his family. At the request of his father he studied law at Utrecht and was admitted advocate July 26, 1766; but London fascinated him and he became too much involved with the social life in which he found himself there to pursue the studies necessary for admission to the English bar before Hilary Term, 1786. He was a dunce, says practicality, not to devote himself exclusively to the law when in it he might have made an eminently successful career; just as he was a dunce to leave Auchinleck — the family title to which had been granted by James IV — with its ten broad miles from portal to highroad and its £ 1600 a year, to seek precarious living in London. He could easily enough have remained at home and become a proper laird, so that when the time came he might (like his son Alexander) have had ten thousand people to accompany him to the grave. Dunce or not, in the eye of practicality, he chose the better part and wrote the greatest of all biographies.

Beauclerk referred to him as the epitome of bores. Johnson once said that it was too bad he had been born so late, for he might otherwise have become immortal through inclusion in the "Dunciad." He endured the gibes of his father; the complainings

of his wife; the annoyance of Lady Cork; the hatred of the Duchess
of Argyle, resulting from his having been on the opposing side in a
law case; the persecution of Lord Lonsdale; and the sneers of
Colonel Macleod — attitudes toward him which may be summed up
in a letter which long after his death Sir Walter Scott wrote to
Croker:

> Sir Alexander Boswell was a proud man, and like his grand-
> father, thought his father lowered himself by his deferential
> suit and service to Johnson. He disliked any allusion to the
> book or to Johnson himself, and I have observed that the fine
> picture by Sir Joshua Reynolds was sent upstairs out of the
> living room at Auchinlech.

All this — but in contrast, to show at least his acceptance by people
of prominence — Boswell won his way into the confidence of
Voltaire; he so impressed Rousseau that for some time they corre-
sponded intimately; he captivated Wilkes so far that for years he
remained a familiar acquaintance; he made himself useful to
General Paoli and gained the old patriot's unswerving loyalty;
Queen Charlotte said he was so extraordinary that he would do
something extraordinary; Fanny Burney enjoyed him, but refused
him access to her Diary and her Johnson letters; Mrs. Thrale
suffered him, although later she came to hate him; the Earl of
Chatham failed to do more than smile in a niggardly fashion at his
compliments; but Johnson himself once said, "Sir, if I were to lose
Boswell, it would be a limb amputated"; and in a letter to Boswell
dated August 27, 1775, wrote:

> Never, my dear Sir, do you take it into your head to think
> that I do not love you; you may settle yourself in full confi-
> dence both of my love and my esteem; I love you as a kind
> man, I value you as a worthy man and hope in time to rever-
> ence you as a man of exemplary piety. I hold you, as Hamlet
> has it, in my heart of hearts.

And in addition one may point out that during the tour of the
Hebrides he and Johnson spent thirteen weeks together in daily
and nightly contact with no cost to their friendship.

In view of such contradictions and confusions, what is one to think other than what has been thought? It may be that Boswell was "a man of the meanest and feeblest intellect," and that "one of the most extraordinary successes in the history of civilization was achieved by an idler, a lecher, drunkard, and a snob"; only, as Professor Chauncey Tinker suggests, there is always the matter of figs and thistles.

The paradox concerning his biographical fate seems the more confusing when one considers that he was a lawyer and trained to value evidence, that he did, in fact, save letters and documents concerned with his affairs, and journals, diaries, and every kind of record relating to both private matters and his various enterprises — going so far, for instance, upon one occasion (that of his proposal for the hand of Zelide) to request permission to copy the twenty-six page letter if it were not to be returned to him. All this material he seems to have treasured in an ebony cabinet which he inherited from his grandmother, Lady Kincardine; just as, it is now revealed, he stored in a croquet box material which his publisher and Edmund Malone advised against including in the "Tour of the Hebrides." All was mislaid at the time of his granddaughter Emily's marriage and removal to Malahide Castle in Ireland. Everything has now been recovered, however, thanks to the efforts of Lord Talbot of Malahide, great, great grandson of Boswell, and of Colonel Ralph H. Isham, and published, thanks to the editorial skill and high scholarship of Mr. Geoffrey Scott and Professor Frederick A. Pottle. A further discovery of letters at Fettercairn House by Professor Claude C. Abbott, made in 1930, together with the Temple letters, available since 1857, comprises, all told, a body of information such that Boswell should now become as well and intimately known as any man who ever lived, with the possible exception of Johnson himself. The paradox of the "Great Biographer" going unbiographized in spite of his quite definite efforts to guard against so ironical an accident — for he was as fully aware as anyone has ever been that posterity would be interested in him — has been resolved. What is required now is a biographer equal to the task in order that the century and a half old story of the dunce and the unequaled contribution to literature may be corrected. And yet, no matter how admirably the material is handled, will Boswell's reputation be changed? — One remembers Hazlitt and his comment upon the world when it has made up its mind! Be that as it may, whatever some future biographer may demonstrate the character of Boswell to have been, there can be no two opinions about the character of his book.

The idea of writing Johnson's life seems to have occupied Boswell almost from the time of their first meeting, in 1763. He says himself that he had "the scheme of writing his life constantly in view." The first definite evidence of the undertaking, however, appears in his asking Johnson in May, 1768, for permission to publish the letters at the proper time. The next record concerns Johnson's approval of the particulars of his early life then in Boswell's hands, on March 31, 1772. More than a year later, on Easter Sunday, 1773, when Boswell was dining for the first time at Johnson's house, he asked for further details of Johnson's early life and Johnson told him: "You shall have them all for twopence. I hope you shall know a great deal more of me before you write my life." Johnson was, however, later to say, "You have but two topics, Sir: yourself and me. I am sick of both." Nevertheless he was quite pleased to have Boswell undertake to write his "life," for he had feared that Goldsmith might. Upon one occasion, according to Mrs. Thrale, he had said, "the dog [Goldsmith] would write it best, to be sure; but his particular malice towards me, and general disregard for truth, would make the book useless to all, and injurious to my character." In pursuance of his purpose, furthermore, in the "Tour of the Hebrides" Boswell records under the date of October 14, 1773:

I shall lay up authentic materials for "The Life of Samuel Johnson, L.L.D.," and if I survive him I shall be one who shall most faithfully do honour to his memory.

And on April 30, 1776, he wrote to Mrs. Thrale asking that she give him some of her records of Johnson's sayings, which request that lady refused with little ceremony.

It was not until after Johnson's death in December, 1784, however, that the actual composition was begun, and by that time many years of association and steadfast purpose lay behind the writing. Boswell's genius in human relationships, together with a literary training which recent developments show to have been considerable, contributed largely; but the secret of the "Johnson" — analyze it how you will; study the difference between the rough notes and the finished sentences; point to the concreteness and authenticity of detail; discover the devices by which the spirit of the age is revealed as a setting for the subject — the secret of the "Johnson's" success is wellnigh the secret of perfection, despite certain present-day critics, notably Mr. Hesketh Pearson, who apply to Boswell the word "artist" in its pejorative sense.

But the years that went into the composition of such a work, short as the time was in proportion to its quality — Hill complained indeed, that it took him twelve years to edit what Boswell had taken only six to write — were to him a continued agony. The tenor of his life came to be bound up in the success of his book. His wife had died; the future of his family was not secured; his health, impaired by dissipation, was failing rapidly; and his spirits were alternately elated and depressed, the whole condition becoming aggravated as he approached the end of his task by the knowledge that other men were busily engaged upon a similar work, just as earlier he had feared that Goldsmith might undertake it. In spite of everything, however, he persevered. He knew that no one else possessed comparable material; in amassing it he reached even to the point where he admitted that "collecting so much of his conversation [has] made the World shun me as a dangerous companion." As the work grew under his hand he became convinced that his was the best plan any biographer had ever adopted, and that complete fidelity to the facts as he knew them and perfect loyalty to the friend whom he had loved would make his book unique.

Toward that latter end, therefore, he fixed his aims. How indefatigably he labored, how meticulously he checked and rechecked his material, he himself in the "Advertisement to the First Edition" suggests:

> Let me only observe, as a specimen of my trouble, that I have sometimes been obliged to run half over London, in order to fix a date correctly; which when I had accomplished, I well

knew would obtain me no praise, though a failure would have been to my discredit.

How infinitely painstaking he was to preserve the character and personality of Johnson becomes plain from letters written, according to the deductions of Professor Tinker, in the year 1788. Following, for instance, is a passage from a letter to Bishop Percy:

> I am ashamed that I have yet seven years to write of his life. I do it chronologically, giving year by year his publications, if there were any; his letters, his conversations, and everything else that I can collect. It appears to me that mine is the best plan of biography that can be conceived; for my readers will, as near as may be, accompany Johnson in his progress, and, as it were, see each scene as it happened.

In a letter to Temple he speaks further of his plan and conveys something of his hopes.

> I am absolutely certain that *my* mode of biography, which gives not *only* a *history* of Johnson's visible progress through the world, and his publications, but a *view* of his mind, in his letters and conversations, is the most perfect that can be conceived and will be *more* of a *Life* than any work that has ever yet appeared.

And, again in commenting to Anna Seward upon the "variety of publications" that Johnson had inspired — one of which, William Cooke's "Life of Samuel Johnson, LLD.," had appeared only nine days after Johnson's death — he contrasts his own:

> I flatter myself it [the "Life"] will exhibit him more completely than any person, ancient or modern, has yet been preserved, and whatever merit I may be allowed, the world will at least owe to my assiduity the possession of a rich intellectual treasure.

In another letter to Temple he expresses his fatigue and discouragement and yet communicates something of his faith in ultimate success:

> You cannot imagine what labour, what perplexity, what vexation, I have endured in arranging a prodigious multiplicity of materials, in supplying omissions, in searching for papers

buried in different masses — and all this besides the exertion of composing and polishing. Many a time I thought of giving it up. However, though I shall be uneasily sensible to its many deficiencies, it will certainly be to the world a very valuable and peculiar volume of biography. . . . Would that it were in the booksellers' shops.

He was never seriously in danger of giving up, however; for as time passed and one by one his various enterprises failed — including the unfortunate attempt to stand for Parliament — he concentrated more intensely upon the "Life." Then, too, he enlisted the aid of Edmund Malone, to whom he read aloud portions of the MS. as he proceeded and from whom he received countless valuable suggestions. In the end, so confident of success had he become that he refused an offer of £1000 from George Robinson, the bookseller, for the copyright, preferring to issue the work himself under the aegis of Dilly, trusting to the public for recompense; and the sequel shows that he was wise. The first edition of 1750 copies, issued May 16, 1791, was half depleted in two weeks. In three months the public had bought 1200 copies; in the spring following, the second edition was in preparation, the first having brought Boswell £1550, although two years later he complains in the Journal that the sale had diminished and he was much discouraged. In fact he received during his own life £2500 in all for his work.

No great reward, surely, for having composed one of the most remarkable of books — and hardly any other phrase suffices. For, while it seems to violate every principle of biographical writing, it actually violates none. There is no doubt that Boswell was diffuse. James Field Stanfield, for instance, in his "Essay on Biography," published in 1813, characterizes the "Life" thus,

> Boswell's "Life of Dr. Johnson," though reprehensible for its egotism, culpable concealments, and indiscriminate admiration, stands perhaps foremost as the most copious mass of biographic matter that has ever been laid open:

and although one disagrees with the thought of the subordinate clause he can but approve the main statement, qualifying it, however, as he remembers Lockhart's accumulation. Yet despite his diffusion, Boswell made use of hardly a detail that points away from the reality that was Johnson.

[ 168 ]

Candid, likewise, there is no doubt he was, although the "Monthly Review" could remark that Johnson's "enemies had judiciously left the office of biographer to his friend." He refused Hannah More's suggestion that he "mitigate some of the asperities of our most revered and departed friend." He protested that he would "not cut off the doctor's claws or make his tiger a cat to please anybody." And he went so far as to display, in the words of Miss Seward, "the darker as well as the fairer side of the medal," even if in doing so he was at times compelled to reveal the snubs which he himself had suffered, although, to be sure, he is not so self-revealing here as he had been in the "Tour of the Hebrides." But snubs were not all he revealed. In the course of reanimating his great subject, proposing to himself to follow Bale's device of recording *acta, dicta, consilia, et scripta,* he perforce included more of himself — his antagonism toward Mrs. Thrale, for instance, as revealed in his subtly contrived portrait of her — than any previous biographer had done. Certain animadversive remarks on the part of others, contemporary and of early subsequent date, like Stanfield's "reprehensible egotism," for instance, further indicate something of the attitude toward his self-inclusion — although today, and for decades past, this same self-reference has been eagerly relished. In short, granted that he violated certain tenets of eighteenth century taste, the very liberties he took helped in making the book what it is, proving, as is universally to be proved of genius, that he who can "break rules constructively" should be licensed to do as he pleases. Boswell's "Johnson" is a biographical masterpiece; by some strange coincidence the ideal subject inspired the ideal treatment.

How acceptable the work has been, innumerable readers and scores of editions have now testified — even translation into German, Swedish, and Russian. Boswell's boast that his work would exhibit Johnson "more completely than any person, ancient or modern, has yet been preserved," is not a boast but a simple statement of fact. It remains only for him to become in his turn the subject of a "life" on a par with his merit. The materials, at least, are now at hand with which to compensate for the errancies of his detractors. At all events, figs have never yet grown from thistles.

# 15—Malone and the "Dryden"

*No one sees further into a generalization than his own knowledge of details extends. —* William James.

*For generals, not explicated, do but fill the people's heads with empty notions and their mouths with perpetual unintelligible talk: but their hearts remain empty and themselves are not edified. —* Jeremy Taylor.

IN SPITE of Havelock Ellis' comment, in his review of the "Dictionary of National Biography," that

> Biography is, or should be, at least as much of a science as ethnography; it is a description of the life of an individual just as ethnography is the description of the life of the race. It is a science in which, when we approach it seriously, both anthropology and psychology are found to have their concern,

one is tempted to retain the idea that a science of biography must remain forever impossible; it is only by variation from the norm that an individual becomes memorable. None the less, in biography as in every other record of human achievement, we can do no better than hearken with the Thessalonians to Paul's admonition, "Prove all things; hold fast to that which is good." For individual variation, like everything else which can be judged, must be checked and balanced if in the end we are to know what to hold fast as good. Therefore, because of this checking and balancing that an author must undertake, biography may be thought of as taking on something of the aspects of science — in the weighing of material and the sifting of evidence, that is — but such science, once it has served its purpose as the solvent of truth, must give place to art, for art alone can bring the whole to life.

Only after centuries, however, did biographers become aware that the available methods of science were indispensable. In fact, not until Edmund Malone applied them in his "Life of Dryden," published in 1800, did scientific methods come into their own; but even then they would not have done so had such methods not previously proved their worth to historians in general. Although Voltaire and Montesquieu had long since pointed out the difference between biography and history, and in spite of the futility of Carlyle's attempt to make one the summation of the other, nevertheless there remains enough in common between them so that the same methods may be applied in both — a fact which biographers were slow to grasp, but once having grasped it they proceeded accordingly.

For the matter of that, historians themselves had not been too quick in recognizing the obvious. The seventeenth century was well under way before anything like science in the analysis of material became evident. And yet there was ample precedent, even so obvious a one as that set by Plutarch, who in his "Nicias" set forth:

> And such things as are not commonly known and lie scattered here and there in other men's writings, or are formed amongst the old monuments and archives, I shall endeavor to bring together; not collecting mere useless pieces of learning, but adducing what may make his [Nicias'] disposition and habit of mind understood.

But in addition there were Thucydides and Polybius in antiquity; Ibn-Khallikan and Ibn-Khaldun during the middle ages; Machiavelli and Guicciardini in the renaissance — these, besides the Englishmen like John Leland, Matthew Parker, Robert Cotton, Thomas Bodley, and later Dugdale, Madox, Wilkins, and Rymer, had all been occupied with tracing and classifying if not analyzing and interpreting the spores of human enterprise. It was left for Jean

Bolland, however, and the "Acta Sanctorum" begun in 1643, and still continued (with the expectation that 1975 will see the end), and for Jean Mabillon, the Benedictine monk of St. Maur's in Paris, and his "De Re Diplomatica," which in 1681 established the science of Latin palaeography and laid down the principles for the study of medieval archives — it was left for these scholars and their associates to stress properly the application of science in historical study and gain for it the recognition it so richly merited. These men were not innovators perhaps as much as they were discoverers; knowing the practice of ancient historians and influenced by the restless spirit of their century they refined upon what they knew to the extent of their powers. And in so doing they prepared the way for the appearance a century later of the man who is usually credited with having brought the evolving methods to a state very nearly approaching perfection — Friederich August Wolf.

Wolf, in 1795, published the "Prolegomena to Homer," a work, based upon all available material scientifically weighed, analyzed, and interpreted, which essayed to demonstrate that the "Odyssey" and the "Iliad" were not the work of one man whom the world called Homer, but of a succession of men throughout succeeding generations. It is not the thesis that is important but the method by which it is developed. Granted the premises, and to grant them has proved easy enough for many eminent scholars, the demonstration is irrefutable. So effective was Wolf's method, in fact, that it gave rise to a school of classical research, among the followers of which were, first, August Boeckh, Wolf's most brilliant student, and, later, Barthold Georg Niebuhr, who in 1810, delivered a course of lectures in Berlin upon the history of Rome which discussed critically the early legends and stressed Roman institutions and social characteristics rather than, as former historians had done, the acts and influence of celebrated men. His work was published in 1827–1828 and the first volume translated into English by Connop Thirlwall and Julius C. Hare in 1828. (Hare later wrote the "Life of Sterling" to which Carlyle objected with his own "Life.") Hence Niebuhr became a pioneer in applying modern scientific methods to historical study.

Among biographers, likewise, no one prior to the eighteenth

century group represented by the Society of Antiquaries, can be considered scientific in the treatment of data. This group had been founded in 1572 by Matthew Parker, but was suppressed after the death of Elizabeth, and re-established in 1717.

Dryden, to be sure, could not be termed unscientific in his use of the Plutarch material, and Anthony Wood had labored with the utmost patience over his "Athenae Oxoniensis." And, too, John Toland had striven for accuracy and objectivity in writing the "Life of Milton," which he issued in 1698. Nevertheless nothing properly scientific appeared until after the turn of the eighteenth century.

Then it was that, in parallel with the rise of the novel, the perfection of the periodical essay, the development of the newspaper, the thousand and one other responses to the ever-increasing demand for information on the part of a people avid for education, biography shook itself free from complete dependence upon a relationship between author and subject and in certain instances became absorbed in studying personalities of the past. Technique was thus augmented and scope increased. Among the first of the scholar-biographers was Samuel Knight, one of the most enthusiastic members of the Society of Antiquaries. His "Life of Colet" was published in 1742, and his "Life of Erasmus" in 1726, which, although by no means recapturing the personalities of either of the great renaissance humanists, succeeded in presenting newly discovered facts concerning both men in such fashion as to remain authoritative for decades. Following Knight's work John Lewis edited William Roper's "Life of Sir Thomas More" (1729) so expertly that his became the basis for all subsequent editions. Besides this he wrote a "life" of Caxton (1737), and one of John Fisher (1738), after having issued in 1723 "The History of the Life and Sufferings of John Wicliffe."

As the century progressed more and more men became engaged in scholarly biography and their practice became ever more and more scientific as succeeding works contributed by trial and error to developing method. A catalogue of representative men and books — a matter most effectively set forth by Professor Mark Longaker in his "English Biography in the Eighteenth Century" — would include William Oldys and his work with the "Harleian Miscellany" in 1744, his editing the "Biographia Britannica" in 1747–1760, and his "Life of Raleigh," published in 1736; David Malet and his "Life of Bacon," 1740; Conyers Middleton and his "Life of Cicero," 1741; Ferdinando Warner and his "Life of Sir Thomas More," which, current with John Jortin's "Life of Erasmus," was issued in 1758; William Hayley and the "Life of Milton," 1794; and finally Edmund Malone and his "The Critical and Miscellaneous Prose Works of John Dryden with an Account of the Life and Writings of the Author," 1800.

The first paragraph of the "Account" defines Malone's attitude and purpose — to delineate the man, not the poet:

> So few are the notices which have been transmitted to us concerning the great poet . . . that Dr. Johnson, who at an early period had mediated writing his Life, soon abandoned the project, in despaire of finding materials sufficient for his purpose. Many years afterwards, however, having undertaken a general review of the lives of the most eminent English Poets, he enriched his volumes of biography with an account of this author, in which are displayed such comprehension of mind and accuracy of criticism, such vigor of expression and luxuriancy of imagery, that of the various masterly Lives in his admirable work, that of Dryden is perhaps the most animated and splendid; so splendid, indeed, that a competition with such excellence can be sought only by him who is actuated by a degree of confidence in himself, which I beg leave most strenuously to disclaim. Having, however, as he himself told me, made no preparation for that difficult and extensive undertaking, not being in the habit of extracting from books and committing to paper those facts on which the accuracy of literary history in a great measure depends, and being still less inclined to go through the tedious and often unsatisfying process of examining ancient registers, offices of record, and those sepulchers of literature, publick repositories of manuscripts, he was under the necessity of trusting much of his own most retentive memory, which furnished him many curious and interesting particulars concerning the most famous English Poets, collected during the course of a long life; but he was frequently, as in the present instance, obliged to rely

for incidents and dates, on such information as had been transmitted by preceding biographers.[1]

Having as early as 1776 become interested in ferreting out detail
concerning Goldsmith, and having in 1779 published his "Attempt
to Ascertain the Order in which the Plays of Shakespeare Were
Written," and ten years later issuing the eleven volume edition of
Shakespeare, Malone was one among the most scholarly men in
England. In 1790 he was free to undertake a new project. He
thought of re-editing the "lives" and works of some of the older
poets, Pope, perhaps, or Dryden, to include such gleanings as his
editorial experience had shown him to remain. Among the friends
whom he consulted were Lord Hailes, who encouraged him to
proceed, and Lord Claremont, who in June, 1794, wrote thus:

> If a new edition be wanted of Dryden's critical prose works,
> I know of nothing better worth republishing. The matter is
> for the most part excellent; the manner incomparable through-
> out. There cannot be a better antidote against our modern
> innovation in style than his compositions — perspicuous, grace-
> ful, elegant, humorous, and easy. His life will also be very
> acceptable, as nothing of the kind worth reading has hitherto
> been written.

On the strength of such encouragement he seems to have set to
work, permitting himself, however, to be interrupted by the com-

---

[1] "It is observable, that when once an errour has found a place in any
original biographical work, it is generally transmitted from age to age by
succeeding biographers, and, according to a modern author, this is a very
laudable mode of proceeding. To correct false dates, to ascertain the births
or deaths of eminent men, the number of their children, and the nature and
extent of their property, or in any other way to throw new light on their
history, by examining Parish-Registers, Tomb-stones, or Wills, the documents
in the Herald's Office, or the Inquisitions *post mortem* in the Chapel of the
Rolls, is, we are told, an invasion of the sacred rights of the dead, and little
less than profanation. Unfortunately, all the accounts of Dryden and his
works were one continued tissue of inaccuracy, errour, and falsehood. Very
little has been handed down, and of that little the greater part has been
untrue. With the aid, therefore, of original documents, to rectify these mis-
statements, to illustrate the history of our author's life and writings by such
intelligence as I have been able to procure, and to dispel that mist of confusion and errour in which it has been involved, shall be the principal object
of the following pages." — Malone.

position of his four hundred page letter to Lord Charlemont, "An inquiry into the authenticity of certain papers attributed to Shakespeare," in exposure of the Ireland forgeries, and so was not ready to go to press with the "Dryden" until early in 1799.

Like all contributory accomplishment, the "Life of Dryden" was the product of its age and of the characteristics of its author. The end of the eighteenth century saw Europe in the confusion wrought by thought-shaking change. The stage was being set for greater development in all departments of human activity during the coming century than had accumulated during ten centuries preceding. Naturally biography was to bear its part (it must be remembered, however, that only in the use of the historical method was it affected; Boswell's "Johnson" has been equaled by no subsequent work) and, as opportunity seldom goes ungrasped, there was a man ready to grasp what the times provided.

Edmund Malone was born October 4, 1741, in Dublin, of a long line of distinguished men. His father, Edmund, had been a lawyer and a member of several parliaments; his grandfather, Richard, likewise a member of the Irish bar, had served King William with eminent success in a series of negotiations in Holland. Early members of the family are set forth in the 7th volume of Archdall's "Peerage of Ireland." He himself was educated privately in Dublin until in 1756 he entered the University whence he proceeded Bachelor of Arts. From the beginning he showed extraordinary abilities as a student, "being assiduous in acquiring general information" — but only that which could be accurately obtained. He went about his study in a systematic fashion, first concentrating upon the chronology of the work in hand, the history and character of the author, the feelings and prejudices of the period involved; then he gathered collateral information which tended to illustrate the subject and the cast of his author's thought. In his way he acquired not only a wide range of general knowledge but also the habit of ordered and exact thinking which was to serve him so well in later life. In 1763 he became a student in the Inner Temple and four years later was called to the Irish bar; and in all probability he would have followed his family tradition and become a noted lawyer had not a fortune been bequeathed him and so made it possible for him to devote his talents to literary study, which, after all, was the pursuit of his choice.

The better to satisfy his tastes, therefore, he went to London and soon found himself in the midst of the finest literary minds of the day. Burke and Johnson, Reynolds, Goldsmith, Garrick, and Fox, all made him welcome to the famous Literary Club. Here it was that he met George Steevens, the stormy petrel of the group, who quarreled with everybody but whose service in the editing of Shakespeare could hardly be spared and without whose assistance Johnson could not, except with vastly more effort than he was willing to expend, have composed his "Lives of the Poets."

Steevens immediately recognized Malone as a kindred spirit in enthusiastic admiration for Shakespeare and enlisted his aid in supplementing the edition of the plays which he had previously issued — which Malone accomplished in 1780 by adding two volumes containing additional notes, the poems, and seven of the plays. In this way did Malone embark upon his career as a literary editor and scholar.

His work with Steevens completed, he nevertheless continued his researches in the subject, feeling that although much had been done much more required doing. In fact, he discovered so much material that was new and so many errors that had persisted for years that he determined to appear as editor in his own right, even though in so doing he incurred the jealous dislike of his old friend Steevens and later called forth Charles Lamb's impatient "the wretched Malone" in this gentle author's "Detached Thoughts," apropos of the incident of the Stratford Statue. None the less he persevered and in November, 1790, published his work, a text of Shakespeare with notes and emendations, which must still be consulted by Shakespearian students. To characterize so vast a work in a word or two would be presumptuous; one can, however, point out that Malone treated more than 100,000 lines and made 1654 emendations — yet his critics were able to indicate only thirteen errors, five of which were later shown not to have been errors at all. A further instance of the accuracy of his scholarship is, of course, his exposure of the Ireland forgeries in 1796, mentioned previously.

The work of the scholar is usually remote from the general reader except as it furnishes material which other men may use, and Malone's contributions are not excepted. Subsequent "lives" of Dryden, like Sir Walter Scott's, have been by far more widely read, for instance, but they could probably never have been written had he not prepared the way; in fact, Scott says as much at the outset of his work. "It would be hard," he wrote, "to produce facts which have escaped the accuracy of Malone, whose industry has removed the clouds which so long hung over the events of Dryden's life." And much the same comment may be made concerning the Shakespearian studies: Malone discovered much new material, made many corrections, and pointed the way toward better understanding, but very few readers of "Hamlet," for instance, know of their debt to him. On the other hand, his work with Boswell on the "Life of Johnson" has not gone unrecognized by the public. So popular a series of books as the Modern Library includes the Malone edition of Boswell's great work.

His relationship with Boswell, as a matter of fact, was probably more intimate than that with any other member of the Literary Club, except perhaps with Sir Joshua Reynolds, one of whose executors he became and whose writings he edited with a memoir. And Boswell was not slow to profit by Malone's talents, as is clear from his letters and the statements he made during the time in which the "Johnson" was under way. He consulted Malone constantly, relying upon him not only for advice as to form and arrangement but also for material — which Malone seemed always ready and eager to supply. A word of Boswell's to Temple, dated January, 1789, illuminates the relationship:

> Whenever I have completed the rough draft, by which I mean the work without nice correction, Malone and I are to prepare one-half perfectly, and then go to press.

When the great biography was finished and had been received in a manner highly gratifying, Malone continued his interest in it, and after Boswell's death in 1795 he took over the task of seeing subsequent editions through the press, adding many notes of his own, including additional letters as they came to light, and rendering the text as perfect as possible. In this way he assumed responsibility for the third, fourth, fifth, and sixth editions, the third usually being accepted as definitive. As a fitting sequel to these practical indications of his friendship, in 1812, when he knew his own end was near, he turned over the materials for his final edition of Shakespeare to James Boswell, the younger, with the request that he complete the work — which he did, issuing it, with a memoir of Malone, in 1821.

Careful as was his work with the Shakespeare material and valuable as his help was in the composition of the "Johnson," it is his own "Dryden" that best illustrates his accurate scholarship and his enthusiasm in the search for the last item of illuminating detail. A sentence or two drawn at random from the text, with accompanying footnotes will set forth something of his practice:

> "The Hind and the Panther," the longest original poem that our author ever wrote, consisting of near two thousand lines, was the employment of part of the year 1686 and 1687; for from an entry in the Stationer's Books, it should seem to have been ready for the press in January, 1686–8.[1]

Just as the foregoing instance indicates his reliance upon documents, the following shows his eagerness to correct error:

> All the biographers of Dryden have said, that on the death of D'Avenant, in 1668, he was appointed Poet Laureate. But it appears from his Letters Patent, a copy of which will be found in the Appendix, that he did not obtain the laurel till August 18th, 1670. With respect, however, to the emoluments of this office, and that of Historiographer Royal (which had become vacant by the death of James Howell in 1666, and was also granted to him), the patent had a retrospect.[2]

Throughout, the work is as completely specific in detail as research could make possible. Horace Walpole called the effort "inde-

---

[1] In the last leaf of that volume of the Stationers' Registerers which begins with 29 January 1682–3, is the following entry;
"Jan 12, 1686, i.e. 1686–7, Md. That Mr. Jacob Tonson enters this Caveat — that noe person enter the poem called the Hind and ye Panther.
Witn. J.T."
[2] All Dryden's biographers have erroneously represented him as not possessing this office till the accession of James the Second.

fatigable," and no other word is more suitable. Malone establishes the spelling of the name "Dryden" as such rather than "Driden," "Dreydon," or "Dreyon." He apologizes for his inability to determine the precise date of the poet's baptism. He shows that he was born in the parish of Aldwincle All-Saints in Northamptonshire, although it was more natural to believe him born at Lichmarch, the home of his grandfather, Sir Eramus Dryden — and seven footnotes support his conclusion. He ridicules the "Corina" account of Dryden's funeral. Altogether he leaves neither page, nor it would seem stone, unturned in this search for fact. Not only this, but the reader is never in doubt as to the source of the fact — the pages of his text average two footnotes each, not a few of which exceed a hundred words. The result, however, is inevitably a work of reference, not a reanimation of its subject.

It goes without saying that Malone's "Dryden" is not a work glowing with the spark of life; no one will probably ever thrill over the excellence of the style or the reality of the personality communicated. In fact, from the time of its appearance in 1800 until the present the criticism has often occurred that Malone has so persistently sought trifles that Dryden is submerged beneath a welter of but slightly related detail. All this is as may be. The fact remains, however, that after the work had had time to make itself felt, the scientific approach and a resulting exactness became vital to biography, and it is Malone's right to a niche in the temple that he was among the first to make it so.

# 16—Washington Irving

*A biographer, like a dramatist, has no place upon the stage. When he has made his bow to his audience and has spoken his prologue telling what he will try to exhibit, it is his duty to retire to the wings, to raise the curtain and leave the play to the actors.* — Freeman.

FOR a biographer to write the "life" of a man whom he has not known in the flesh is, obviously enough, to be handicapped from the start. Nevertheless, if he undertakes such a task and can follow it through to the end, remaining free from the effects of personal impact, and emotionally disengaged except for the enthusiasm natural to an artist, he may have a decided advantage. There can be no doubt that the "lives" at the head of the canon were written in accordance with Carlyle's "secret" of the "graphic" — as set forth in his comment upon Boswell:

> To have an open loving heart, and what follows from the possession of such. Truly it has been said, emphatically in these days ought it to be repeated: A loving heart is the beginning of all knowledge. This it is that opens the whole mind, quickens every faculty of the intellect to do its fit work, that of knowing; and therefrom, by sure consequence, of vividly uttering-forth. Other secret for being "graphic" is there none, worth having: but this is an all-sufficient one.

Not far down the list, however, stand the names of works only less notable. It may be that the "Johnson," the "Macaulay," and the "Scott" will never be equaled; but granting them precedence, even the most discriminative must acknowledge the claim upon remembrance of Walton's "Hooker," Dryden's "Plutarch," Johnson's "Cowley," Goldsmith's "Nash," Forster's "Goldsmith," and Lee's "Shakespeare," to point out but six of several score equally worthy of mention, all which were synthetically composed from vicarious rather than actual experience. For, wanting the knowledge that springs from Carlyle's "open loving heart" and the understanding that is gained through Johnson's "eating and drinking and living in social intercourse" with his subject, a biographer can, none the less, very nearly achieve the graphic in his "uttering-forth" if he combine the science of recognizing the originality, the uniqueness, and the essential reality of the life before him with the poetry of interpreting that life in terms of the common humanity which animated its pilgrimage through the world. It is this last, this combination of science and poetry, which when justly balanced functions as the next best substitute for personal impact; and so, freed from the effects of what all too frequently is emotional blindness — instance after recurrent instance having proved subversive of truth in the interest of family, official, ethical, or selfish ends — proceed on the side of art to reclaim merit from oblivion.

It is the "just balance" that is all-important, naturally — too much science and the defects of a Malone obtrude between reality and realization; too much poetry and the imperfections of a Maurois appear to make one wonder how, if Shelley is Ariel, he could have written as he did; or if, indeed, he was himself, then who is Ariel? Hence, neither fact nor interpretative imagination should dominate; but in proportion as fact pertains and imagination interprets fairly, so must they be fused in order that graphic representation ensue — a fusion which is as necessary to the biographer's integrity of effect as his disentanglement of the demonstrable from the insubstantial or his ability to write a quick and cogent English.

Lacking the "open loving heart" of Carlyle's dictum on the one hand, and lacking the "just balance," on the other, Washington Irving is, in spite of such lack, significant in the annals of biography — if for no other reason than that he was among the first Americans to achieve success in the form. His major "lives" — the "Columbus," the "Mohamet," the "Goldsmith," and the "Washington" — all fascinate by the charm of their poetry even though they may disappoint because of the flaws in their science. The manner of their reception upon appearance was enthusiastic enough — both at home and abroad. There was no doubt of the graphic in the art of the portrayals. As the years have accumulated since, however, graphic though the "lives" were adjudged when issued, their focus becomes less and less sharp under the light of recent scholarship — defects appear and become increasingly apparent when Irving's poetry and his science are weighed upon the steelyard of objective analysis. Perhaps the author of the "Knickerbocker History," of "The Sketch-Book," of "Bracebridge Hall," and the "Alhambra," and the creator of Geoffrey Crayon should not have undertaken to write "lives"; his gifts lay in revealing himself rather than the characters of other men, in allowing his own gentle nature and generous philosophy, at work upon the riches disclosed to his informed perceptions, to flow from him in a style as artless in effect as in development it was carefully wrought. Perhaps — to be more nearly concrete — he should have limited himself to reflecting, as he did upon occasion, the spirit of an elder English age, transplanting its culture to advancing America, and to the creation of inimitables like Ichabod Crane, Katrina van Tassel, and Rip van Winkle, instead of attempting a form so alien to him as biography — with its confining gyves and fetters. Attempt it he did, however, and although his work is not of highest rank, yet with such exceptions, possibly, as Cotton Mather's "Magnalia Christi Americana"; the "Life of Charles Brockden Brown," usually associated with William Dunlap, the dramatist, as author; some of the sketches in Jeremy Belknap's "American Biography"; and the work projected by Jared Sparks in the "Library of American Biography," what Irving wrote in the form must be considered as the earliest authentic life writing produced in America and, until the quite recent past, the best.

His apprenticeship was served in writing the four essay "lives" which appeared in the "Analectic Magazine" during his own editorship, in 1813–1814. These comprised laudatory accounts of the personalities and exploits of Captain James Lawrence, of Lieutenant Burrows, of Commodore Perry, and of Captain David Porter. They are all short and, except for the patriotic sentimentality of the style

[ 183 ]

as inspired by the fervor of enthusiasm aroused by the victories of the War of 1812, they were not inconsiderable as such work went at the time—they are surprisingly better, for instance, than any of the fifteen similar sketches which James Kirke Paulding wrote about the same time. These naval warriors were idols, and rightly so; but they were not the creatures of romance which such phrasing as Irving used suggests. When, describing Lawrence, for instance, he writes of the "silent melancholy of [his] proud and noble heart"; when he speaks of the "amiable disposition" of Burrows and the "silent broodings of [his] wounded spirit"; and when he characterizes the effects of the redoubtable Perry's exploits—as pointed out by Dr. Stanley Williams in his "Washington Irving"—thus:

> Mothers no longer shrunk aghast, and clasped their infants to their breasts, when they heard the shaking of the forest or the howling of the blast—the aged sire no longer dreaded the shades of night, lest ruin should burst upon him in the hour of repose, and his cottage be laid desolate by the firebrand and the scalping knife—Michigan was rescued from the dominion of the sword, and quiet and security once more settled on the harassed frontiers, from Huron to Niagara,—

when he writes in this fashion he is merely permitting feeling so to outweigh fact that the result is almost tristfully sentimental, and he is contributing to the worst of the earlier American manner. These sketches, however, are redeemed by being extraordinarily good hero tales. Irving could write; he had the gift of high narrative; there can be no question of his art, of his ability, as his subsequent life writing demonstrates, to "utter forth" in such fashion that he satisfied the uncritical at home, in England, and later, through translation, in continental Europe.

The first authentic expression of his ability as a biographer—if one thinks of the "Analectic" sketches as apprentice work—was "A History of the Life and Voyages of Christopher Columbus," published in 1828, a work of history and drama, fact and fiction, science and poetry commingled—to the delight of the ten thousand, if to the despair of the few. Irving wrote it during 1826–27, following his appointment by Alexander Hill Everett to an embassy post in

Madrid. The inception of the idea is suggested by an entry in his Journal dated January 30, 1826:

> Received letter from Mr. Everett, attaching me to embassy at Madrid. Inclosing passport and proposing my translating voyage of Columbus.

At the time he was at something of a loose end in France, having dropped most of his earnings from previous writings in speculative ventures concerned with steamboats and Bolivar mines. Hence, the appointment and the suggestion were not only timely but stimulating; so much so, in fact, that they provided a background and an opportunity for him to compose a work requiring concentrated effort, close judgment, and unremitting patience — qualities which heretofore had not been demanded of him. The sequel was that for quite two years he confined himself to a single room, with but the briefest of holidays, prosecuting relentlessly his difficult and baffling task. How intensely he applied himself and with what result is revealed in a letter to his friend Storrow, written June 12, 1826:

> I am absolutely fagged and exhausted with hard work. For nearly three months I have been occupied incessantly with my work; sometimes all day and a great part of the night in defiance of all rules I had set myself and at the risk of my health. I never worked so hard, nor so constantly for such a length of time; but I was determined not to stop until I had made a rough draft of the whole work. I have succeeded in so doing. To finish it up and make all the necessary additions, amendments, and illustrations will be a work of time and labor.

The occasion of Everett's suggestion had been the work of the eminent Spanish historian, Martin Fernandez de Navarette, in collecting, collating, and editing documents concerning the discovery of America. It was upon Navarette's work that Irving based his own, together with material made accessible to him by Obadiah Rich, the American Consul at Madrid, a distinguished collector and bibliographer; by the Royal Library; and by the Jesuit College of San Isidor. Navarette's work, however, remained his chief source — and the use he made of it became the cause of the difficulty as well as the fame which later accrued. For, although the "Columbus" and the other of his writings about Spain, "The Conquest of Granada," "The Alhambra," and the lesser works contributed largely to his reputation, and led indirectly to his being selected by Daniel Webster in 1842 as Minister to Spain, critics and historians at home and in Europe fell upon him as having done nothing more than translate Navarette and done that badly. It was a matter which his election as corresponding member to the Real Academia de la Historia could not overcome — nor even, indeed, the opinion of Navarette himself as expressed in a letter to Irving, dated April 1, 1831:

> I congratulate myself that the documents and notices which I published in my collection about the first occurences in the history of America, have fallen into hands so able to appreciate their authenticity, to examine them critically, and to circulate them in all directions; establishing fundamental truths which hitherto have been adulterated by partial or systematic writers.

In fact the matter has not yet been satisfactorily offset. Irving steeped himself in the materials available to him, becoming immersed to the point at which the accumulation overflowed and poured from him as transformed by his own consciousness. Naturally, because he was an artist rather than an historian trained in methodology, the work was what it was — poetic, imaginative, dramatic, but not scientific, not even accurate as the letter of the documents at hand had made possible, in spite of the objectivity aimed at as indicated in the Preface:

> In the execution of this work, I have avoided indulging in mere speculations or general reflections, excepting such as naturally arose out of the subject, preferring to give a minute and circumstantial narrative, omitting no particular that appeared characteristic of the persons, the events, or the times; and endeavoring to place every fact under such a point of view, that the reader might perceive its merits, and draw his own maxims and conclusions.

However, if the letter was ignored, the spirit was exploited to the full — imparting that quality of romance which has so long sustained his work in public favor.

The popular approval accorded the book at the time of its appearance is summed up in the opinion expressed by the "Edinburgh Review" for September, 1828:

> This, on the whole, is an excellent book; and we venture to anticipate that it will be an enduring one. Neither do we hazard this prediction lightly, or without a full consciousness of all that it implies. We are perfectly aware that there are but few modern works that are likely to verify it; and that it could not be extended with safety to so many as one in a hundred even of those which we praise. For we mean not merely that the book will be familiarly known and referred to some twenty or thirty years hence, and will pass in solid binding into every considerable collection; but that it will supersede all former works on the same subject, and never itself be superseded. . . . Mr. Irving has written the history of the greatest event in the annals of mankind, with the fulness and feeling it deserved; and has presented us with a flowing and continuous narrative of the events he had to record, far more luminous and comprehensive than any which previously existed, and yet much less diffuse and discursive than the earlier accounts, from which it is mainly derived; the while without sacrificing in any degree the intense interest of personal adventure and individual sympathy, he has brought the lights of a more cultivated age to bear on the obscure places of the story; and touched skillfully on the errors and prejudices of the times — at once to enliven his pictures by their singularity, and to instruct us by their explanation or apology.

And how well the work has upheld the reputation established by the early comments is suggested by the remarks of Dr. Edward Hayes O'Neill of the University of Pennsylvania in his "A History of American Biography," published in 1935. "We have learned a great deal more about Columbus than Irving knew," he writes,

> but Irving has seldom been found wrong. He developed a method for this book which he used for all of his later biographical writings. He made a careful study of his sources, digested the material, and then wrote his narrative. Scholars are inclined to scoff at this method because it eliminates foot-

notes and the rest of the critical apparatus. Irving was not writing for scholars and critics; he was writing for the intelligent reading public, which wants the results of scholarship rather than the methods.

Irving's *Columbus* is a full and rapid narrative of Columbus' life, his geographical studies, his attempts to secure aid for his project, his disappointments, his final success. The reader is carried along from one point to another with such ease that he feels he is actually with the Genoese. History and biography are so artistically combined that one is hardly conscious of the amount of history that is in the book or of the amount of research that went into the making of the book. This is historical biography at its best.*

This is perhaps excessive praise. However, the "Columbus," especially the concise edition which Irving was forced to make under the threat of piratical venture, has become an important item, finding even today its share of eager readers. The faults of its science are softened if not obscured by the rightness of its poetry. Scholars, historians, and critics may complain that Navarette was paraphrased, echoed, translated, exploited, what they will; they may also point out errors in places and dates, errors even in transcription. More than a century has passed and the book is still read, however, bearing out, it is not too much to conclude, Southey's opinion as expressed to Murray, the publisher, after he had read the manuscript, an opinion, incidentally, which helped Murray in deciding to undertake publication:

> I return [Southey wrote] the MS. of Columbus' Life by this day's coach. It appears to me to have been compiled with great industry and to be well conceived, presenting a most remarkable portion of history in a popular form, and therefore likely to succeed; not for the ability displayed in it, but because the book is interesting and useful.

Irving's success no doubt grew out of the intense interest that has always existed in connection with Columbus, his romantic exploit and his subsequent disillusionment — this together with the romantic

---

* Included by the courteous permission of the publishers of E. H. O'Neill's "A History of American Biography," the University of Pennsylvania Press.

character of the author himself and his reputation as among the first American citizens of the world. If the book were better history, or even better biography it could hardly have been more human and hence more directly appealing. Biography so early in America has little to show more fair.

In December, 1847, the "United States Magazine" announced,

> The life of Mohammed by Washington Irving! What visions of delight flood the mind at the thought! What stores of long-buried lore, rescued from the dust of the ages by so experienced a literary delver, may we not reasonably hope to see!

With such exclamatory enthusiasm was the "Mahomet" awaited. To be sure, by the middle of the century Irving was a figure of international celebrity; his fame had extended so far that he and his works had been included in the textbooks and curricula even of European schools. Hence the news of a forthcoming book was news indeed. In addition to the interest in no matter what he chose to write, there was at the time a very great interest in the subject of his current selection. Between 1843 and 1865, for example, an unprecedented preoccupation with Mohamet and all that concerned him was finding expression in the works of German, English, and American scholars, like Gustav Weil, for instance, J. L. Merrick, Aloys Sprenger, and William Muir. And so, ever aware of the trend of popular taste, Irving bethought himself of an early work which had grown out of his studies of the Moorish material incidental to his "Columbus," but one which Murray, his publisher, had read in 1831 with no enthusiasm whatever. Only now, sensing awakening demand, Irving determined to revise the hastily composed early version. He could hardly have failed to read Carlyle's lecture, and he knew of the accumulating scholarship on the subject, especially of Weil's "Mohammed der Prophet," a translation of which he eagerly sought. Demand and inclination, therefore, coinciding, Irving availing himself of the added material at hand, brought his work up to date in his own fashion and published it in 1849–1850 as "Mahomet and His Successors."

"His own fashion" is particularly applicable, but in this instance, perhaps more apparent than in any other of his historical writings, not his best fashion. Rich in legend and romance though the subject was, he seems not to have taken advantage of the opportunities thus provided. The many books which had appeared naturally created controversy by presenting conflicting evidence, but he avoided all participation in the current disputes. He even omitted, for the most part, any mention of basic sources. The work, as a result, is more or less a paraphrase, or free translation, of modern language renderings of ancient Arabian history. The second-hand sources obtrude and the effect is that of many books combined, each contributing something, but the whole wanting the impression of assimilated unity.

Nevertheless, the "Mahomet" is not a dry and arid waste. The life story of the Prophet, which makes up about a third of the work, concentrates upon his career and the religious following and political empire he created. The familiar stories of his birth, his journey to the Seventh Heaven, his love for Maruyah, the revolt of the harem, and his dramatic end are recounted with no little spirit, the outgrowth of Irving's untarnishable narrative style, sustained by the inextinguishable romance of the old legends. There is missing, undoubtedly, the charm of "The Alhambra" and the stirring qualities of "The Conquest of Granada." The customary Irving poetry shines through, however, and the gentle irony — this last being especially noticeable in connection with the supernatural element. And the same atmosphere pervades the account of the twelve caliphs which comprises the remainder of the work. The matter of Arabian ethnology is avoided — a question which any writer on the subject, it would seem, could hardly ignore — and little or no space is devoted to Islamic theology and philosophy. Instead, exciting affairs like the siege of Damascus and of Baabek are projected in scenes suitable for some barbaric canvas; anecdotes of Khaled and Calous are dramatically unfolded; and the dim, almost mythical exploits of the Moslems during the invasion of Persia flash momentarily and then fade out, in the softened outlines of the "long ago and far away."

Irving makes no pretense at scholarship; indeed he states in his preface: "The author lays no claim to novelty of fact, nor profundity of research." But then his public did not require scholarship at his hands. In place of controversial didacticism he tells old tales—inimitably. Instead of documentary history he supplies a pleasantly ironic, faintly humorous mingling of fact with fable and fancy so effectively contrived that a critic in the "North American Review" for October, 1850 wrote:

> We are glad to see the theme in the impartial and generous hands of Mr. Irving, by whose efforts, not more romantic than just, it is prevented—preserved, we would hope,—from a final subsidence into the Hades of voluntary and self-seeking deceivers. Mr. Irving possesses the rare power—fruit of genial sympathy and most honest intent—of throwing his own mind into the mind he steadfastly contemplates, so as to see with its eyes, understand with its understanding, and feel with its passions. Some lack of potential passion in his own nature is, perhaps, rather an advantage than the contrary, when he assumes the position of an observer and faithfull reporter; for if we miss the imposing strength imparted to a partisan bias or sectarian malignity, we are also protected from the prejudices which are so apt to cloud the vision. . . . Besides this enviable impartiality, the biographer of Columbus and now of Mahomet, possesses a magic equal to that of the 'wise Cornelius,' who by 'gramarye,' could show in his 'mirror broad and high,' the absent and the dead, characters typically employed, and wearing the full appearance of life.

And no less flattering was the opinion of the "Literary Gazette" for April 13, 1850:

> For variety, adventure, and characteristic traits of a singular people, and the wonderful imposition of a strange religion upon the world, it is hardly possible to imagine a more stirring narrative.

In our own day, however, opinion has shifted somewhat. Dr. Stanley Williams—whose "life" of Irving, incidentally, must remain the background for no matter what comment upon Irving—considers the "Mahomet" hack work; Dr. Edward O'Neill says that it "is a charming story, charmingly told"; and Professor Dana Merrill remarks that Irving's work "stressed the pictorial surface of the time and did not seek the underlying philosophical bases of events"

— opinions far removed from the exclamatory enthusiasm of the "United States Magazine" ninety years ago. However, although below the "Columbus" in quality and unacceptable as authoritative in Islamic affairs, "Mahomet and His Successors" has its place — if no where else, among the best American biographies of escape.

Composed concurrently with the "Mahomet" but issued some four months before is "Oliver Goldsmith: a Biography." In fact the years 1849 to 1859 must be considered among the most industrious of Irving's life. He was carrying on the duties of Minister to Spain in a manner highly gratifying to the State Department besides publishing an average of a volume a year — more than enough, surely, to nullify the lay conception, still very much alive, that he was "an elegant idler." It is true, of course, that this decade was a period of fruition, almost everything he issued having resulted from plans and activities which had occupied him for many years. For not only was the "Mohamet" the revision and expansion of a work undertaken much earlier, but both the "Goldsmith" and the "Washington" were likewise culminations of projects begun as long since as the 1820's which needed only time and opportunity to take proper form.

These last differ widely, however. The "Washington" grew out of a lifelong ambition and became fittingly, the climax of his long career. The "Goldsmith," on the other hand, may almost be called another piece of hack work — and this in spite of the place it occupies even today in popular estimation. From one point of view it may be thought of as an evolution. Twenty-five years before it appeared as, according to Dr. O'Neill, "a life of Goldsmith that has not yet been superseded," Irving composed his first version of it. During the winter of 1823 while in France he had been approached by the Galignam brothers, booksellers and publishers in Paris, who were particularly interested in bringing out English works. They invited Irving to edit a collection of British classics and compose biographical introductions for each writer included. Beginning ambitiously enough and intending to include the "lives" and works of Rogers, Campbell, and Goldsmith as a start, he completed only the "Goldsmith."

He himself said that it was nothing more than "a mere modification of an interesting Scottish memoir." The fact that he could find no better materials than this — in 1823 no authentic "life" existed — should have pointed him toward a task which, one is tempted to think, would have absorbed him. There had been dozens of references to the kinship supposedly existing between Irving and Goldsmith: they still continue for the matter of that. Resemblances are pointed out linking the two both in spirit and in art. In keeping with the habit of relating English and American writers on the basis of fancied similarities, just as Cooper became the "American Scott" and Bryant the "American Wordsworth," so Irving became the "American Goldsmith." Furthermore, G. W. Greene, an early biographer of Irving, commented that

> They have the same quick perception of the ludicrous, and the same tender simplicity in the pathetic. There is the same quiet vein of humor in both, and the same cheerful spirit of hopefulness.

And these are but trifling indications of the relationship. The scores of references to Irving's reliance upon Goldsmith, the essayist, for mood and attitude, if not for suggestions in the choice of material for writings of his like the "Salmagundi Papers" tend to show a debt of considerable proportions. Not any of such influence or kinship, however, is sustained by a close comparison. Dr. Stanley Williams has shown the emptiness of such speculation by pointing out the catholicity of Irving's indebtedness and by showing the utter difference between the American minister to Spain and "poor Poll." If this were not enough, why, one may ask, did not Irving seize upon the Galignam assignment as an opportunity to rescue his mentor from the comparative obscurity into which the half-century since his death had thrown him? The answer no doubt is the same as it would be had it concerned any other of Irving's writings except possibly the "Washington" — he considered Goldsmith a subject to be handled for replenishing his purse and nothing more. The best way at the time was to make use of the sketch to be found in "Ballantyne's Novelist's Library," which he called "an interesting Scottish memoir."

If the first version did not approach adequacy — he was content with merely fifty-six pages of crudely prepared text — neither did the second. This last he wrote in 1840 for "Harpers' Family Library," basing his work upon the previous sketch and adding something from Prior's "Life," which had appeared in 1837. Again, however, the "Goldsmith" was nothing more than hack work. Looking about for a subject, he had thought of Byron, whom together with other English celebrities he had come to know intimately — he disdained the "Cockney School," however, having once declined an introduction to Hazlitt — and then of further Spanish studies. But seizing the opportunity afforded him by the Harpers to edit a two-volume collection of Goldsmith's writings with an introduction, he became engaged at once upon the task; only, this time he devoted 186 pages to the work.

The first paragraph of the third, and final, attempt defines its atmosphere and Irving's attitude better than anything else can do — if one reads it remembering that again the author is trying to please his public and make some money rather than repay a mythical obligation:

> There are few writers for whom the reader feels such personal kindness as for Oliver Goldsmith, for few have so eminently possessed the magic gift of identifying themselves with their writings. We read his character in every page, and grow into familiar intimacy as we read. The artless benevolence that beams throughout his works; the whimsical, yet amiable views of human life and human nature; the unforced humor, blending so happily with good feeling and good sense, and singularly dashed at times with a pleasant melancholy; even the very nature of his mellow, and flowing, and softly-tinted style, — all seem to bespeak his moral as well as his intellectual qualities, and make us love the man at the same time that we admire the author. While the productions of writers of loftier pretension and more sounding names are suffered to moulder on our shelves, those of Goldsmith are cherished and laid in our bosoms. We do not quote them with ostentation, but they mingle with our minds, sweeten our tempers, and harmonize our thoughts; they put us in good-humor with ourselves and with the world, and in so doing they make us happier and better men.

The book is a long, highly wrought biographical essay — in no wise to be considered a definitive "life of Goldsmith," an honor which must even yet be accorded Forster's book. As a matter of fact Irving used both Prior and Forster as the basis for his work. And so well did he write — though again the predominance of poetry over science prevents authoritativeness — that he quite detracted from Forster's fame in particular, a fact not passed over lightly in Forster's ironical comment in his second edition:

> Mr. Washington Irving, who has done me the honor to copy it the ["Jessamy Bride" hint] and many other things from the first edition of this biography, goes somewhat too far in accepting the suggestion as if it were an ascertained fact . . . with whatever success for romance-loving readers, less pleasantly, it must be admitted, for sober seekers after truth.

And justly might Forster complain. He had with all his skill in historical research and with his great gift in lucid interpretation presented the facts in connection with Goldsmith and his career in conclusive fashion only to be attacked by Prior (whose "Goldsmith" had recently appeared) on a charge of what amounted to plagiarism. Forster counter-charged in a manner eminently satisfactory, and the matter was closed. As a sequel, however, he had to accept Irving's work; for his answer to Prior that the facts concerning a man were common property to be handled as a biographer thought just, neutralized any serious objection he may have wished to make. But his acceptance was as shown in the foregoing.

Forster's is the better "Goldsmith"; but Irving's is the much more popular. Forster was as scientific as his opportunities, the materials available, and his manner made possible; Irving, using the facts thus provided proceeded to temper them with sentiment and so fix his "Life" in the public mind that his poetry is a part of lay awareness, while Forster's researches are respected as contributions to scholarship. The book is an example of Irving's own "mellow, and flowing, and softly-tinted style"; but the hero is a Goldsmith of romance. The use made of Mary Horneck, for instance, exemplifies much. Disregarding both Prior and Forster in their discreet reference, Irving develops a mere hint into a sentimental episode which lives — and will in all likelihood continue to flourish — as the story of the "Jessamy Bride" (nickname for Mary Horneck), hanging, in Forster's phrase, "a poetical wreath above her grave." And in similar manner similar liberties are taken; everywhere the "graphic" is in evidence, but it is rendered less real than it might have been by the intrusion of "the insubstantial" among "the demonstrable" — a defect the more insidious because the more easily absorbed by the uncritical.

How effective Irving's "Goldsmith" was is echoed in contemporary reviews, like that in the "Athenaeum," for instance, which praised it because of the beauty of "the personal portrait"; and that in the "London Critic," which proclaimed it "Goldsmith, the man, as he really was." But more especially perhaps it was the opinion expressed in "Graham's Magazine," November, 1849, that defined the contemporary attitude:

> From no living person could we have expected a more delightful biography of Goldsmith than from Washington Irving, and, accordingly, we have one, written closer to the heart and brain of its subject, than any other in English literature. . . . With exquisite refinement of thought, and simplicity of narrative, it exhibits the gradual growth of Goldsmith's mind and disposition under the tutorship of experience, and so clear in the representation, that the dullest eye cannot miss seeing the essential features of the character, and the dullest heart admiring them.

With hardly a dissenting voice raised at the time of its publication, therefore, and with a concensus of admiration from that day to this, Irving's "Goldsmith" is, none the less, more nearly of the heart than of the mind.

When at last he turned to "the Washington," it was to approach the climax of his career. He was old and ill, but from his early youth he had worshiped the man for whom he had been named by his mother, a nurse in the Revolutionary War. And the thought of writing Washington's "life" seems to have been constantly with him; his Journals contain frequent references to the undertaking, and as early as 1825 he had begun to make notes for it, although at that time he had refused to consider pursuing the task seriously, saying to Constable, the Edinburgh publisher, who urged it upon him, "I stand in too great awe of it."

As a matter of fact, he had always realized the difficulties of such a work: research among the thousands of documents, the tremendous amount of correspondence necessary, the close study of the biographies already written, but particularly the examination of Washington's own writings. Nevertheless, despite the obstacles involved, despite his accumulating years and growing illness — catarrh and asthma affected him with increasing intensity toward the end — in 1851 he commenced the work with sufficient freedom and wrote steadily on until it was finished.

There can be not the least doubt that he labored with the greatest attention to detail as he proceeded with this the most significant of his biographies. He read everything extant, made innumerable visits to the places concerned — from Saratoga to Sulgrave Manor. There can likewise be no doubt, however, of his dependency upon the researches of Sparks, who, himself protested against what is all too mildly acknowledged in Irving's Preface. "I have also made use," wrote Irving,

> of "Washington's Writings," as published by Mr. Sparks; a careful collation of many of them with the originals having convinced me of the general correctness of the collection, and of the safety with which it may be relied upon for historical purposes, —

in comment upon which Sparks said,

> I think he might have given a more full account of that work in his preface, especially as he was to draw so largely from it.

The reliance upon Sparks is, indeed, so close that H. B. Adams in his "The Life and Writings of Jared Sparks" points out that "Irving could no more have written his 'Life of Washington' without the aid of Sparks than he could have written his 'Columbus' without the help of Navarette."

Notwithstanding, "the shaping spirit" of Irving's imagination — sustained by his love of the subject, and communicated by the grace of his style — has so permeated no matter what material he drew upon that his "Washington" has remained the ideal characterization of the national hero. And it was natural that Irving's "Life" should be accepted as the definition of the Washington tradition. When as early as 1834 it became known that he was at work upon it, editors and critics alike voiced the opinion that he was inevitably the proper person to undertake it. His position as a representative American was firmly established, his literary powers were adjudged as of the first rank, his nonpartisan attitude was well-known — he himself expressed it as "I wish to stand in my history where Washington stood, who was of no party" — and the stories of his love for the first president were of common remark. Hence, when the volumes began to appear, filled as they were with detail, anecdote, the heroic deeds of patriots, character sketches of statesmen (particularly sketches like that of Hamilton), accounts of dramatic events and of spiritual as well as political and military triumphs — when the volumes began to appear, each sustaining the quality of its predecessor as they followed one another at almost yearly intervals from 1855 until 1859, the last being issued just eight months before Irving's death, the applause was universal. The "Washington" was immediately adopted for school use. No patriotic speaker failed to mention it. The periodical press welcomed it, for although the "Westminster Review" for October, 1856, remarked that it found

> rather material for a history of the war, than a biography of the greatest man who has appeared in this world since Oliver Cromwell,

the "North American Review" had, three months before, characterized it as

> less didactic and political than Marshall's, less historical and official than that of Sparks, and more familiar and minute than either.

It, in fact, led a chorus of approval which continued for more than thirty years among critics and historians and continues until our own day among the sentimentally disposed — although in the words of Dr. O'Neill,

> Much has been discovered and published concerning Washington since Irving's time and consequently his book has been

superseded, but it cannot be ignored either as biography or as literature.

Not any of Irving's work is to be "ignored either as biography or as literature." If his science is outweighed by his poetry, at least the poetry is of high order. He set a pace in American literature and was among the first to give it distinction. He wrote because not to write would have been with him unthinkable. Depend upon the work of other men he did; he was none the less original, and as Carlyle once wrote, "The world loves its original men, and can in no wise forget them."

# 17—Lockhart and Scott

> To find out the great men, to clean the dirt
> from them, and place them on their proper
> pedestals. — Carlyle.

THE office of biography as a hoarstone of friendship is obvious
enough; there are, as has been said repeatedly, few "lives"
within the canon which did not emanate from this nearly divine
among human relationships, no matter how infrequently it may
have attained in particular instances to the perfection suggested by
Montaigne in referring to his love for Etienne de la Boétie, as

> In true friendship, of which I am a good judge, I give
> myself to my friend more than I draw him to me. Not only
> would I rather benefit him than that he should benefit me,
> but also that he should benefit himself rather than me; he
> benefits me most when he benefits himself.

But scarcely any of such records, not even Mason's "Gray," proceed more directly out of sentiment than the "Memoirs of the Life
of Sir Walter Scott, Bart.," by his son-in-law, John Gibson Lockhart,
published in 1836–1838. The work is at once a monument to
friendship, an exposition of the character and career of the most
illustrious author of his day, and a masterpiece from the hand of a
man who had he not composed it would very probably have been
neglectfully permitted, like hundreds endowed with greater gifts,
to sink into the oblivion of Lethe. It is easily said that so patent a
subject as Walter Scott and so close a relationship as was Lockhart's
with him — productive as it was of understanding and, incidentally,
of completely adequate material — could hardly fail of eminent suc-

cess. It is likewise easy to point to the certainty of large reward, for, although it was understood that the proceeds would be applied toward liquidating Scott's debts, Cadell allowed Lockhart a generous fee. None the less, something more profound was needed before the earthly reality of the famous novelist could be perpetuated — from the glamour of his personality, through the celebrity of his self-wrought position, to the utter sadness of his last days. And the need was provided out of the deep and lasting friendship which Lockhart felt for Scott — an emotion which began with the elder man's kindness to the young writer at their first meeting, was augmented by the latter's inclusion in the family at Abbotsford by reason of his marriage with Scott's daughter Sophia, and was sustained and rarified by a thousand ties which triumph and poignant grief contrived.

Such spiritual kinship, moreover, was the more real for being natural, based as it was, in addition to the exigencies common to their lives, upon their love of letters and their pride in being Scotsmen. Scott's expression of nationalism, for instance, was not more successful than Lockhart's conception of it was vital. In fact, Lockhart would have liked nothing better than to become a Scottish novelist like Galt. But, try as he did in his youth, as a fiction writer he had to remain content with "Valerius," a novel of ancient Rome (so classical in style that, as Andrew Lang points out in the "Life of Lockhart," "one is always turning it into Latin prose"), and with three other works in the form, not one of which has been distinguished. Fortunately he had not to depend upon fiction; his talents lay in another direction — in journalism of a high order which he developed, and in poetry of a lesser sort which he did not. Through everything he wrote, however, runs the thin red line of his love for Scotland, whether of Scottish character, as in "Reginald Dalton," "Adam Blair," and "Gilbert Earle"; of Edinburgh society, as in "Peter's Letters"; of native politics, as in the critical essays for the "Quarterly"; or of his friend, as in the "Memoirs."

Not that he was militantly Scottish. He was proud of his race and of its accomplishments, as became a Lockhart of the Lee, and lost no opportunity to show his pride; but his literate temperament held him for the most part in check — the temperament which linked him to Scott much more closely than did their common racial bonds. If occasionally Lockhart found himself in difficulties, as when, for instance, he persisted in remaining loyal to Blackwood and his magazine in spite of the disapproval of both Scott and Christie; when he was suspected of attacking Keats and Leigh Hunt; when he became involved in the affair with John Scott, editor of the "London Magazine"; in the curious episode of "The Chaldee Manuscript"; and in the religious disagreements with the "Edinburgh Review" and some of its contributors — if he sometimes became the center of involvements like these, it was partly because of partisanship growing out of the bitter rivalry for literary prestige and political preferment which developed during the early part of the century. On the whole, however, Lockhart is not to be thought of as one thinks of Gifford, whom he succeeded as editor of the "Quarterly," or of Jeffrey, Sydney Smith, and Lord Brougham of the "Edinburgh Review." He was what he was, and one need be no "apostle of approval" to "hang out a bush" for him. As in its obituary article of December 9, 1854, the "Times" could remark,

> So acute, unsparing, and satirical was his intellect that, had Lockhart been endowed with that alone, he would have been the most brilliant but the most dangerous of men; but so strong, upright, and true were his moral qualities also that, had he been a dunce in attainment or a fool in wit, he must still have been recognized as an extraordinary man, —

so can we accept him. The old quarrels have been silenced; the old wounds have lost even their scars. Lockhart was a giant among biographers, and Walter Scott's good friend.

> The evil stars
> Are set and gone; and we must turn our eyes
> On suns that are, and shine.

As is oftener true than not in comparable relationships, the beginning of the friendship was also, in a manner, the beginning of the biography. Lockhart describes the first quite simply. "It was during the sitting of the General Assembly of the Kirk in May, 1818," he wrote, that I first had the honor of meeting him in private society: the party was not a large one, at the house of a much-valued common friend — Mr. Home Drummond of Blair Drummond, the grandson of Lord Kames. Mr. Scott, ever apt to consider too favorably the literary efforts of others, and more especially of very young persons, received me, when I was presented to him, with a cordiality which I had not been prepared to expect from one filling a station so exalted. This, however, is the same story that every individual who ever met him under similar circumstances has had to tell. When the ladies had retired from the dinner-table, I happened to sit next to him; and he, having heard that I had lately returned from a tour in Germany, made that country and its recent literature the subject of some conversation. In the course of it, I told him that when, on reaching the inn at Weimar, I asked the waiter whether Goethe was then in the town, the man stared as if he had not heard the word before; and that on my repeating the question, adding *Goethe der grosse dichter* (the great poet), he shook his head as doubtfully as before — until the landlady solved our difficulties by suggesting that perhaps the traveller might mean "the *Herr Geheimer Rath* (Privy Counsellor) *Von Goethe.*" Scott seemed amused with this, and said, "I hope you will come one of these days and see me at Abbotsford; and when you reach Selkirk or Melrose, be sure you ask even the landlady for nobody but the *Sheriff.*"

At the time Lockhart was twenty-four, having been born in 1794 at Cambusnethan, and a tall, very handsome man. He had been educated at the high school in Glasgow and at the university there, proceeding to Balliol College, Oxford, however, in 1808, upon a Snell exhibition. Here he took a degree with highest honors in 1813, at an age when most young men are just beginning to study. His distinction had been won in the Classics, but he had also begun his life-long interest in Spanish and German literature and developed a leaning toward writing — although fully intending to follow the law as a career. Returning to Glasgow after graduation, he lived more or less remote from the tumultuous life about him, sharing none of its interests, suffering, in fact, the usual fate of one whose formal preparation for life has been ended too soon.

After two years, however, he removed to Edinburgh, reading law until his admission to the Scottish bar in 1816, and indulging his literary talents by acting as one of the chief contributors to "Blackwood's" along with John Wilson, soon becoming known, because of the trenchant wit which colored his critical comments, as "the Scorpion," corresponding to Wilson's "the Leopard," and Blackwood's "Ebony." In fact, he thus took on the character by which he continued to be known throughout his life, the result partly of his native shyness and partly of his having tried to establish himself too early and without sufficient funds in an intensely complicated society — of which he wrote:

> Edinburgh, even were its population as great as that of London, could never be merely a city. Here there must always be present the idea of the littleness of all human works.

How unjust such a reputation was it is only necessary to remember certain of his virtues to establish — his loyalty to "Maga," for instance, because it was the means of his commencing authorship when the law failed to produce for him more than £50 a year; his life-long friendship with Christie; his ideally happy marriage with Scott's daughter; his intense love for his children, especially "Littlejohn," for whom Scott wrote "Tales of A Grandfather"; and his devotion to Scott himself. Authors might fear him, being misled by

> the laugh about the screwd up mouth, that fules ca'd no canny, for they couldna thole the meanin' o't,

and Harriet Martineau might say that he lived "amidst the explosions of friendships, formed in flattery and broken off by treachery," and that "free and constant friendship he never enjoyed, nor seemed to desire." Furthermore, Charles Sumner, among others, might say, "Lockhart has not a friend"; none the less, Allan Cunningham could write, "There is a heart in Lockhart when one gets through the crust"; and he himself in a letter to his sister during 1819 could say that locks of his black hair were in such demand that he feared baldness. And finally, Scott, soon after the meeting at Drummond's invited him to Abbotsford, and went on long walks with him. He engaged him to furnish material for the "Edinburgh Annual

Register" which had been solicited of himself. He evidently saw the innate fineness beneath the coldness that protected Lockhart's diffidence — although he had a dislike of Lockhart's reputation as one of the "Maga" group, all of whom Scott disliked, especially Blackwood. It has been suggested, of course, that Sir Walter's encouragement of the younger man was in the interest of Scott's dynastic ambitions — an alliance with a Lockhart of the Lee was anything but insignificant in his eyes. However that may be (and one cannot remain unaware that Scott looked upon his writing more or less as a means of attaining worldly success rather than artistic distinction, leaving nothing undone that would aid such attainment), nevertheless the association formed on that memorable occasion in May, 1818, endured until Scott's death in 1832, and has now become immortal through Lockhart's realization of it in the "Memoirs."

To say, as was said in an earlier passage, that the beginning of a friendship is — when the final expression of it is a notable "life" — the beginning also of the biography, is to fall not far short of defining the source of whatever excellence the work may possess, for there is no gainsaying Dr. Johnson's famous "Nobody can write the life of a man but those who have eat and drunk and lived in social intercourse with him." In order, therefore, to suggest something of Lockhart's inevitability as the biographer of Scott, it is only necessary to refer to a letter of Sophie Scott Lockhart to her husband written during her father's last illness,

> I used to think it was both selfish and wrong, my marrying; but when I hear papa talk of you, and see the comfort you are to him, dear Lockhart, I feel I can never be grateful enough to you.

In no other place is a better definition of the developed relationship to be found; Lockhart understood and was understood. Furthermore, Mrs. Lockhart in her letters provides some suggestion of the biographer's eagerness in undertaking and completing his enormous task. In March, 1836, for instance, she wrote to Cadell, the publisher:

> Knowing how anxious you are for the "Life," I cannot help writing you a few lines to tell you it is fairly begun, and

Lockhart working as hard at it as ever you could wish. He has been arranging it so long in his mind that, now fairly commenced, he will not be long about it; and he has read to me, and continues to do so, what he writes, and I am much mistaken if anything in our time will come up to it in interest, style, or as a picture of manners just passing away. I cannot speak enough of the interest he has contrived to give to the genealogy, the least promising part, and you may believe the rest is not behind hand.

Provided thus as he was with talent, with sympathy, with interest, and, not less essentially, with material — the collection of documents in his possession was to be spoken of in terms of weight, not number — Lockhart proceeded to achieve the best work of his career and to contribute a masterpiece to biography.

For to term it anything less is to fail through understatement. Professor Hugh Walker called it "an achievement which has very rarely been rivalled." George Saintsbury referred to Boswell's "Johnson" as "the only possible rival" of the "Scott," and continues by commenting that

> the taste and spirit of Lockhart's book are not less admirable than the skill of its arrangement and the competency of its writing; nor would it be easily possible to find a happier adjustment in this respect in the whole annals of biography.

And Leslie Stephen said that it might "safely be described as, next to Boswell's "Johnson," the best in the language."

In the Preface, Lockhart sets down formally the character of his undertaking:

> In obedience to the instructions of Sir Walter Scott's last will . . . I consider it my duty to tell the story truly and intelligibly: but I trust I have avoided any unnecessary disclosures; and, after all, there was nothing to disclose that could have attached any sort of blame to any of the parties concerned.

Further on he defines his procedure:

> I have endeavored to lay before the reader those parts of Sir Walter's character to which we have access, as they were

indicated in his sayings and doings through the long series of his years — making use, whenever it was possible, of his own letters and diaries rather than of any other materials — but refrained from obtruding almost anything of comment. It was my wish to let the character develop itself.

And in a letter written January, 1837, to Will Laidlow, Scott's faithful amanuensis during the last years and author of the highly interesting "Lucy's Flitting," he comments upon his purpose with such sincerity that one cannot but agree with Andrew Lang's comment that the statement "is, in itself, a sufficient reply to some of the censures urged, at the time of publication, against Lockhart's work." The letter contains, among less pertinent material, these passages:

> My sole object is to do him justice, by so contriving it that he shall be, as far as possible from first to last, his own his-toriographer, and I have therefore willingly expended the time that would have sufficed for writing a dozen books on what will be no more than the compilation of one.
>
> A stern sense of duty — that kind of sense of it which is combined with the feeling of his actual presence in a serene state of elevation above all petty terrestrial and temporary views — will induce me to touch the few darker points in his life and character as freely as the others which were so pre-dominant; and my chief anxiety on the appearance of the book will be, not to hear what is said by the world, but what is thought by you and the few others who can really compare the representation as a whole with the facts in the case.
>
> *          *          *
>
> Out of these confused and painful scraps [the last few letters] I think I can contrive to put together a picture that will be highly touching, of a great mind shattered, but never degraded, and always to the very last noble, as his heart con-tinued pure and warm as long as it could beat.

An additional expression of Lockhart's regarding the composition of the book occurs in the body of Volume IV in connection with the advice he had received from various persons urging the Boswell-ian technique of including recorded conversation. As a matter of fact, quite out of keeping with the romantic attitude, which decried Boswell and all his works, the "Memoir" of Scott is the first important work of the nineteenth century to follow Boswell's crystallization of the autobiographical method. The author's preoccupation with this method is indicated in the just quoted passage, "that he shall be . . . his own historiographer," although he did not make a point of conversation, for the reasons that

> I never thought it lawful to keep a journal of what passes in private society, so that no one need expect from the sequel of this narrative any detailed record of Scott's familiar talk. What fragments of it have happened to adhere to a tolerably retentive memory, and may be put into black and white without wounding any feelings which my friend, were he alive, would have wished to spare, I shall introduce as the occasion suggests or serves; but I disclaim on the threshhold anything more than this . . . To report conversations fairly, it is a necessary prerequisite that we should be completely familiar with all the interlocutors, and understand thoroughly all their minutest relations and points of common knowledge, and common feeling, with each other. He who does not, must be perpetually in danger of misinterpreting sportive allusion into serious statement.

To attempt to estimate so vast a work except in the most general fashion is futile. One may, however, point out that certain passages reveal Scott as a personality of romance, certain others as a fallible human being. In the description of his struggles to complete "Count Robert of Paris," for instance, when weakened by disease, and of the beginning of "Castle Dangerous" under much the same conditions; in the narrative of the disturbances at Hawick and Jedbourgh, the journey to Yair Ashestiel, to Traquair, to the Douglas tombs, and of the warning by death of Bosthwickbrae, one sees the "Shurra," the humorist, the boon-companion, the poet who "with half his heart inhabits other worlds." But it remains for two scenes in particular to reveal Lockhart in the fulness of his reverence and the simplicity of his style. The first, a simple anecdote, concerns a dinner party of young advocates, Lockhart among them, and Scott while he was writing "Waverly":

We had adjourned to a library which had one large window looking northward. After conversing here for an hour or more, I observed that a shade had come over the aspect of my friend, who happened to be placed immediately opposite to myself, and said something that intimated a fear of his being unwell. "No," said he, "I shall be well enough presently, if you will only let me sit where you are, and take my chair; for there is a confounded hand in sight of me here, which has often bothered me before, and now it won't let me fill my glass with a good will." I arose to change places with him accordingly, and he pointed out to me this hand which, like the writing on Belshazzar's wall, distracted his hour of hilarity. "Since we sat down," he said, "I have been watching it — it fascinates my eye — it never stops — page after page is finished and thrown on the heap of MS., and still it goes on unwearied — and so it will be till candles are brought in, and God knows how long after that. It is the same every night — I can't stand the sight of it when I am not at my books." — "Some stupid, dogged, engrossing clerk probably," exclaimed myself or some other giddy youth in our society. "No, boys," said our host, "I well know what hand it is — 'tis Walter Scott's."

And the second is one of the finest death scenes in biography even though one suspects that certain details were invented, for it has been shown that Scott remained unconscious during these last days:

As I was dressing on the morning of Monday the 17th of September, Nicholson came into my room, and told me that his master had awoke in a state of composure and consciousness, and wished to see me immediately. I found him entirely himself, though in the last extreme of feebleness. His eye was clear and calm — every trace of the wild fire of delirium extinguished. "Lockhart," he said, "I may have but a minute to speak to you. My dear, be a good man — be virtuous — be religious — be a good man. Nothing else will give you any comfort when you come to lie here." He paused, and I said, "Shall I send for Sophie and Anne?" "No," he said, "don't disturb them. Poor souls! I know they were up all night — God bless you all." With this he sunk into a very tranquil sleep, and indeed, he scarcely afterward gave any sign of consciousness, except for an instant on the arrival of his sons. They, on learning that the scene was about to close, obtained a new leave of absence from their posts, and both reached Abbotsford on the 19th. About half-past one P.M., on the 21st of September, Sir Walter breathed his last, in the presence of all his children. It was a beautiful day — so warm that every window was wide open — and so perfectly still, that the sound of all others most delicious to his ear, the gentle ripple of the Tweed over its pebbles, was distinctly audible as we knelt around the bed, and his eldest son kissed and closed his eyes. No sculptor ever modelled a more majestic image of repose.

The hundred years that have passed since the publication of the first edition have served to fix more and more firmly Lockhart's "Life of Scott" in its place among the great biographies. The change of taste from that which frowned upon even Mason's tempered candor in the "Gray" and sixty years later objected to Lockhart's, as exemplified in Harriet Martineau's calling his work "a precious bequest to posterity . . . purged as we hope it will be of whatever is untrue and unkind, and rendered safe as it is beautiful" — the change of taste to that of our day has aided rather than hindered plain speaking. We, as a matter of fact, agree with Scott himself in point of view, according to his expression of it in one of his letters to Miss Seward:

> Biography loses all its interest with me, when the shades and lights of the principal character are not accurately and faithfully detailed. I can no more sympathize with a mere eulogist than I can with a ranting hero on the stage.

And one remembers also Scott's amusement at Queen Elizabeth's demand that Zucchero paint her portrait with no shadows on the face, an attitude which recalls by contrast Cromwell's insistence that Sir Peter Lely was not to cover the famous wart with court-plaster. No, all thought of defect arising from mention of fallibility has passed. Scott was, unquestionably, at fault when during the postwar inflation he overextended his credit. However, his pen and his indefatigable energies cleared him from all blame in the matter, and his estate became finally unencumbered when Cadell took over the copyright and the profits accruing from Lockhart's work.

It is not this sort of criticism that one nowadays has to offer; one can read the whole 2500 pages and not need to be a Scot of Andrew Lang's quality to enjoy them — Andrew Lang, who wrote:

> To a Scott, and a Scot of the Border, the book has the charm of home, and is dear to us as his own grey hills were dear to Sir Walter.

It is, rather, the fact of these same 2500 pages, the sheer bulk of them, that causes one to wonder if perhaps compression, a more discriminate selection, would not have added quality by sharpening somewhat the focus.

Lockhart seems to have expected such criticism, and defended himself against it by insisting that Scott was so celebrated a man that no amount of material was too great. Nevertheless, he referred to his work as a "compilation"; and it seems to be just that. For instance, Frederick Harrison once wrote of it:

> Lockhart's book is not a *Life* (he does not so describe it); it is certainly not a work of art, it is too long and spun out with too many letters and diaries of other persons, and Lockhart is in truth neither a Joinville nor a Boswell, and worst of all, Scott himself had no great gifts as a writer of letters or journals. Byron was immensely his superior in this, and so, as Scott naïvely told Lockhart, he gave up poetry because Byron beat him. And yet, though neither Lockhart nor Scott had any genius in biography — Scott's own early fragment might be written by any one — and though the letters are often goody-goody commonplace, and the diaries cited are not literature at all, still I find Lockhart's *Memoir* the fascinating record of a glorious genius in a great spirit.

And no less a man than Thomas Carlyle — himself a Scotsman, and the firmest friend Lockhart had in London — set forth something of the same idea in what is the most understanding of the contemporary reviews:

> The work is not so much a composition as what we may call a compilation well done. Neither is this a task of no difficulty; this too is a task that may be performed with extremely various degrees of merit: from the *Life and Correspondence of*

*Hannah More,* for instance, up to this *Life of Scott,* there is a wide range indeed. To picture forth the Life of Scott according to any rules of art or composition, so that a reader, on adequately examining it, might say to himself, "There is Scott, there is the physiography and meaning of Scott's appearance and transit on this earth; such was he by nature, so did the world act on him, so he on the world, with such result and significance for himself and us:" this was by no manner of means Mr. Lockhart's plan. A plan which, it is rashly said, should preside over every biography. . . . Scott's biography, if uncomposed, lies printed and indestructible here, in the elementary state, and can at any time be composed, if necessary, by whosoever has a call to it, —

the corollary to which and, incidentally, the expression of our own taste in the matter, has been the appearance in 1938 of a compressed and highly wrought "life" of Scott by Sir Herbert Grierson, one based, however, upon Lockhart's work.

But in spite of Lockhart's lack of plan, in spite of the enormous length of his book, in spite of what seems almost a labyrinth of facts, persons, places, letters, journals, diaries, and direct comment, abundance never becomes attenuated into the superfluous and so the chief figure is seldom lost sight of — the quality which has caused every critic during the long century just passed to temper his views. At times, to be sure, the image of Sir Walter becomes obscured; but it never fades, and in the end a sense of reality pervades the mind of the reader, a feeling of being in the presence of personality at its highest, as detail after detail finally falls into place to create the semblance of "that day" called Scott.

# 18—Carlyle's "Life of John Sterling"

*When life is framed in death the picture is
ready to hang.* — Henry James.

SELDOM has the life of a comparatively obscure figure been
written by an author of the first rank. Usually the contrary is
true. However, when such a life does appear, almost invariably it
is a work of distinction. Samuel Johnson's "Life of Richard Savage"
is one instance in point, and Goldsmith's "Nash" is another. But
the clearest example is Thomas Carlyle's "Life of John Sterling,"
one of the most sympathetically understanding of biographies and
quite the simplest piece of Carlyle's prose. Johnson wrote of an
unfortunate friend and achieved one of the best things in the "Lives
of the Poets." Goldsmith touched to splendor a shabby soul and
added to his own fame. But Carlyle reanimated one for whom the
world was all too much; and although he himself called the work
"a poor tatter of a thing," his biographer Froude said: "It is perhaps
the most beautiful biography in the English language," an opinion
which almost a century has sustained.

Within the limits of its intention the "Life of Sterling" attains its
end — it is probably the best illustration we have of the "glorification
of the imperfect," or of genius at liberty to choose its material as
against mediocrity concerned with the obvious. Both theme and
mood are early established. In the Introductory Carlyle writes:

> I have remarked that a true delineation of the smallest man,
> and his scene of pilgrimage through life, is capable of inter-
> esting the greatest man; that all men are to an unspeakable
> degree brothers, each man's life a strange emblem of every

man's; and that human portraits faithfully drawn, are of all pictures the welcomest on human walls;

and as the theme is suggested and the mood set, so the narrative proceeds. It is as well a revelation of Carlyle, however, as it is a life of his young disciple. For the "Sage of Chelsea" felt impelled in order to explain Sterling's attempts at adjustment to reveal directly more of himself than hitherto he had done — a necessity inextricably involved with the relationship linking the two and with the forces moving Carlyle to write.

Sterling's life was all too short — born on the Island of Bute in 1806, he died of tuberculosis in 1844 — to connote more than a promise of achievement. Nevertheless it was long enough for him to exercise something of the exceptional magnetism he possessed so that not only did he attract and hold the affection of so unpredictable a critic of men as Thomas Carlyle (one does not soon forget, for instance, the comment upon Charles Lamb or the inexplicable remark about Cardinal Newman), but he also drew about himself as the center of a literary group men like Tennyson, Connop Thirwall, Allan Cunningham, J. S. Mill, Thackeray, Lord Houghton, James Spedding, Sir Francis Palgrave, and a score more equally discerning, who in 1838 named themselves the "Sterling Club." It was personality, however, rather than accomplishment, being, not doing, that made him unique. The admiration he won in his own circles is evident from a letter written to him in his last illness by his friend Mill:

> There are certainly few people living who are capable of doing as much good by their conscious and unconscious influence as you are, and I do not believe you have even had an adequate conception of the extent of the influence you possess, and the quality of good which you produce by it. Even by your mere existence you do more good than many by their laborious exertions.

Birth and parentage, schooling at Llanblethian, Paris, and London, with university training at both Glasgow and Cambridge open Carlyle's story. There follows notice of Sterling's unsuccessful editorship, with Frederick Maurice, of "The Athenaeum," some account of his early writing, and mention of "Arthur Coningsby," the Wertherian novel which, sent by Mill, had caused Carlyle to hope some day to know the author. His interest in the book seems to have been aroused by the "prefigurement" he saw in it "of an opulent, genial, and sunny mind, but misdirected, disappointed, experienced in misery." The high point of Part One is the half contemptuous, half compassionate chapter on Coleridge (in a letter to Hare, Sterling once wrote, "To Coleridge I owe education"). In it is presented Sterling's quest for answers to the metaphysical problems with which his day was engrossed and which Coleridge, in the opinion of many, was able to supply; for at the time he was comfortably at home with the Gilmans on Highgate Hill discoursing in his inimitable fashion and trying to provide a key to the absurdly conceived problem which he posed as "the sublime secret of believing by the reason what the understanding has been obliged to fling out as incredible." The result was, as a following section points out, that in his enthusiasm for the transcendental, Sterling, together with his cousin, Captain Robert Boyd, as financial backer, espoused the cause of General Torrijos and the Spanish exiles in their efforts to return to power — only to remain the sole survivor of that ill-fated conspiracy, Boyd, even Torrijos himself, having been executed on the Plaza at Malaga.

As an effect of his broken dream of aiding the persecuted Spaniards he turned to marriage and travel, visiting with his "blooming, kindly, and true-hearted Wife" — the former Suzannah Bonton — the British West Indies, and there because of slowly fading health spending some fifteen months upon the island of St. Vincent, where he acted as manager of a sugar plantation belonging to his mother. But the "strangling oppressions of his Soul" grew too heavy; illness and the lack of success in certain efforts towards relieving the condition of the slaves forced him to give up the enterprise. Solution and relief lay in Europe, if anywhere. Part One, therefore, ends with his return to England and a visit to Germany in 1833, where at Bonn he met his old friend and one time tutor, Julius Hare, rector of Hurstmonceux in Sussex and translator with Connop Thirwall of Niebuhr's "Roman History." Still in search of the substantials he resolved, under the encouragement of Hare, to deepen his theological studies, which he had dropped upon leaving Cambridge without a degree; and in the course of time he did so and became Hare's curate. For some months he found peace at Hurstmonceux, where he established his wife and small son Edward, while according to his own conceptions striving with all his might, as Carlyle puts it, "not to be a moonshine shadow of the first Paul."

Part Two completes the story. Sterling occupied his curacy just eight months. Ill-health, the old disturbances, doubts, misgivings as to the authenticity of his pursuit of the ideal beginning to assail him, he grasped at his gathering illness as an excuse — disease was becoming sufficiently aggravated to warrant his action, naturally; but it seems to have been characteristic of him always that he chose the ostensible instead of the underlying as a determining factor — and went up to London to consult physicians. While there he came to a decision and in sorrowful agitation wrote to Hare resigning his curacy. "It was during this expedition to London that I first saw Sterling," writes Carlyle:

> At the India House, incidentally, one afternoon, where I found him in company with John Mill, whom I happened like himself to be visiting for a few minutes. The sight of one whose fine qualities I had often heard of lately was interesting enough; and on the whole proved not disappointing, though it was the transition of dream into fact, that is, of poetry into prose, and shewed its unrhymed side withal. A loose, careless-looking thin figure, in careless, dim costume, sat in a lounging posture, carelessly and copiously talking. I was struck with the kindly but restless swift-glancing eyes, which looked as if the spirits were all out coursing like a pack of merry, eager beagles, beating every bush. The brow, rather sloping in form, was not of imposing character, though again the head was longish, which is always the best sign of intellect; the physiognomy in general indicated animation rather than strength.

For a time he retained his home in Sussex, but finally, ever restless, he wandered to London and lived in Bayswater. Here he preached occasionally. Carlyle heard him once, "in some new College-chapel in Somerset House (I suppose what is now called Queen's College)." Most of his time, however, he spent in reading and writing and in cultivating many friendships. Carlyle characterizes him at this time in a vivid passage:

> He was full of bright speech and argument; radiant with arrowy vitalities, vivacities, and ingenuities. Less than any man he gave you an idea of ill health. Hopeful, sanguine; nay he did not even seem to need definite hope, or much to form any; projecting himself in airy pulses like an aurora borealis, like a summer dawn, and filling all the world with present brightness for himself and others. Ill health? Nay, you found at last it was the very excess of *life* in him that brought on disease. This restless play of being, fit to conquer the world, could it have been held and guided, could not be held.

None the less it was ill-health stalking him like Nemesis that shaped the remaining years. In the summer of 1836 he moved to Bordeaux and prospered in the mild air of southern France, but an outbreak of cholera pushed him on. He went to Madeira, then to Italy, and returned home in 1839 to settle in "the dry, dogmatic air of Clifton for a time," only to move to Falmouth, and then in the end to Ventnor on the Isle of Wight where he had built a house, characterized by him in a letter to Carlyle as one

> which promises to be as good as a wise man needs, and far better than most wise men ever enjoyed on earth.

Soon after his coming to London from Hurstmonceux, John Wilson of "Blackwood's" had opened a correspondence with him and paved the way for his entrance into that magazine. From time to time he contributed dramatic ballads, like "The Sexton Daughter," and "The Onyx Ring"; and detached thoughts like the analogical "Crystals from a Cavern," "Thoughts and Images," and "Sayings and Essayings." In addition, J. S. Mill upon becoming editor of "The London and Westminster" had invited his contributions. He wrote for Mill a number of literary essays on Montaigne, on Simonides, on Coleridge, Milton, Burns, Tennyson, and best of all his work of the kind, the article on Carlyle. These writings, together with those contributed to "The Athenaeum" and a number of other journals; an abortive play, "The Tragedy of Strafford" —

called "colossal" by Ralph Waldo Emerson, to whom it was dedicated, but called "trash" by Carlyle; the equally futile poem "Election" and the Orlando-like "Coeur-de-Lion" — these and the brightly vivacious letters make up the body of his literary work. There was no outward success for him, however. Friendships, the devotion of his growing family, the love of his mother, the sympathetic regard of his brilliant but blustering father, he had and retained. But from the world came little save misunderstanding, except that this last led indirectly to Carlyle's biography and so in the end to remembrance.

And remembrance as fixed by Carlyle is more than a little akin to that cherished by those who knew Sterling. He moved his friends to feel, not, it seems, to think; their hearts were stirred, if not their understanding. Melancholy arises from the contemplation of a lively soul in a sickly body, for something of the influence thus obscurely engendered by sickness and solitude at work upon the judgment communicates itself to those in sympathy with the sufferer. A condition more or less comparable may have been operative upon Carlyle, the most sensitive and the most articulate of the Sterling intimates; at least Carlyle's characterization is decidedly more personal than any other of his writings.

Their first meeting, as has been set forth, occurred in Mill's office at India House; but each had known of the other. Carlyle's reading "Arthur Coningsby" had made him "hope perhaps, one day, to know him," as he himself records; and Sterling had been one of the small group at Cambridge, including Thackeray, Tennyson, and Arthur Hallam, called "The Apostles" that, studying "Sartor Resartus" when it first appeared, became Carlyle's first disciples, despite their disagreement with certain of the ideas expressed. They likewise objected — being all trained classicists — to the tortured style, which Thackeray characterized as "choking double words, astonishing to the admirers of simple Addisonian English," and of which Sterling once complained that it was "heightened — and plethoric" in its fulness, and on the basis of which, in 1836, he was to reject "The Diamond Necklace" for Mill's "Review." They believed that they perceived in "Sartor" the expression of a man brilliant beyond any that they had hitherto encountered, one also who was unable to lie, or even to equivocate, insisting upon saying what he was convinced was the truth, regardless of consequence. Such qualities, as they conceived them, appealed at once to Sterling, and he, snatching the opportunity afforded by the meeting in Mill's office, introduced Carlyle, in turn, to his father, Edward Sterling, known as the "Thunderer" and then editor of the "Times" — in the 1830's the most powerful journal in the world. The elder Sterling offered Carlyle a position as staff correspondent. But Carlyle, knowing that he would be hiring out his mind, shackling it at a price, and preferring to remain his own master, declined the offer. Journalism always seemed to him to deny the moral worth of sincere opinion; he went so far once as to refer to it by the phrase "the yellow eye of journalism."

A friendship was begun, nevertheless, which soon became intimate. In fact the intimacy was such as to move Carlyle to write to Emerson:

> There is a man here called John Sterling, whom I love better than anybody I have seen since a certain sky-messenger alighted to me at Craigenputtock and vanished in the Blue again;

and

> He flings too much sheet-lighting and unrest into me when we meet in these low moods of mine, and yet one always wants him back again: 'No doing with him or without him, the dog!'

In Sterling, Carlyle saw an eager mind anxious for truth — an impression drawn from the thoughtful "Arthur Coningsby" — and truth, as the whole course of his life testified, was his own abiding quest, however wrongly he might conceive of it. And for Sterling, Carlyle represented the means by which his own weakness might be made strength, an "idleness," as he later said, "like trying to jump off one's shadow." For just as at Oxford the Tractarians were looking backward toward the beginnings of Christianity, many of them following Newman into Catholicism as a result, so there was at Cambridge a group that looked back toward Luther and on toward Schleiermacher, hoping to align revelation with reason (though Luther himself denounced reason in unspeakable terms)

[ 219 ]

and so provide a clear way through the spiritual murk that surrounded their thought. Coleridge was the high priest of the movement, as was previously said; but a few in the group, among them Sterling, thought that in Carlyle's utterances lay an inkling at least of the solution. How mistaken they all were need not be stressed here — a friendship flourished, to become enshrined in a book that at all events was a labor of love.

It was not the first life of Sterling to appear, however. Some time before his death Sterling appointed Carlyle and his friend Julius Hare as his literary executors, widely at variance though they were in character and outlook. In the end he had had small opinion of his own writing; in fact, he burnt much of it and suppressed more, as, in Carlyle's words, "looking steadfastly"

> into the silent continents of Death and Eternity, a brave man's judgments about his own sorry work in the field of Time are apt to be too lenient.

Nevertheless some of it had been published: it was this that he wished his executors to have charge of. When the time came, it was agreed, Carlyle being engaged at the time with Cromwell's letters, that Hare should prepare a selection of the works together with a biographical sketch, a task upon which he entered with some uncertainty as to its effects, saying later in answer to criticism:

> I did not undertake it without counting the cost nor without much hesitation and reluctance. No other work I ever engaged in caused me a hundredth part of the painful anxiety. Besides I could not but forsee the likelihood that I myself should incur blame and might give offense to many pious persons which my office rendered it a special obligation to avoid . . . Nor was any other qualified to speak of the most interesting, most energetic, happiest, and best period of his life, that which he spent in the active labours of the ministry. . . . Had the picture of his ministerial life been left out the whole would have been sadly distorted . . .

Accordingly, in 1848, four years after Sterling's death, the volume appeared, "John Sterling's Essays and Tales, with Life" by Archdeacon Hare.

The book had, however, an unfortunate bias; Sterling had been active in Anglican orders during only eight months of his thirty-eight years, yet Hare confined his "Life" almost entirely to that period. Furthermore, since Sterling had not been free from tinges of heresy, Hare, as editor, not being able to overcome either his natural tendencies or the bent of his ecclesiastical position, dwelt at length upon the matter. Heterodoxy, therefore, became the prime interest of the treatment, and it was so heavily stressed as to appear to have been the very essence of Sterling's experience. As a consequence the Anglican press, at the time very active in ferreting out heresy, seized the opportunity and so branded Sterling's reputation — not omitting to attack Hare, incidentally — that it could not have been more thoroughly discredited had he been convicted by an ecclesiastical court. The "Record" carried the attack to extremes, for instance, by violently attacking the Sterling Club on the basis of its name alone. "The noble Sterling," indignantly wrote Carlyle, who himself acknowledged no form of Christianity as embodying the truth,

> a radiant child of the empyrean, clad in bright auroral hues in the memory of all who knew him, — what is he doing here in inquisitorial *sanbenito,* with nothing but ghastly spectralities prowling round him, and inarticulate screeching and gibbering what they call their judgment on him.

However much Carlyle disagreed with his fellow-executor's work, he did nothing immediately, having no taste for such controversy. It was February, 1851, before he set to work, urged by Sterling's friends and by his brother Anthony. Then he reread Sterling's letters, sought information among his surviving relatives, and in three months completed his task.

Carlyle's opinion, as earlier pointed out, was that the book was a thing of tatters. Yet, upon its appearance it was more admired than anything else he had done. In fact, he was chagrined by the popularity of this his least characteristic work. The tranquillity of it was a surprise, not more than ten sentences of vituperation occurring in 344 pages. Heretofore Carlyle had trumpeted across the roofs of England in prophetic blasts, how prophetic our own day realizes upon recalling his words:

What does history show but the story of noble structures raised by the wisdom of the few and gradually undermined and destroyed by the proflicacy and ignorance of the many!

Here, however, he showed himself gentle, gentle and tender, in revealing the soul of a friend. There was no tinge of the rubric hues of "The French Revolution," the volume which to Sterling was a "breathing epic, a book that makes the heart ache." Gone, too, were the hollow laughter of "Sartor," and the violence of "Chartism." The nearest approach to the "Sterling" in manner and tone is the early "Schiller"; but it lacks entirely the evidences of emotional engagement. For emotional engagement is apparent throughout the "Sterling," sustained by an almost lyric quality now and again darkened by an in-dwelling sense of loss so poignant that the mood becomes nearly comparable to that of "Lycidas," "Adonais," or "Thyrsis," as suggested by the final paragraph:

> Here, visible to myself for some while, was a brilliant human presence, distinguished, honorable, lovable amid the dim common populations; among the million little beautiful, once more a beautiful human soul: whom I, among others, recognized and lovingly walked with, while the years and hours were. Sitting now by his tomb in thoughtful mood, the new times bring a new duty to me. 'Why write the Life of Sterling?' I imagine I had a commission higher than the world's, the dictates of Nature herself, to do what is now done. *Sic prosit.*

"A well-written life is almost as rare as a well-spent one," Carlyle wrote upon one occasion — but he was forgetting his own "Sterling."*

---

* Since in this book the religious note was perforce definitely touched upon, it will be of interest to recall here the words of Francis Thompson on Carlyle's view of Christianity as "a dissolved or dissolving myth, the spirit of which survived, awaiting incarnation in some new and modern *mythus.*" To supply this reincarnation, the poet says, was Carlyle's futile effort. He could increase the yearnings in men's hearts but could not fill them. Sterling's failure to look steadfastly at religion and see its saving grace lay at the root of his failure to adjust to the exigencies of life. — Ed.

# 19—John Forster

*The biographer has this problem set before him:
to delineate a likeness of the earthly pilgrimage
of a man.* — Carlyle.

*Read no history, read only biography, for it is
life without theory.* — Disraeli.

THE literary fate of John Forster, like that of Boswell, aptly
illustrates the paradox that, just as "a prophet is not without
honor save in his own country," a biographer is seldom himself the
subject of biography. As concerns Boswell, of course, the chances
are that ample recompense will be made for the century and a half
of misconception now passing. But nothing comparable is assurable
to Forster. True, he was not of the stature of Boswell either as a
biographer or as a personality. Nevertheless he was a man whose
career, according to the requirements derived by Sidney Lee in his
"Principles of Biography" from the characteristics of Greek tragedy,
exhibited all "the seriousness, the completeness, and the magnitude"
necessary for full portraiture; and as a personality on a par with his
contemporaries now thought of as eminent he fell but little short
of the distinction set forth by Leslie Stephen, first editor of the
"Dictionary of National Biography," as essential for life record. His
own day rewarded him with wealth and position, and posterity
has honored him by respecting his writing; and the story of his
career is not without significance in Victorian literary history, for
at least three of his "lives," the "Goldsmith," the "Landor," and the
"Dickens" are ranked among the best the period produced.

Percy Fitzgerald, one of his closest friends and the author of what is probably the best account of him — "John Forster," published in 1903 — said that his ambition was to attain high place in letters, an aspiration which, although posterity has denied it fulfillment as the expression of genius, cannot be judged as having failed of effecting the utmost in terms of his endowment. For humbly reared, he accomplished his measure of success through sheer force of natural energy, enthusiasm, and self-cultivated abilities.

He was born April 2, 1812, at Newcastle, the eldest of four children to Robert and Mary Forster. Robert Forster was a cattle dealer in a small way and while never prosperous was none the less able and generous enough to aid the large family of his wife's sister Anne, who having married an artisan named Gilmour on a guinea a week found long before their eighth child was born that such slender means were far from adequate. Mary Forster, too, was kindly and charitably disposed, "a gem of a woman," one who was later described by T. H. S. Escott in a "Fortnightly" article as a woman "whose mere presence and bearing diffused a general conviction of sound sense, disinterested sagacity, and an assurance that no confidence reposed in her would be misplaced." Hence from the beginning John Forster by the example of his home was encouraged in the ways of kindliness and generosity which became a part of the magnetism that was to draw about him some of the most vital personalities of his time, testimony of which traits a cousin, James Gilmour, one of the children who owed much to Forster's parents and whom the older boy took under his protection, was long afterward to give. "How kind he was to me," Gilmour is reported by Richard Renton in "John Forster and His Friendships" to have said,

> when we were boys together. He would sacrifice much to give me pleasure. . . . He followed in the footsteps of my aunt, his mother. . . . But even as a boy his outward manner was apt to be misunderstood by strangers, yet he always seemed to have the power to turn desirable acquaintances into friends.

The quality of his mind, likewise, made itself early apparent. In the old grammar school in Newcastle he became head boy, being thought of as something of a prodigy in the classics by the headmaster, the Reverend Edward Moises. At the age of thirteen he published a little sketch — now lost — in a local paper; and two years later, upon being remonstrated with because of his liking for the theater, he wrote an essay, "A Few Thoughts in Vindication of the Stage." It was a justification of his taste on moral and religious grounds — an exposition of his thinking more than a little suggestive of precocity, as the following excerpt reveals:

> He who first observed that religion was the strongest pillar of the state, that laws divested of its support were powerless, has probably, without knowledge or intention, defended the theater on its most advantageous side. . . . The laws, it may be said, busy themselves only about negative duties; religion extends her succours to actual affairs.

A further indication of his interest in the theater — one which points toward literary ambition, however, rather than dramatic ability — is the two-act play, "Charles at Tunbridge, or the Cavalier of Wildinghurst," which he wrote in 1828 and which the Newcastle Theater management produced in a benefit performance for Thomas Stuart, a highly popular provincial actor. This schoolboy activity, strained and artificial though it was, had one important and deciding result. It induced the boy's uncle, John Forster, a man of some property, to undertake responsibility for his namesake's further education. Accordingly, in October, 1828, Forster entered Cambridge. In November, however, for reasons not now clear he began to study law at the newly established University College in London. Two years later he joined the group of students reading in the chambers of Thomas Chitty, afterwards a noted judge and legal authority. The law Forster found attractive enough and, Chitty becoming especially interested in him, he might well have developed into a distinguished practitioner. In fact, one of his friends, the Reverend Whitwell Elwin, editor of the "Quarterly Review," in comment upon his probable success, remarked in later years,

> In one particular — the zest with which he would have espoused the interests of his client, — he would not have been surpassed by any advocate alive or dead.

He did not pursue his legal study far enough, however, to be admitted to the bar although he remained with Chitty for several years. Literature claimed him so completely that, before he was eighteen, contributions to Newcastle and London periodicals were bringing him an income sufficient for his needs without the allowance from his uncle.

Gifted as he was, and inevitable as a literary career seemed for him, his personal attributes, particularly his genius for friendship, aided in making his entrance upon it as easy as it was natural. When he went up to London, for instance, he came at once to know two members of his law class, James Emerson, later Sir James Emerson Tennent, and James Whiteside, who subsequently became famous as a Lord Chief Justice of Ireland. The three were accustomed to gather in Forster's lodgings at 17 Penton Place, Pentonville, and there over suppers of "oysters, fog, and grog, the fog being tobacco smoke," to engage in endless discussions of literature, law, history, and politics, no doubt led by Tennent, who was even then writing his "History of Modern Greece," "Letters of a Midshipman," and "Letters from the Aegean," all which were published while Tennent was still a student. Quite early, too, Forster became acquainted with Leigh Hunt, perhaps through the offices of Henry Colburn, the publisher, who kept open house in Bryanston Square for both notables and aspirants in literary affairs. Hunt became attracted to Forster and encouraged him in his writing, establishing a friendship that endured until Hunt's death in 1859. One mark of its quality is a comment which Forster made after the funeral: "He influenced all my modes of literary taste at the outset of my life"; another was the gift to Hunt of an original "Tatler" paper, which brought forth a characteristic letter:

> I need not repeat to you how highly your gift is valued. I have been carrying it about the house with me like a child who has a picture book given it. . . . I persuade myself that Steele may have had the identical copy in his hand, perhaps Pope, perhaps my Lady Suffolk.

But the most tangible expression of Forster's feeling perhaps — aside from his undertaking a more or less profitable subscription edition of Hunt's poems — was the "unwearied thoughtfulness" with which he aided "the deliberate and strongly formed convictions of Macaulay," according to Thornton Hunt, in the matter of the crown pension which was granted in 1847 to the aging poet and critic.

Among his early triumphs in friendship also was his conquest of Charles Lamb, whom he first met in 1831. Lamb seems to have been drawn to him immediately; at all events he was soon writing in his inimitable manner,

> If you have lost a little portion of my good will it is that you do not come to see me oftener,

and some time later,

> Dear Boy,
>    I am sending you the original Elias, complete. When I am a little composed, I shall hope to see you and Procter here; maybe, may see you first in London.

Besides, Lamb confessed that this "tall, ardent, noticeable young fellow" was among those he "herded with whenever possible." Talfourd, in the "Final Memorials," testified to Lamb's affection — and incidentally to Forster's rapidly developing position in literary London — by noting that the younger man was one of his guests at the famous "hare dinner," "a friend of comparatively recent date, but one with whom Lamb found himself as much at home as if he had known him for years."

As a matter of fact Forster's being included in such a group at the time — he was twenty-two — was only partly due to his social talents; he was already becoming a miscellaneous writer whose work found ready welcome. At the age of twenty, for instance, he had become dramatic critic of "The True Sun," the newspaper for which Charles Dickens made his first appearance in the reporters' gallery of the House of Commons. It was, indeed, a circumstance leading to the most famous of Forster's friendships, the contributing incident to which seems to have been Forster's interest in a speech Dickens made in support of a group of striking reporters — and in the end to the most famous of his biographies, the "Life of Dickens." A year later Edward Moxon made him editor of his newly acquired "Reflector," a weekly journal, which Leigh Hunt guided through four numbers, but which Forster could sustain through only three. Not all such enterprises, however, were so short-lived, for he soon joined the staff of "The Examiner," at first as dramatic and literary critic, but finally becoming editor, a position which he held until 1855, exhibiting a taste so discriminating that Whitwell Elwin said of him, "It may be doubted whether in a single instance he overlooked the first faint dawn of coming power." Among the instances of this ability, it may be pointed out, were his accurate estimation of Alexander Smith's "A Life's Drama" and his recognition of Browning. Forster, in fact, was the first and, for a time, the only favorable reviewer of "Paracelsus" — the manuscript of which now in the Forster collection in South Kensington Museum bears the inscription: "To John Forster, Esquire (my early understander), with true thanks for his generous and seasonable confession of faith in me. R. B." So marked was its editor's appreciation of new writers, indeed, that "The Examiner," according to Henry Morley,

> soon became conspicuous for the swiftness and decision with which it called attention to a new book, or a new play, or a new actor that gave signs of a true power. . . . Again and again the hearts of earnest men leapt out towards him who had been the first to know the meaning of their utterance, and with bold emphasis had been the first not only to call the world to listen, but clearly to set forth reason for his faith in what they said and did.

His critical writing, however, was not confined to the pages of "The Examiner"; he became a contributor to most of the influential periodicals of his day, the "Athenaeum," the "Edinburgh Review," and the "Foreign Quarterly Review" among them. In fact he became editor of that last in 1842, and succeeded Dickens as editor of "The Daily News" in 1846 — all this before taking over the editorship of "The Examiner" in 1847, a position he retained until 1855, when, receiving appointment as secretary of the lunacy commission at £ 500 a year and in 1861 as a commissioner at £ 1500, he gave up his journalistic career entirely and turned to incidental writing, particularly to the biography from which his fame arose. Then, too, at this period he married the widow of Henry Colburn, the publisher, subject of Charles Lamb's pun, "Coal-burn him in Beelzebub's deepest pit," who had been among his earliest London friends. Forster took up residence with her at 46 Montague Square, a house which Colburn had bequeathed her together with other property of considerable value. Here he remained until in 1862 he built a "handsome stone mansion at Palace Gate, with its beautiful library room at the back, and every luxury of lettered ease." And here it was that he accumulated the 18,000 books, the manuscripts, and objects of art which now compose the collection in South Kensington Museum.

With his developing success as journalist, critic, and editor had come an ever increasing circle of friends. Fitzgerald characterizes him in his prime:

> We find him as the common referee, the sure-headed arbiter, good-naturedly giving his services to arrange any trouble or business. With him friendship was a high and serious duty. His warm heart, his time, his exertions were all given to his friend. No doubt he had some little pleasure of his office, but he was in truth really indulging his affections and warm friendships.

And James Fields, in "Barry Cornwall and His Friends," adds certain realistic details to the characterization:

> He looked full of energy, and his whole manner announced a determination to assert that nobody need prompt him. His voice rang out loud and clear, upstairs and down, everywhere through his premises. When he spoke, nobody required an ear trumpet. The deaf never lost a syllable of his manly utterances.

As a matter of fact, almost the only jarring note in the record of the esteem in which he was held is the comment of Barron Field, who, writing to Crabb Robinson about a possible biographer for Charles Lamb, suggested Moxon, saying that Talfourd would "write too fine," and adding, "Heavens preserve us from a monster named Forster!" Nevertheless when Talfourd wrote his "Memorials" Forster contributed in no slight degree. Elwin, however, in a sentence, sums him up both socially and professionally perhaps better than any one else has done. "No stress of work," he wrote, "could induce him to forego the charms of good fellowship."

Yet the stress of his work was heavy, for besides his periodical writing, which followed the customary paths of such work, the same decades (1830–1855) that saw his advance as a critic saw also his development as biographer. In this capacity, incidental though it was at first to his profession as journalist, he reached his abiding place in literature. And yet no small part of his success is attributable to the artlessness with which, while allowing "no stress of work" to interfere with his enjoyment of "good fellowship," he none the less contrived to make the one contributory to the other.

In the fourth paper of John Hawkesworth's "Adventurer" occurs a passage that in commenting upon the subjects of life writing furnishes also, if a bit obliquely, a hint of the biographic consciousness itself. "Biography," it runs,

> would always engage the passions, if it could sufficiently gratify curiosity: but there have been few among the whole human species whose lives would furnish a single adventure; I mean such a complication of circumstances as holds the mind in an anxious yet pleasant suspense, and gradually unfold in the production of some unforeseen and important event; much less such a series of facts as will perpetually vary the scene, and gratify the fancy, with new views of life.

And it is just this ability to sense the dramatic and to communicate it with judgment, realism, and yet a suggestion of glamor, that imparts to biography its sustaining worth. If there are "few among the whole human species whose lives would furnish a single adventure," as Hawkesworth had it, there are even fewer capable of appreciating anything but the obvious in human adventure. Yet some there are who can. These are they who keep bright the annals of personality, the biographers whose understanding of human motive, human achievement, and human worth has rendered them only less vivid in memory than the men whose deeds they celebrate — high among whom John Forster should find place. It may be, of course, that "the subject of biography is really its object," as some one has recently said; yet it is difficult to think of Forster thus scientifically disposed. For in the long list of his "lives" — he wrote many, so many in fact that he may almost be considered the first among "professional biographers" — there is scarcely an item that does not project the humanity of its subject, the dimensional presence of the man, "a likeness of" his "earthly pilgrimage." Such stress may sometimes fail of effectiveness — as it does in his early "lives," those of the seventeenth century liberals, for instance, there having been only a limited amount of authentic material available in his day and he scorned to use the merely traditional. Such stress, however, is clearly intended, and falls short not so much because of Forster's failure to recognize essentials as because of a paucity of fact and of his fallibility as a literary artist. None the less, with these works Forster, at twenty-seven, came to be classed among the chief historians of Stuart and Commonwealth England.

The years during which the early "lives" appeared, those of John Eliot, Thomas Wentworth, Henry Vane, Oliver Cromwell, and some of the lesser Commonwealth figures — 1836 to 1839, that is — were also the years during which he collected material for "The Life and Adventures of Oliver Goldsmith." The book came out in 1848 and ran immediately into several editions; it was the first of his significant "lives." Six years later he revised the work, adding much that had to do with Goldsmith's day and with the men with whom he lived and worked, and changing the title to "The Life and Times of Oliver Goldsmith." As such it has remained authoritative, its position of honor now being that it introduces the beautiful Cunningham edition of Goldsmith's works.

The personality of the Grubb Street hack, "who touched nothing he did not adorn," and who became the friend of Johnson, Burke, Reynolds, and Boswell, emerges, vivified by Forster's understanding. One shares with the booksellers who employed him and with the friends who loved him their impatience at Goldsmith's improvidence. Yet his luckless, quite futile attempts to change his ways, his amusing vanity and contradictory distrust of himself, together with his generosity and his genius, excite ready sympathy in the reader just as those same traits aroused it in the hearts of his famous contemporaries. Forster extenuates nothing; weakness, frailty, every fault is set forth, not in criticism or in pity so much as in definition of the ultimate triumph possible to erring humanity.

[ 231 ]

Forster dedicated the "Goldsmith" to Charles Dickens as to one who could well sympathize with the hardships and misery endured by its hero. The dedication brought the following expression of appreciation from Dickens — with its altogether fruitful suggestion, as the sequel proved:

> I cannot sufficiently say how proud I am of what you have done, or how sensible I am of being so tenderly connected with it. . . . I desire no better for my fame, when my personal dustiness shall be past my control of my love of order, than such a biographer and such a critic. And again I say, most solemnly, that literature in England has never had and probably never will have such a champion as you.

The reference to Forster as a champion of literature grew out of his basic conviction that authors had never been accorded their proper place in society, an attitude which he frequently set forth but which is perhaps best defined in the "Goldsmith" — no doubt because the career of Goldsmith is the best of all illustrations of the conditions involved: "Another object of this book," wrote Forster,

> has therefore been to point out that literature ought long ago to have received from the state an amount of recognition which would, at least, have placed its highest cultivators on a level with other and not worthier recipients of its gratitude. . . . More than ever it is felt as national opprobrium that such of our countrymen as have achieved greatness either in literature or in science, should have struggled into fame without the aid of English institutions, by waging continuous war against disparagement and depression, and in sheer defiance of both, forcing their reluctant way. . . . The world will greatly be the gainer when the biography of the man of genius shall no longer be a picture of the most harsh struggles and mean necessities to which man's life is subject, exhibited as in shameful contrast to the calm and classic glory of his fame. With society rests the advent of that time.

Dickens was pleased, naturally, with the dedication — so well pleased in fact that he immediately decided that Forster should be his biographer, and the public approved of the "Goldsmith" to such an extent as to demand four editions, as has been said. The appearance of the book, however, was the signal for an accusation on the part of Sir James Prior, published in "The Athenaeum" for June 16, 1848, that Forster had unscrupulously taken all the facts relating to Goldsmith from Prior's biography of him, and that Forster's direct contribution did not exceed two pages. Forster's denial, printed in "The Literary Gazette" of July 29, 1848, and included in the preface to the second edition — an edition which carried also the comment upon Washington Irving's use of Forster's work — while amusing in its vehemence is none the less interesting because of the light it throws upon a point of ethics in biographical writing. The gist of Forster's argument is contained in the following:

> The question broadly raised was whether any man, who may have published a biography, contributing to it certain facts as the result of his own research, can lay claim to the entire beneficial interest in those facts, nay, can appropriate to himself the subject of the biography, and warn off every other person as a trespasser from the ground so seized. . . . No man can hold a patent in biography except by a mastery of execution unapproached by competitors. He only may hope to have possessed himself of a subject who has exhausted it; or to have established his originality in dealing with facts, who has so happily disposed and applied them as to preclude the chances of more successful treatment by any subsequent writer.

The ensuing passage comprises a spirited and exhaustive exposure of Prior's methods, pointing out Prior's — and incidentally his own — dependence upon Cooke, Glover, Percy, Davis, Hawkins, Boswell, and other contemporary commentators for the most important particulars of Goldsmith's life; but indicates also that, unlike Forster, he had made no reference to his obligations, had, on the contrary, made pretensions to originality which the most casual examination could expose. Furthermore, concerning himself and his purpose, Forster had this to say:

> The reader will do me the justice to remember that any apparent depreciation of the labors of a predecessor in the same field with myself has been forced on me. Why should I now conceal that the very extent of my sympathy with the purpose of this biography had unhappily convinced me of its

utter failure at his hands; and that for this reason, with no dislike for him, but much love for Goldsmith, the present biography was undertaken? It seemed no unworthy task to rescue one of the most fascinating writers in the language from one of the dullest books, from a post-humous admiration more harassing than any spite that vexed poor Goldsmith while he lived, from a clumsy and incessant exaltation far worse than Hawkin's absurd contempt or the amusing slights of Boswell.

Before undertaking the most difficult of his "lives," the "Landor," Forster issued a volume of biographical essays containing accounts of Defoe, Richard Steele, Churchill, and Samuel Foote. Significant, moreover, of his instinct to interpret the misunderstood and protect the reputation of the maligned or the unfortunate, as exemplified in the "Goldsmith" — the book which stirred him so profoundly that he rewrote it twelve times before it satisfied him — all four essays were works of reclamation. Likewise he published an enlarged edition of his "Sir John Eliot," probably the best of the earlier "lives," the new material consisting of letters, autobiographical notes, and speeches not previously released by the Eliot family, for he was ever eager to augment fact the more perfectly to sustain truth. The "Landor," however, was written in a spirit somewhat different from that of anything else he had done. Landor had been his friend; Forster was the logical biographer. Possessing, if not in exaggerated measure, at least in some degree, the reticence of the Victorian, he hesitated to make public the unhappy events of Landor's domestic experience. Some incidents, particularly those relating to the last years in Italy, would, if related, cause embarrassment, even distress, to the surviving members of his family. To tell the whole truth about the mercurial temperament of Landor was to risk over-emphasizing the capricious and violent side of his nature; yet nothing less than the truth could be thought of. Forster made up his mind, he tells us, that if this memoir were to be written at all, it should contain a fair statement of truth — a resolution in which he was upheld by Robert Landor, the younger brother of the poet, who furnished much information, especially detail concerning the uncontrolled childhood and youth, and the extremes of joy and disappointment during the early middle years.

Vicesimus Knox, one of the last of the eighteenth century essayists, in the eleventh paper of "Winter Evenings," contributed the following comment to the perennial debate as to biographic inclusions:

> It is said that not only truth, but the whole truth, should be published and left naked for the contemplation of mankind; for as the anatomy of the body contributes to the benefit of human nature, by promoting medical and chirurgical knowledge; so the dissection of characters tends to the development of error, which, by being thus exposed, may be avoided.

It is to be questioned whether Forster was concerned with exposing error in order to insure the avoidance of it. He wrote of seventeenth century liberals because, for him, they represented progress toward the welfare of the downtrodden, and of eighteenth century characters like Defoe and Steele because he felt that they had been treated unfairly by posterity. But Landor had been his intimate friend; he saw no reason why his memory should be smirched in order that society should benefit. Having entered upon the task, however, delicate though it was, such was his integrity and such the depths of his compassion for one whom he considered unfortunate, that he brought his best powers to bear upon the subject.

His success, notwithstanding, is doubtful. The image under his treatment is sharp and harmoniously projected. Many who knew Landor well, Dickens in particular, thought that the difficulties had been more than adequately surmounted. But there was disagreement. Although the "Edinburgh Review" said, "Mr. Forster has performed a difficult and delicate task with dignity and affection," "The North British Review," on the other hand, found fault with Forster's attitude toward his subject and characterized certain passages as "bits of ill-natured honesty." And this divergence of opinion has obtained. One is justified in thinking the "Landor" least successful among Forster's major works.

The chief and abiding perplexity lay in the extremes of Landor's complex character. Forster in speaking of his dilemma says:

> Most characters are too narrow for much variety; but in him there was room enough for all changes alike. My own pre-

dominating impression from our years of intercourse, during all of which he was living alone, was that of a man genial, joyous, and kind, and of a nature large and generous to excess; but of a temper so uncontrollably impetuous and so prone to act from undisciplined impulse that I have been less startled upon a closer knowledge to find it said by others, unfaltering both in admiration and tried affection for him, that during hardly any part of his life between nine and almost ninety could he live with others in peace for any length of time; for that, though always glad, happy, and good-natured for a while, he was apt gradually to become tyrannical where he had power, and rebellious where he had it not; and I here, therefore, candidly state so much, to be always kept steadily in view, that hereafter there may be less danger of doing unconsciously some injustice to others in the desire to be in all things just to so remarkable a man.

In his attempt to mitigate the effect of what his conscience required him to include Forster lays to lack of early training the blame for Landor's failure to adjust himself properly to society. He was, for instance, neither disciplined at home in childhood nor by a profession in later life. He wrote with no other aim than to please himself — "What he did best and worst," said Forster, "he did, in his earliest as in his latest life, for the satisfaction of his own will or pleasure." Yet to all appearances, everything was in his favor. He had family position, an independent fortune during most of his life, a superb education and the surroundings of culture, in addition to extraordinary talents. He traveled constantly during long periods, settling for a time now in France, now in Italy, now roving as a soldier of fortune in Spain, but sooner or later always returning to live for a short year or two upon his estate at Llanthony. But the extravagance of his action and the searing rashness of his speech rendered any association insecure. At his best no one was more pleasing or ingratiating. He could be gentle. He was quick to forget injuries and to recover from disappointments. And his frequent tumultuous laughter carried everything before it in a cleansing flood of good humor. Nevertheless he would in an instant become aflame with an anger that consumed all vestiges of the charm which but a moment before had seemed his dominant trait.

Leigh Hunt once visited him in Italy and as a result of the experience, in trying to convey some impression of him at the time, summed him up as "a stormy mountain pine that should produce lilies."

Having presented the man as he had known him personally and as Robert Landor's recollections and anecdotes, besides the great mass of correspondence available, had enlarged his knowledge, Forster hoped that he had supplied the means by which his readers could strike a balance between good and ill, saying that although

> never had so masculine an intellect been weakened by so violent a temper, so many durable thoughts degraded by so many momentary humors, and such masterly discrimination of praise and blame been made worthless by so many capricious enmities and unreasonable likings,

none the less

> what is really imperishable in Landor's genius will not be treasured less, or less understood, for the more perfect knowledge of his character.

Thirty-three years of unbroken friendship lay behind the "Dickens"; and, as has been stressed repeatedly, friendship is the leaven of life writing. The work, as a result, is Forster's best. He had the memory of countless intimacies in terms of which to weigh and consider the mystery that was Charles Dickens. With him he had weathered the vicissitudes as well as enjoyed the triumphs that had come during the long years since their first meeting in the offices of the "True Sun." Out of no less experience could have come so authentic an interpretation. The story is told as far as possible by means of what Dickens himself had written. The sparkling personality is revealed, according to Carlyle, through "bits of autobiography unrivaled in clearness and credibility, those clear and sunny utterances of Dickens' own." Running through the whole, however, binding it together, imparting to it the essentials of human reality is the warm, pulsating presence of Forster himself — for here as elsewhere in biographic accomplishment of high significance, the author, although sometimes unawares, reveals himself only less completely than he portrays his subject.

Conclusive though the "life" has come to be esteemed, upon the appearance of the successive volumes in 1871, 1872, and 1873, with a two-volume revision in 1874, a deluge of adverse criticism descended. So confusing, if not contradictory were the reports, however, that if Forster had been able to begin all over again he could not, even then, have used them to advantage. It is the fate of genius that supreme examples defy delineation. Much remains undisclosed concerning Shakespeare, for instance, and Goethe; and no one has yet caught and confined the soul of Lincoln within the covers of a book, not even Carl Sandburg. Spirits like these could become realities only to equals, but with them there is no equality—for, as Goethe had it, *Du gleichst den Geist, dem du begreifst.* What record is possible must remain no more than approximate; "the world knows nothing of its greatest men," said Sir Henry Taylor in "Philip Van Arteveldte." Of lesser men record can be satisfactory; the closer biographer and subject approach each other in potential, the better the result, except perhaps when the former exceeds the latter, as instanced by Johnson and Savage or by Carlyle and Sterling, when there can be no failure. The fact that Boswell reached toward perfection in the "Johnson" and that Lockhart attained such heights as his "Scott" reveals him capable of, augurs many degrees less difference in stature between author and subject in these instances than in any other point of comparison. To be able to understand and record greatness is, in a measure, to share it; or as Sydney Dobell noted in his Journal:

> Biographies, other than of the less by the greater, or of equals by equals, are really not biographies at all, and resemble those huts which the Archian cottar builds with the broken pillars of a Grecian temple.

In the Dickens-Forster relationship there was decidedly more of equality than their respective reputations suggest; if the one was worthy of the world's remembrance, the other was worthy to sustain him there—by reason of his sensitive appreciation. That his work falls short of the first order is plain, but that its fault is inadvertent is untrue; Forster contributed to it the best he had to give, and the defects of his book were the result of omission dictated by his day

[ 238 ]

and his reluctance to give pain, a matter which becomes sharply focused as defined in a comment made by Dickens' sister-in-law, Georgina Hograth:

> Mr. Forster was the only person with the material and authority to write the biography; but it was written soon after Mr. Dicken's death, and a great deal could not be said then which becomes possible as the years go by.

For it was in connection with his treatment of Dickens' domestic affairs that much of the criticism arose — the name Ellen Lawless Ternan, for instance, appears only in connection with the will, which is relegated to an appendix. To say anything about such matters was, naturally, to touch upon the delicate, and yet there could be no entire avoidance. Victorian taste, besides the rights of the Dickens family to the inviolency of its sorrow (there should be a tradition among biographers that survivors in the family of the subject be spared the pain of precipitate revelation), prohibited inclusion of detail which Forster in the course of his intimate association could not have helped learning. The resulting comments by critics were almost bizarre in their failure to agree: he had written too familiarly, he had been too formal; he had used too many trifling items, he had revealed nothing intimate; he had stressed Dickens' father, he had overstressed Dickens' mother; he had shown himself blind to his subject's faults, holding him up as a paragon; he had proved a traitor to his friend, representing him as "an excited, restless, hysterical, self-engrossed, quarrelsome, unreasonable egotist." Obviously comment like this is worse than useless.

A second fault attributed was that Forster had had too much to say about himself, limiting his use of letters only to those which had been written to him; showing himself as the constant companion, adviser, and confidant of Dickens — to the exclusion of those perhaps who would have liked to share mention as basking in the warmth of the great man's regard. One reviewer, for instance, complained, and not it seems without some personal feeling:

> But Mr. Forster cannot keep himself out of his book for a moment. He forgets that nobody cares anything about John Forster or about anyone else, except in great subordination to

the subject of the biography. . . . If there was much of anything in the life of Charles Dickens worth telling, the life of that person has yet to be written. This one may be prolonged even to four volumes — giving to Mr. Forster from some quarters a certain temporary reputation and it may be, the more volumes there are, the more money will be made by the present biographer.

In reply to his critics — for the intervals elapsing between the appearance of the several volumes provided opportunity — Forster included in a late chapter an explanation of his purpose, range, and attitude. "To give," he wrote,

> to the memoirs what was attainable of the value of autobiography, letters to myself such as were never addressed to any other of his correspondents, and covering all the important incidents in the life to be retraced, were used, with few exceptions, exclusively. . . . Such were my limits, indeed, that half even of those letters had to be put aside; and to have added all such others as were opened to me would have doubled the size of my book, and not contributed to it a new fact of life or character, and altered materially its design. . . . It is the peculiarity of few men to be to their most intimate friend neither more nor less than they are to themselves, but this was true of Dickens; and what kind or quality of nature such intercourse expressed in him, . . . the letters to myself in these volumes could alone express. Gathered from various and differing sources, their interest could not have been the interest of these; in which everything comprised in the successive stages of a most attractive career is written with unexampled candour and truthfulness, and set forth in definite pictures of what he saw and stood in the midst of, unblurred by vagueness or reserve. Of the charge of obtruding myself . . . I can only say that I studied nothing so hard as to suppress my own personality, and have to regret my ill success where I supposed I had even too perfectly succeeded.

It is an interesting exception to the generally observed practice of biographers that Forster, in spite of the number of "lives" he wrote, offers almost nothing to be added to the body of biographic technique. He follows whenever possible the autobiographical method, but has no critical comment to make, unless one considers an early paragraph in the "Goldsmith" which merely alludes to accepted uses. In fact he seldom defines his intention in writing particular "lives." Had he done so in connection with the "Dickens," had he said at the outset, for instance, that he professed to write of Dickens only as he himself knew him and as the documents in his possession revealed him, he could no doubt have forestalled much of the adverse opinion that was voiced. He took for granted that he was the logical person to portray Dickens and, aware that his material was authentic, he confidently proceeded in his work. Although in his own time objection did arise, he has met with popular acceptance in our day.

Mr. J. W. T. Ley, a noted Dickensian, who has recently edited the Forster "Life," sums up today's opinion by considering the book sympathetic, balanced, and yet sufficiently detached in spirit to present Dickens in the round; and he indirectly indicates Forster's effectiveness by having found few details to add — remaining content with explanations which time alone made necessary — and by making few, if any, corrections of fact. In a phrase, one may conclude that Forster's "Dickens," particularly in the Ley edition, must stand as the best "life" of the novelist, just as it is to be accepted as the best of the friend — in life they shared a rare and sunny friendship, and now they share a common niche in our remembrance, aptly illustrative of George Santayana's comment that "Our friends are that part of the human race with which we can be human."

One more "life" remained for Forster to undertake. His health was failing rapidly. None the less for years — since 1838, when he had undertaken but given up the writing of the life and times of Queen Anne — he had been interested in Jonathan Swift. He had spared no pains in the accumulation of material and was in position, because of fresh information he had acquired, to compose, not a restatement of the facts about Swift, but a re-evaluation of the man. More than 150 new letters had come to light; authentic additions to the fragmentary autobiography had been discovered, besides scattered pieces of unpublished prose and verse, and the original MS. of the "Journal to Stella." In addition he had obtained a large paper copy of the first edition of "Gulliver's Travels," interleaved for alterations and additions by the author, and containing, besides all the changes, erasures, and substitutions adopted in the later editions, several interesting passages which had not yet been given to the world. With such material, and equipped by his long experience, Forster could, perhaps, have reanimated the great satirist as no one even yet has done.

Unfortunately his health gave way and he was able to complete only the first volume, which dealt with Swift's early life, from his birth to the time of his enlistment in the Tory cause under Henry St. John and Robert Harley, the years 1667–1711, no more than enough to suggest what the completed work might have been.

Sick though he was, he saw the volume through the press, however, and then ceased work altogether. Growing rapidly worse and suffering intensely, he died February 1, 1876, of a gout of the chest, the circumstances being perhaps best described by Carlyle in a letter to his brother John, dated February 5:

> I am just returned from Kensal Green and poor Forster's funeral, which has occupied me in personal activity for all the morning, but which I don't think has done me any special damage, great as have been the confusions, fasheries, and chaotic sorrows and reflections connected with it and him, ever since his sudden removal from among us. Nobody, I believe, expected so sudden a death. I had called at the door on Sunday last and met Dr. Quain just stepping out, who told me cheerfully that Forster, who had been suffering much in previous days, was a shade better. Tuesday morning following, Quain was sent for hurriedly between eight and nine; and before twelve, appeared here, and by cautious degrees informed me, with considerable emotion of his own, that poor Forster was no more. It is the end of a chapter in my life, which had lasted, with unwearied kindness and helpfulness wherever possible on Forster's part, for above forty years. Today, contrary to expectations, I found myself next after Lord Lytton, constituted chief mourner.

# 20—Trevelyan and Macaulay

*The portrait speaks and lives; I have found the man.* — Sainte-Beuve.

AMONG the most telling of nineteenth century comments upon biography is one to be found in the Gladstone review of Trevelyan's "Life and Letters of Lord Macaulay." It appeared in the "Quarterly Review" soon after the work was issued, in 1876. "A peculiar faculty and one approaching to the dramatic order," wrote the great Liberal,

> belongs to the successful painter of historical portraits and belongs also to the true biographer. It is that of representing personality. In the picture, what we want is not merely a collection of unexceptionable lines and colours so presented as readily to identify their original. Such a work is not the man, but a duly attested certificate of the man. What we require, however, is the man and not merely the certificate. In the same way, what we want in a biography, and what, despite the etymology of the title, we very seldom find, is *life*. The very best transcript is a failure, if it be a transcript only. To fulfil its idea, it must have in it the essential quality of movement; must realize the lofty fiction of the divine Shield of Achilles, where the upturning earth, though wrought in metal, darkened as the plough went on, and the figures of the battle-piece dealt their strokes and parried them, and dragged out from the turmoil the bodies of their dead.

And in the columns of the same periodical not ten years later appeared the same insistence, in Mowbray Morris' review of Froude's "Carlyle":

> It seems hard to doubt the truth of the portrait. The man that many, perhaps, who never set eyes on him in the flesh have fashioned out of his works, it may not be; but that this is the true and theirs the counterfeit likeness, is surely writ large on every page, and with the man's own hand.

This cry for living likeness in biography is perennial — "lives" must stand forth as *picturae loquentes;* they are effective only if the "portrait speaks and lives." Boswell, Lockhart, and Trevelyan, all three — and English biography has no more vital work than theirs to show — succeeded because in their hands facts became the key that unlocked nature. Action, speech, and recorded thought, the projection of the man as formally and informally he projected himself, made up the material upon which they depended, agreeing instinctively that nobody can "pronounce *ex cathedra* on the whole structure and complexion of a great mind," and hence in no wise presuming to explain the miracle of the soul, its obscurities, its secret processes, as frequently seems to be the ambition of present-day biographers, those especially who have had recourse, for instance, to "arrested developments," "Oedipus complexes," and "alcoholic syndromes" in their efforts to explicate the inexplicable. The three men whose works stand at the head of the canon relied for reality upon nothing more than the ascertainable facts, the disengagement of the personalities which were Johnson and Scott and Macaulay from their surrounding mass of humanity, but with purpose to uplift humanity itself — for as Phillips Brooks once said,

> The supreme blessing of biography is that it is always bathing the special in the universal, and so renewing its vitality and freshness.

The idea is well founded upon a Johnson who could burst forth with "She is an odious wretch" in condemnation of the young proselyte to Quakerism, Jenny Harry, and yet carry home upon his back and take care of her, a forlorn victim of vice, poverty, and disease; upon a Scott who could lay himself open to charges of doubtful dealing in the hope of founding a great estate and yet remember to bring home from Paris a pocketknife as a present for his gilly; or upon a Macaulay who could blast the reputation of harmless Robert Montgomery and yet record in his Journal:

> Mrs. . . . . . . . . again, begging and praying. "This the last time; an execution, etc., etc." I will send her five pounds more. This will make fifty pounds in a few months to a bad writer whom I never saw.

In a multitude of outward acts recorded and in an accumulation of impulses thus self-revealed lie the materials from which reanimation springs, but only at the hands of genius — as the position accorded Boswell, Trevelyan, and Lockhart in the hierarchy attests.

And such position has been accorded Trevelyan with scarcely a dissenting voice; the only question which is raised concerning him is whether or not he should outrank Lockhart. His work has occasioned less adverse criticism than that of any other major biographer, even that of Boswell. A "Quarterly" reviewer, with the Croker episode in mind, complained: "Does Mr. Trevelyan think that Lord Macaulay's fame will be enhanced by publishing to the world such a raucous tirade?" Yet beyond this no one has commented upon him in such terms, for instance, as those applied by an anonymous reviewer to the author of the "Johnson" — "A Boswell may crawl along at the heel of mediocrity and amuse whole generations with his twaddle and tattle."

The story of Macaulay's "joyous and shining pilgrimage" is unique in many ways, not the least of which is the mere fact that it is the story of a "joyous and shining pilgrimage. Life records are replete with high achievement; the happiness and satisfaction, however, that permeate Trevelyan's pages are elsewhere far to seek. And it is this quality which, in large part, makes for the work's distinction; or as a review in the "Edinburgh" concludes,

> It only remains to acknowledge the skill and candour with which Mr. Trevelyan has executed a very delicate and difficult task. So much of the life of his illustrious uncle was spent within the sanctuary of domestic life that it was impossible to make it entirely known to posterity without lifting those veils of privacy which are commonly drawn closer by ties of kindred and personal affection. But it was good fortune to have nothing

to conceal, and nothing to relate that was not amiable, honourable, and true. Details sometimes trivial in themselves, add to the reality of the picture, and we do not doubt that these volumes will be read throughout the world with a curiosity and an interest only to be surpassed by the success of Lord Macaulay's own writings.

The domestic happiness alluded to — for although Macaulay never established a family of his own, he found a supreme happiness in relationships with his sisters and their families — and the success achieved by his writings were real enough. The permanent value of his writings, however, suggested in the review, is questionable. "Every schoolboy knows," that in his own day — although John Sterling spoke of his writing as "mock turtle nutriment" — he was held in the highest esteem both as a critic and as an historian; so highly esteemed was he, in fact, that augmented editions of the "Edinburgh" were required whenever his articles appeared, and the publishers of his "History," Longmans, retain even today in their archives a canceled royalty check in the amount of twenty thousand pounds drawn to his credit. None the less posterity admires his writing chiefly for its color, the clarity and aggression of his sentences, and the logic of his structure, thinking little of his opinions and respecting his handling of history not at all. Furthermore, his political services are all but forgotten. His years in Parliament bore fruit at the time, as his appointments in the War Office and to the Supreme Council of India indicate. But the magnetic presence and mellifluous voice that drew members from lounge and corridor no longer dominates, and the reports like those upon the status of military affairs, the lack of freedom in the India press, the minutes upon education, all so carefully weighed and so crisply yet urbanely phrased, have long since gathered dust. Macaulay himself still lives, however, and will continue to live, in the vibrant pages of his nephew's book, not because of what he did so much as because of what he was — a personality. In fact, it might have been that without the book remembrance would have been much different. Macaulay was, it is remembered, a member of the nationalistic partisan school and as such was not much given to that spirit of "divine meditation" which gives the cue to remembrance. Or as Lord Morley put it,

I could not imagine him as meditating, as modestly pondering and wondering, or possessed for as much as ten minutes by that spirit of inwardness which has never been wholly wanting in any of the kings or princes of literature with whom it is good to sit in counsel.

And as Walter Bagehot held:

Men of genius are in general distinguished by their extreme susceptibility to external experience. Finer and softer than other men, every exertion of their will, every incident of their lives, influences them more deeply than it would others. From a peculiar sensibility, the man of genius bears the stamp of life commonly more clearly than his fellows; even casual associations make a deep impression on him; examine his mind and you may discern his fortunes. Mr. Macaulay has nothing of this. You could not tell what he has been. His mind shows no trace of change. What he is, he was; and what he was, he is.

Hence, biography once more becomes not merely the record of accomplishment, but, as in the "Johnson" or the "Scott," it resolves itself into what it should always be, "the likeness of a man," although in the present instance it is a likeness such as only a sympathetic nature, influenced by the "ties of kindred and personal affection," with "nothing to conceal and nothing to relate that was not amiable, honorable, and true," could create. Completely at variance with Emerson's "Shakespeare is the only biographer of Shakespeare," Trevelyan held it would have been

as hard to compose a picture of the author from his "History," his "Essays," and his "Lays" as to evolve an idea of Shakespeare from "Henry the Fifth" and "Measure for Measure";

or as Samuel Johnson was never weary of insisting,

Lives can only be written from personal knowledge, which is growing every day less and less, and in a short time is lost forever;

and as William Roscoe Thayer seems to emphasize,

Given life, the first impulse of life, the incessant triumphant impulse is to manifest itself in individuals. From the beginning, there has never been a moment, or the fraction of a second, when the universe or the tiniest part of it, became abstract.

Such — to repeat — was the "pilgrimage" of Macaulay that only an intimate could appreciate it, for it was as a kinsman as well as an intimate that Trevelyan proceeded, even going so far as to stress the fact upon the title page of his book, by printing above his name the phrase "By his nephew." The kinsman as biographer has seldom proved successful, as a glance at the long list of "lives" written by sons and daughters, nephews and nieces will show, no doubt for the reasons set forth by Sir Sidney Lee:

> Those who live in domestic relation with eminent men rarely see in the true perspective what is most worthy of remark about them. They tend to set in the forefront of their picture his domesticities, his domestic virtues. They take a domestic pride in his public service, with the detail and significance of which they are usually very imperfectly acquainted. They have knowledge peculiar to themselves — a partial knowledge which is only of biographic value when it is thoroughly fused with the whole available stock of biographic material. It may sound harsh to say that biography has no place for the widow's tears or the orphan's cry. On the other hand, the family bias often cherishes esoteric prejudices which may lead to the omission of essential facts.

With Trevelyan, however, no such impediments seem to have existed; at all events, some fortunate alignment of circumstance took shape in which the ability to see clearly — and "clearness of vision is the beginning of art" — to estimate justly, and to record beautifully combined to reveal the personality of a man about whom there was nothing to conceal, little to palliate, and much to admire, if not to reverence. With what distinction all this was done the Gladstone review, again, bears witness:

> To write the biography of Lord Macaulay was a most arduous task. Such seems to have been the conception with which it was approached; nor is it belied by the happy faculty with which it has been accomplished. Mr. Trevelyan had

already achieved a reputation for conspicuous ability; and the honour of near relationship was in this case at least a guarantee for reverent and devoted love. But neither love, which is indeed a danger as well as an ally, nor intelligence, nor assiduity, nor forgetfulness of self will make a thoroughly good biography without the subtle gift of imparting life. By this it was that Boswell established himself as the prince of all biographers; by this we believe Mr. Trevelyan has earned for himself a place in what is still a scanty roll. . . . He has executed a congenial and delightful office in exhibiting *ad vivim* the personality of which the world knew little, and of which its estimate, though never low, was, as has now been shown, very far beneath the mark of truth.

Unquestionably, remembrance of Macaulay the man is so much more important than that of Macaulay the essayist, the historian, or the statesman, in spite of Sir Henry Taylor's "His looks always seemed to me the most impudent contradiction of himself that nature ever dared to throw in a man's face." Different from most subjects of biography, Macaulay had few friends and no intimates outside his family except Ellis and perhaps Macvey Napier, neither of whom could have served to write his biography, and so a relative was inevitably the choice. There was, then, no one else so well equipped as George Otto Trevelyan, the son of Macaulay's favorite sister, Hannah, and himself a favorite.

But kinship provided no more than the condition in which knowledge of characterizing detail became possible. Trevelyan had, in addition to affectionate understanding, both the literary taste and the writing experience necessary to the task. Hence he brought to it a ripeness of style and a discrimination in the balancing of effects gained through arduous study at Harrow and later at Cambridge, and through the composition of classical imitations like "The Cambridge Dionysia" and "Horace," and his chastely restrained letters from India, which, published in 1864 as "The Competition Wallah," began his reputation in literary London.

However, it was his intention to make politics his career. Entering Parliament, therefore, Trevelyan supported Gladstone, under whose tutelage he might rapidly enough have risen to not undistinguished heights. But soon disagreeing with his patron's policy, in the matter of Church Schools particularly, he resigned his office in protest — and so delayed for ten years any possibility of advancement. The Eastern question arising, however, he seized the opportunity to side with Gladstone against Disraeli, believing sincerely that the latter was wrong. As a result he was made Civil Lord of the Admiralty in 1880, Chief Secretary for Ireland in 1882, and Secretary for Scotland in 1885. Moreover, on returning to Parliament in 1887, he continued to represent his constituency, Bridgeton, until 1897, when he retired to his estates, living part of the time at Wallington, part at Welcombe, and part in London. He had married in 1869, Caroline Phillips, daughter of a Manchester merchant, and the marriage was in the tradition of happiness which seems to have been the lot of all the members of his family.

Writing, rather than politics, was in reality his closest interest, and so, beginning as he did with echoes from the classics, he continued during the remainder of his long life to write — in spite of the point of view once expressed by him in a letter to Henry Holland:

> The secret of my life is that I had a craving for literature, like that of some people for drink, and, till it was worked off, I could settle to nothing. Perhaps the most perfect simile would be that of a young man who is desperately in love, gets over it, and then goes about his business in peace afterward.

In the end, consequently, it was authorship, not public service, that became the basis of his fame. In truth had he never composed the "Macaulay" he might have achieved fame by the "Early History of Charles James Fox," published in 1880; but more particularly, perhaps, by "The American Revolution," issued in parts between 1899 and 1914, a work which exerted a vital influence in bringing about a clearer understanding on both sides of the Atlantic. Notwithstanding, it is the "Macaulay" by which he is best known. The "Fox" is a work of art which shows Trevelyan's peculiar habits of thought and exhibits his style at its height, but it is a picture of society rather than the portrait of a statesman; and "The American Revolution," influential though it was and authoritative as it has come to be recognized, has not the breath of life which animates the great biography. His son, George Macaulay Trevelyan, records in the memoir of him, that there were many who thought that Parliament should require the completion of the "Fox," while the "Revolution" brought Trevelyan the intimate friendship of Theodore Roosevelt and the plaudits of American historians like Rhodes and Van Tyne. It was the "Macaulay," however, that brought him the approval of John Morley (who half in jest said that the nephew's "Life" was better than the uncle's "History"), of Leslie Stephen, and of James Anthony Froude; but best of all, perhaps, of Carlyle, who, in a letter of congratulation written the day after he had finished reading the book, said,

> I have nowhere found in any biography, not even in Boswell's "Johnson," a human life and character more clearly, credibly, and completely brought home to the conception of every intelligent reader; nor have I, it is to be added, in all my reading found any human character that is to my notion more singular and unique. . . .Your own part of the affair I think you have performed to admiration; nothing hidden and yet no offense given; an excellent brief History of the period, as well as of its speaking man.

George Macaulay Trevelyan, the son of the author and Macaulay's grand-nephew, who, besides the memoir of his father, has written a long list of historical and biographical studies, the latest of which is "Grey of Falloden," calls the "Life" "the most important undertaking" of his father's career. It was not begun until his powers had matured and his experience of both life and literature had ripened, and after, it may be noted, he had steeped himself in Carlyle's "Sterling," his choice among biographical writings. In fact he delayed the start so long that his mother, who wanted very much to see her brother's "life" written while she was alive to read it, died three years before it appeared. However, when it finally came out, the evidences of completeness, of integrity not only in fact but in feeling as well, and of fully developed artistic consciousness, were apparent throughout.

Two years were devoted to pouring over the eleven volumes of Macaulay's Journal, to assembling letters, to recalling and arranging the details of the long uncle-nephew relationship, and to the writing of the modest volumes. The design of the work is, without doubt, the best that could have been adopted. Macaulay was no such talker as Johnson; hence to have recorded his conversation would have been to do him small justice. And his was not the celebrity of Scott, of whom, it will be remembered, Lockhart remarked that "no amount of material were too great." To have contrived, therefore, to let Macaulay characterize himself by discriminate selection from the letters and the Journal — realizing as only Trevelyan could that he was at his best in private — and to unify the whole by political and personal exposition in a luminous style, so that the whole life, from cradle in Birchin Lane to tomb in Westminster Abbey, stands revealed, was to take the better way. The work, as a result, to paraphrase Leslie Stephen, is neither "too long" nor "too idolatrous." "Its 950 pages," according to an early review, are "too few rather than too many," and its integrity, according to William Roscoe Thayer, is the outgrowth of

> a perfect interweaving of biography and history, balance, discretion, a rare skill in summarizing, ample quotation from letters and journals but not too ample, and a sufficiently intimate portrayal of Macaulay as a public man, and especially as a son, brother, uncle, and friend.

In short, it draws upon the techniques of both Boswell and Lockhart in creating a "living image" by tempering the physics of history — to borrow a suggestion from Sidney Lee — which determines the power of man in the mass, with the chemistry of biography, which analyzes the mass and resolves it into constituent elements.

Trevelyan sets down his purpose in the opening paragraphs:

> He who undertakes to publish the memoirs of a distinguished man may find a ready apology in the custom of the age. If we measure the effective demand for biography by the supply, the person commemorated need possess but a very moderate reputation. . . . It may, therefore, be taken for granted that a desire exists to hear something authentic about the life of a man who has produced works which are universally known, but which bear little or no indication of the private history and personal qualities of the author. . . . To gratify that most

legitimate wish is the duty of those who have the means at their command. His life-like image is indelibly impressed upon their minds, . . . although the skill which can reproduce that image before the general eye may well be wanting. But his own letters will supply the deficiencies of the biographer. . . . Such letters could never have been submitted to an editor unconnected with both correspondents by the strongest ties: and even one who stands in that position must often be sorely puzzled as to what he has the heart to publish and the right to withhold. . . . Such as in all points he was, the world, which has been so indulgent to him, has a right to know; and those who best love him do not fear the consequences of freely submitting his character and his actions to the public verdict.

And how well the purpose was fulfilled is suggested by a passage from one of his own letters, written almost fifteen years afterward:

I have been reading the Life of my uncle out loud to the boys. The feeling of our respective families about him is the most curious instance of family "solidarity" that I know. It is certain that, in 1930, there will be several men with a lively personal feeling of affection towards a man who was born in 1800;

for the "several men" have come to be all those who read the book, a body that must increase so long as we agree with Carlyle that "man is perennially interesting to man"; even though we cannot agree with him that "there is nothing else interesting."

# 21—Froude and Carlyle

*The necessity of complying with the times and of sparing persons is the great impediment of biography.* — Johnson.

THE abiding question in biography concerns the code of inclusion. As taste veers in the ever shifting current of approval and disapproval, what one day demands the next disdains. In the beginning there was no debate; the code was simple—whatever tended to perpetuate the subject in memory as a pattern of high virtue was set forth, all else forgotten. In such circumstances whom to discuss and what to include were almost self-selective. But as, more and more, men became occupied with ethics as well as morality, with temporal success in addition to spiritual attainment —sometimes indeed to the complete exclusion of that last—more and more did they inquire into the causes and results of their progress through the world. Whom to discuss has always presented less difficulty than what to include; society's predilections are easily apparent, and the biographer's subject is, in a manner, chosen for him. None the less points of view regarding choice of subject have differed somewhat. Sir Sidney Lee, for instance, in his article, "National Biography," wrote:

> Professionally the biographer cares little or nothing for the evolution of society. From the mass of mankind he draws apart those units who are in a decisive degree distinguishable from their neighbors. He submits them to minute examination, and his record of observation becomes a mirror of their exploits and characteristics from the cradle to the grave.

But W. H. Teale in his "Lives of English Laymen," on the contrary, said:

It has been truly observed by Pliny that of the actions which most deserve the attention of mankind the most splendid are not always the greatest. With equal truth may it be said that the characters of men who occupy the loftiest stations are not the most generally instructive. Elevated far above ordinary mortals, and concerned with duties assigned to few, the benefit of their example must be necessarily circumscribed. It is therefore by contemplating those who tread the ordinary paths of life, and are occupied in duties which concern the great bulk that lessons of the most universal applications may be learned. For with such the many feel sympathy, and their conduct comes home to most men's business and bosoms. In a word, while the exploits of the hero, the achievements of the states-man, or the discoveries of the philosopher belong to a very small section, the pursuits of the private citizen are those of the great mass of the community. Hence the biographer is bound, would he produce the good which his labors are calculated to effect, to select examples of imitation of humble calling, as well as from the high-born, the brave, or the wise.

What to include, on the contrary, has caused interminable argument. Our own day seems to insist upon the "last full measure" of inti-mately revealing detail. But the years before had likewise their opinions. Pepys, for example, thought Margaret Newcastle "a mad, conceited, ridiculous woman," and Newcastle himself "an ass to suffer her to write what she writes to him and of him." The "Monthly Review" held that Thomas Gray was "a man of singu-larities too violent for the commerce of society" — hence Mason should have had less to say about his character and opinions. For half a century the pros and cons of Lockhart's disclosures concerning Scott caused contention. And so the question remains — perhaps to be listed among those called eternal. At least there can be no solution as long as jesting Pilates in every age recreate the past according to their own image.

Whatever may be the ultimate decision, as yet there has been only confusion. Would it not be better, for instance, to know why Shakespeare bequeathed to Ann Hathaway his "second best bed"?

Surely we think none the less of Dr. Johnson when we learn of his devotion to Tetty, or even when we discover that his portrait once decorated the label of Barclay's beer. And if Queen Elizabeth's psychophysical parallelism were more sharply defined for us, would it not be easier to understand the fate of Essex? Or, how far short of appreciating John Donne must we fall so long as we know as little as we do about the causes behind his vagaries. We understand John Keats much better for our knowledge of Fanny Brawne; Milton more completely because of recent studies of his blindness; and Mary Lamb more sympathetically if we consider her mother.

There are limits to be sure. Detail which fails to illuminate or which lacks all qualities of the unique contributes merely to completeness; but even such a point of view as this becomes ponderable in connection with supreme genius. The Freudian device of releasing tendencies which the race has expended some of its best efforts to keep buried in the subconscious may be thought of as contributing to either the mythology or the science of psychology, depending upon one's attitude; there is small doubt, however, concerning the futility of comparable techniques as applied in biography. In reflecting upon the whole matter, nevertheless, one can but agree with Francis Jeffrey's comment on "The Memoirs of Sir James Mackintosh" — reasonably interpreting it — that

> Wheresoever there is power and native genius, we cannot but grudge the suppression of the least of its revelations; and are persuaded that with those who can judge such intellects, they will never lose anything by the most lavish and indiscriminate disclosures,

the while believing with Andre Maurois that "no picture of humanity is fair," and with Samuel Johnson that biography is narrative midway between "the falsehood of fiction" and "the useless truths of history," the result being that confusion approaches close upon chaos.

Among the many centers of controversy concerning inclusion, James Anthony Froude's "Thomas Carlyle" has been perhaps the most provocative. Carlyle died in 1881 and by 1897 some twenty "lives" of him had appeared; yet Froude's, issued in 1882–1884, is the only one that springs readily to mind — no doubt for two reasons. In the first place, no previous work had ever been so frank in its divulgence of personal relationships; and in the second, few works either before or since have been written with greater advantages of authority re-inforced by a style of such suave beauty and such cumulate effect. Upon its appearance, therefore, in the midst of a biographical tradition which Carlyle himself had characterized but a few years before with the contemptuous "bless its mealy mouth," it could hardly have failed — to paraphrase Hazlitt's adaptation from "Coriolanus" — of "fluttering the Carlyleans like an eagle in a dove-cote."

For in the past quarter of the century biography, in a very real sense, lagged behind the great Victorian Age; it could show no Tennyson, no Arnold, no Ruskin, no Browning. There was a small group, to be sure, Trevelyan, Morley, Stephen and the "National Biographers," but the great mass of life writing was wanting in almost everything that might give it distinction, yet the amount produced was staggering, William Roscoe Thayer, for instance, saying of the period:

> When any distinguished citizen, lawyer, judge, merchant, or writer died, it was taken for granted that his clergyman, if he had one, would write his life, unless his wife, sister, or cousin was preferred.

There seemed to be no satisfying the desire to commemorate; just as there seemed to be, likewise, no end to the queue of readers.

The urge to read and to write biography in such quantities after the middle years of the nineteenth century, however, when the earlier interest in romanticism — a mood in no wise conducive to the biographical impulse — was losing its intensity, and when the rapidly increasing stress upon science, falsely interpreted, threatened the ancient faith in the "dignity of man" — at such time the urge to read and to write biography as never before developed inevitably. A natural resemblance links the seventeenth with the nineteenth century; if one was occupied with manifold adjustment to all manner of change in inception, the other was equally involved with such change as it progressed toward fulfillment. The first saw

[ 257 ]

biography achieve popular esteem; the second saw it become commonplace because of inordinate demand — the causes of both lying in man's engrossment with himself and in his paramount instinct, survival.

The Victorian Age trusted to science and to the Industrial Revolution for solutions of all manner of problems, expecting disease and maladjustments of every kind to disappear, and expecting answers to questions that have remained unanswered from the beginnings of thought. As the years accumulated, however, few answers and no panaceas evolved, indeed only further complexities appeared — to end naturally enough in global war. Man had become doubtful of his powers to cope with what he had come to consider a monster of his own contriving and had grown frantic to recapture those qualities that differentiate man from machine. The end was a detrition of the form of biography which only new aspects and fresh conceptions could counteract. Such vitality James Anthony Froude infused by means of his "Life of Thomas Carlyle," only to meet outraged opinion, to fail completely of immediate effect upon the form, but in the end to be accorded his due place as a biographer, after the shouting had subsided to normal speech and contention had given way to just consideration.

Yet for Froude to write as he did was as natural as for his day to object. Although the causes which Carlyle had championed and the ideas which he had put forth have now for the most part either triumphed or been forgotten, one cannot help feeling that some of his forgotten ideas may have kept England out of the Franco-Prussian War, and there can be no doubt of his influence in the tide of Fascism. So, when his long life drew to its close, "The Sage of Chelsea" was, in the minds of hundreds, upon the heights of celebrity. Hence for his disciple, his most trusted friend, to reveal in detail what he had learned during long association and so, in Dryden's phrase, "find the demi-god a man," was indevout and not to be sanctioned. The old man had become almost legendary; to expose him as a mere human being was not to show — as Froude quite decidedly did show — the victory of genius over almost insuperable difficulties, but to degrade him to earthly levels and so rob him of the right to be worshiped like one of his own heroes. The whole becomes a crux — to be best explained perhaps in terms of Froude himself and his comprehension of Carlyle.

There are far more resemblances than differences among men; hence it is uniqueness that fosters distinction — and Froude was unique not only in experience and ways of thought but also in appearance. He was tall, quite tall enough to look over the heads of a crowd, and his face was extraordinarily long, with a nose almost massive, a mouth wide but well cut, and eyes of an immensity that startled, an effect heightened by their seeming redness. These features, together with his intensely black hair and pendant brows, accentuated a manner "strangely mysterious, expressive as it was of indefinable melancholy emanating from some obscure source of enigmatic power."

He attended Westminster, later studying at Oriel College, Oxford, where with his brother, Hurrell, he came under the influence of John Henry Newman and took part in the Tractarian Movement. Upon Newman's conversion to Catholicism, however, he turned toward skepticism, the while Hurrell remained close to Newman, with whom he composed a number of poems for "Lyra Apostolica," and finally wrote three of the "Tracts for the Times." James Anthony Froude, on the contrary, had in 1841 met John Sterling at whose suggestion he came to read Carlyle's "French Revolution," which affected him profoundly. As a result he passed on to the writings of Goethe, Lessing, and Schleiermacher, although sustaining such relations with Newman that the latter asked him to write a "life" of St. Neot for his "Lives of the English Saints." The preliminary researches for this study, however, seem to have put the final strain upon Froude's faith — never vigorous and wholehearted — and in his weakness he drifted from skepticism into agnosticism, and thence into misunderstanding of much of the material that perforce he had to use in his "History," and of much concerning Carlyle that should otherwise have been daylight clear to him. As a result in 1847 under the name "Zeta" he published "Shadows of the Clouds," a statement of his altered views, and two years later his famous "Nemesis of Faith," a book which subsequently he himself described as "sentimental heterodoxy," but which at the moment created so much sensation that he was asked to relinquish the fellowship which Exeter College had granted him in 1842, the book itself being publicly burned as the result of a lecture in the College Hall by William Sewall — the only immediate effect, however, as is so frequently the occurrence, was a demand for a second edition.

In June of 1849 Froude, presented by James Spedding, met Carlyle for the first time. He became at once one of his most ardent followers, submitting himself entirely to the personality and opinions of the older man to a degree which he later characterized in a revelatory passage:

> The practice of submission to the authority of one whom one recognizes as greater than one's self outweighs the chance of occasional mistakes. If I wrote anything, I fancied myself writing it to him, reflecting at each word on what he would think of it, as a check on affectation.

During the remainder of his life he lived under the influence of Carlyle, establishing such relations with him that again was illustrated Dr. Johnson's dictum that eating and drinking and living in social intercourse with his subject is the prime potential in the making of a biographer.

In the meantime Froude had occupied himself with researches into the history of Tudor England, being among the first to work with the then unpublished documents, issuing the result in 1856–1870 as the "History of England from the Fall of Wolsey to the Defeat of the Spanish Armada," a work which, although in competition with Macaulay's tremendously popular "History of England," attained a circulation only less wide. If it excited discussion of his ability as an historian, a matter of some moment when one remembers how he was accused of inaccuracy in handling facts in the "Carlyle," it none the less brought him sufficient renown so that upon the death of E. A. Freeman, incidentally, his most venomous critic, he succeeded him as Regius Professor of Modern History at Oxford — ample evidence of the reputation he had by 1892 acquired. Parenthetically, it was this work that inspired Charles Kingsley to write "Westward Ho!" and Tennyson to compose the "Revenge"; and it was Kingsley's review of it in "Macmillan's Magazine," for January, 1860, that provoked Newman's inimitable "Apologia Pro Vita Sua." From 1860 to 1874, besides, he edited "Fraser's Magazine," writing for it and for other periodicals occasional articles on theology, history, travel, including a number of fables, one of which, "A Siding at a Railway Station," is among the best of its kind. A selection from these writings was made and issued as "Short Studies on Great Subjects" in 1867–1883. His "The English in Ireland in the Eighteenth Century," a controversial work which called forth the ire of Lecky, and which, because of its peculiar point of view — Froude could never write of persecution it seems, without championing the persecutor — antagonized, strangely enough, even the party upheld. In 1874–1875 he visited South Africa. From 1881 to 1884 he was engaged with the material entrusted to him as Carlyle's literary executor. He visited Australia in 1884–1885, setting forth his views and reactions in "Oceana, or England and Her Colonies"; and in 1886–1887 journeyed to the West Indies, publishing the results of his visit in "The English in the West Indies." The remainder of his work consists of his lectures as Regius professor, all but the first series appearing posthumously, for his death occurred in 1894, "The Life and Letters of Erasmus," 1894; "English Seamen in the Sixteenth Century," 1895; and "The Council of Trent," 1896.

Outwardly Froude's experience seems not much different from that of many men whose gifts stop short of genius. Inwardly, however, it was different, and because it was, the "Carlyle" became what it is. Froude's uniqueness lay in his dwelling necessity to lean upon someone else, to submit himself and so draw strength which independently he lacked. In the beginning it was his father upon whom he levied. The elder Froude was an old-style Anglican clergyman — whom Lytton Strachey once characterized as "of hunting tastes and a talent for water colors." Toward him the small boy inclined as toward the sun, in spite of floggings, teasings, and a decidedly expressed preference for the older children. Next came John Henry Newman, fascinating, eloquent, colorful, stimulating, but in something out of harmony with him, else Froude could not have turned to his contrary, Carlyle, the crude, the forceful, the headlong. And it was Carlyle who held him — why may be best inferred from Sir Leslie Stephen:

> He ought (using the word in the artistic sense) to have been a refined and sensitive critic, shuddering at the brutalities of the great human tragedy, where the truest and purest causes can only work by turning to account savage and stupid passions. That might be unpleasantly pessimistic and sceptical but then his pessimism and scepticism show through his superficial enthusiasm. Take your hero as simply the embodiment of great cosmic or providential forces, and you may have some sympathy for his antagonists as for the victims of a pestilence or an earthquake. But Froude at once recognizes the ugly side, and feels bound to condone the offense. The tyranny and persecution are not regarded even as a painful and hideous necessity under the perverse conditions of life, but as somehow justifiable in themselves. He has to defend cruelty and to still the hatred by which it was prompted.*

It was Carlyle's sense of the heroic, the dramatic, that attracted Froude, those qualities which caused his preoccupation with individual men rather than society as the mainsprings in human progress. "History is the biography of great men," wrote Carlyle and the thought became a theme which he repeated with infinite variation. And to Froude he seemed by right to rank in that Valhalla of his own creation among the giants whom he placed there, Odin, Mahomet, Dante, Shakespeare, Luther, Cromwell, Napoleon, and the rest. The first impulse was no doubt obtained from reading the "French Revolution" — that flaming projection of the idea that anarchy and upheaval must result from disturbance unless a strong man appears to dominate the action. From the "Cromwell" he drew sustenance, but from the gothic "Frederick" he probably received further justification of the evolving conception — a king without moral sense, an exploiter of his people, and yet a model. "Defend cruelty, and still the hatred by which it may be prompted" may explain much of Froude's attitude, as it becomes apparent in the "History," especially in the mold of Henry VIII, and, in less degree

---

* Included by the courteous permission of the publishers of Leslie Stephen's "Studies of a Biographer," G. P. Putnam's Sons.

perhaps, as it appears in the "Carlyle." "Take your hero as simply the embodiment of great cosmic or providential forces, and you may have some sympathy for his antagonists as for the victims of a pestilence or an earthquake" may explain more. But "Froude at once recognizes the ugly side, and feels bound to condone the offense," explains the author of the "Carlyle" at work and at the same time accounts for the antagonism he aroused. The Victorian public was not ready for such thinking. Froude dealt in shades as well as tints, his own hero worship misleading him into concluding that everybody was as much interested as he in realizing to what heights Carlyle had risen in overcoming the obstacles that had handicapped him. His talent for the picturesque and his sense of style — just as they had served him badly in the "History" — again led him into effects not in keeping with available fact; at least such was the earliest consensus. There was small understanding of the biographic art in which the scholar's accuracy becomes fused with the philosopher's insight and the poet's expression. His public saw only what it considered faults of character, defects in social address, and unpleasantness in marital affairs and concluded that Froude's conception of the "Sage of Chelsea" was one of a misanthrope at war with his neighbors and cruel to his wife although a man of the highest qualities of heart and mind. As a matter of fact, Froude's idea was to present Carlyle as one of the supreme geniuses of the age, whose disposition as the result of abominable health was at times unconscionably irritable — a characteristic which even his mother recognized, remarking that he was "gey ill to live with"; not to stress the implication in Mrs. Carlyle's exclamation,

> If I might write my own biography . . . without reservation or false coloring — it would be an invaluable document for my countrywomen in more than one particular. But decency forbids!

If his own wish in the matter could have been granted, Carlyle would have had no biography. On October 10, 1843, he recorded in his Journal:

> Someone writes about notes for a biography in a beggarly Spirit of the Age or other rubbish basket — rejected *nem. con.*

What have I to do with their 'Spirits of the Age'? To have my 'life' surveyed and commented on by all men even less wisely is no object to me, but rather the opposite; how much less to have it done *unwisely!* The world has no business with my life; the world will never know my life, if it should write and read a hundred biographies of me. The main facts of it even are known, and are likely to be known, to myself alone of created men. The 'goose goddess' which they call 'Fame!' *Ach Gott!*

Again, dated December 29, 1848, the same idea appears:

> Darwin said to Jane the other day, in his quizzing serious manner, 'Who will write Carlyle's life?' The word reported to me set me thinking how *impossible* it was, and would forever remain, for any creature to write my 'life.' The chief elements of my little destiny have all along lain deep below view or surmise, and never will or can be known to any son of Adam. I would say to my biographer, if any fool undertook such a task, 'Forbear, poor fool.' Let no life of me be written; let me and my bewildered wrestlings lie buried here and be forgotten swiftly of all the world. If thou write, it will be mere delusion and hallucination. The confused world never understood nor will understand me and my poor affairs. Not even the persons nearest to me could guess at them; nor was it found indispensable; nor is it now (for any but an idle purpose) profitable, were it even possible. Silence, and go thy ways else-whither.

Furthermore, in his will, made in 1873, naming John Carlyle, his brother, and John Forster, one of his most intimate friends, together with Froude as literary executors, he repeated the request that no "life" be written: "Express biography of me I had really rather there should be none." Then, too, "Reminiscences" had been composed soon after Mrs. Carlyle's death in 1869, and "Letters and Memorials" of Mrs. Carlyle had been annotated and given to Froude in 1871 with the injunction that no part of the material should be published without "fit editing," which editing would make publication of "nine tenths" of it, "after I am gone," impossible. Nevertheless when in 1880 Froude discussed the possibilities of full length biography to be composed by himself — both John Carlyle and Forster having died — Carlyle approved. Hence when the time came he set to work, publishing "Thomas Carlyle: A History of the First Forty Years of His Life" in 1882; and two years later "Thomas Carlyle: A History of His Life in London."

But who can say with the Wanderer, "I have learned truly the mark of a man?" Froude's greatest gift was as "artist historian." He had no respect for methodology, thinking with Talleyrand, *Il n'y a rien qui s'arrange aussi facilement que les faits,* and remarking himself that "The most perfect English history which exists is to be found in the historical plays of Shakespeare; 'Macbeth,' were it literally true would be faultless" — a point of view fully illustrated in his "History," especially in the descriptions of Anne Boleyn's coronation, of lightning striking St. Paul's, of the preparation for death of the Charterhouse monks, of the sea fight at St. Helena, the murder of Rizzio, and the execution of Mary. Throughout his writing there is a prime emphasis upon the persons involved. His characters are alive and vitally colorful. As an anonymous reviewer commented: "With Froude you may disagree, but you cannot disregard." He may not have known "truly the mark" of Carlyle; in fact Ruskin, Mrs. Ireland, and Skelton alone among his articulate contemporaries agreed with him in his characterization. Charles Eliot Norton might say after reading the letters that they "afford a view . . . different both in particulars and in general effect from that given by Mr. Froude . . . as the real and total Carlyle I myself knew"; Nevinson, in speaking of Froude's treatment of Carlyle's relations with Jane Welch Carlyle, might lament, "Their fate has made the very thought of biography detestable"; such expressions as "Froude's disease" and "Froudacities" might arise from his suspected warping of fact for the sake of effect; Horace Furness might remark that he never wanted to hear of Carlyle again after learning from Froude that Mrs. Carlyle was permitted to scrub the bricks in the yard behind Number 5, Cheyne Row (he should have tempered his opinions with her own attitude toward bread making at Craigenputtock); and Thayer might write, "I cite Froude as the great warning to biographers." Froude may have missed the true Carlyle completely, as innumerable contemporary comments insist.

Nevertheless his own point of view, as set forth in his original Preface, borne out as it is by the book itself, is illuminating:

> In the papers thus in my possession, Carlyle's history, external and spiritual, lay out before me as in a map. By recasting the entire material, by selecting chosen passages out of his own and his wife's letters, by exhibiting the fair and beautiful side of the story only, it would have been easy, without suppressing a single material point, to draw a picture of a faultless character. When the Devil's advocate has said his worst against Carlyle, he leaves a figure still of unblemished integrity, purity, loftiness of purpose, and inflexible resolution to do right, as of a man living consciously under his Maker's eye, and with his thoughts fixed on the account which he would have to render of his talents.*

And a further passage, from the "Duty of His Biographer," an introductory chapter appended to the "Life in London" as an answer to criticism, shows him to have had the courage of his inclusions:

> Had I considered my own comfort or my own interest, I should have sifted out or passed lightly over the delicate features in the story. It would have been as easy as it would have been agreeable for me to construct a picture, with every detail strictly accurate, of an almost perfect character. An account so written would have been admired and applauded, and the biographer, if he had not shared in the praise, would at least have escaped censure. . . . The sharpest scrutiny is the condition of enduring fame. Every circumstance which can be ascertained is eventually dragged into light. If blank spaces are left, they are filled by rumour or conjecture. When the generation is gone, there is no more tenderness in dealing with them; and if their friends have been discreetly reserved, idle tales, which survive in tradition become stereotyped into facts. Thus the characters of many of our greatest men, as they stand in history, are left blackened by groundless calumnies, or credited with imaginery excellences a prey to be torn in pieces by rival critics, with clear evidence wanting, and pre-

---

* Included by the courteous permission of the publishers of Froude's "Life of Carlyle," Charles Scribner's Sons.

possessions fixed on one side or the other by dislike or sympathy.*

Whatever approval or disapproval Froude may have encountered in his own day — the discussion accumulated in magazine articles and even in full-length volumes has now become almost unwieldy — we are far enough away from it all to appreciate that by means of the "Carlyle" he brought biography back to the tradition established in the seventeenth century augmented in the eighteenth, and bequeathed in turn, to the twentieth. He revealed Carlyle without the pageantry of his celebrity, showing him as "a reasonable animal" with all his "scars and blemishes," and yet a hero in one of the greatest of dramas — the conquest of poverty and disease through force of genius. "The worldly hope men set their hearts upon" in Khayyam's bitter quatrain, was for him no more than half fulfilled; hence if "like snow upon the desert's dusty face it lit but a little hour or more," none the less the memory of him as a personality is fresh and will be kept so by means of Froude's great book. So far as his method of biography is concerned we can do nothing less than echo Professor Waldo Dunn, whose "Froude and Carlyle" appeared in 1930, and say, "Froude is right in tendency all the while, and entirely right in the end."

---

* Included by the courteous permission of the publishers of Froude's "Life of Carlyle," Charles Scribner's Sons.

# 22–Sir Leslie Stephen and Collective Biography

*All things are engaged in writing their particular history.* — Emerson.

NO MATTER how highly we may value Boswell's "Johnson," Trevelyan's "Macaulay," and Lockhart's "Scott," there remains an impenetrable veil between us and the reality of the men whom through even these works we have sought to know. Boswell may have thought — and rightly — that his "mode of biography, which gives not only a history of Johnson's visible progress through the world . . . but a view of his mind . . . is the most perfect that can be conceived"; none the less his word by no means nullifies the idea set forth in "Urn Burial" by Sir Thomas Browne:

> The iniquity of oblivion blindly scattereth her poppy, and deals with the memory of man without distinction to merit of perpetuity,

an idea which Emerson two hundred years later was all unwittingly to repeat in his "Literary Ethics,"

> Do not foolishly ask of the inscrutable, obliterated past what it cannot tell — the details of that nature, of that day called Byron, or Burke.

For the past can no more be reanimated than its men and women can be resurrected — "the uttered part of a man's life," wrote Carlyle, "bears to the unuttered unconscious part a small unknown proportion." We can, if our skill be sufficient, reclaim brief moments and understand something of their significance, just as we can, if our sympathy, our command of fact, and our art of communication be adequate, call up vague images of the departed great. But vague they must remain, vague and blurred in outline; we have no powers to bring them more sharply into view.

More perfect science and more capable perception than any we know are needed. Biography must naturally remain among the most imperfect literary forms. Of late, however, as is well-known, a demand has arisen for the scientific approach in life writing and not a few attempts to satisfy it have been made; with the result that, all too frequently, the ignorance of the one has called forth but the pretension of the other. Too much is involved. The half-in-fun-wholly-in-earnest comment of Dr. Harold D. Lasswell in a recent number of a scientific journal most fittingly disposes of the matter to date:

> The central nucleus of those interested in the problem of more adequate human biographies might very well constitute themselves an institute composed of an historian, a sociologist, a political scientist, economist, jurist, humanist, historian of science, of philosophy, a psychiatrist, psychopathologist, doctor of internal medicine, a geneticist, and a psychometrician.

All this is by no means to suggest that what we have is valueless, but to say that perfection is unattainable. We can only continue to add to our methods of collecting facts, to refine upon our techniques for interpreting them, and trust that wisdom will come, remembering that there is no useless biographic knowledge — in fact we have Dr. Johnson's word for this last in "I have often thought that there has rarely passed a life of which a judicious and faithful narrative would not be useful." It is absurd, of course, even to contemplate assembling life records of all who walk the earth. We should, however, have many more than are now available. The "lives" of the great may serve to show us what we might become, but the "lives" of the less show us much better what we are, or as Tolsoy expressed the same idea in "War and Peace":

> It is only by studying the differential quantities in history, together with the homogeneous currents that carry men onwards, and finding the integer, that we can master its laws.

In response to some such needs — as well as to indulge the spirit of national pride — groups of men in various countries have composed biographical dictionaries, of which the Dictionary of National Biography, first edited by Sir Leslie Stephen in the late nineteenth century, is the largest and most comprehensive, but of which there are other valuable examples, among them the "Allgemeine Deutsche Biographie," for instance, "Der Grosse Oesterreichische Hausschatz," the "Biographiskt Lexiconofver Namnkunnige Svenskaman," the "Biographie Universelle," the "Nouvelle Biographie Generale," the "Biographie Nationale de Belgique," and the "Dictionary of American Biography."

But many years before any of these works was conceived, biographical lexicography had had its beginning. Early during the English Renaissance there sprang up a hardy race of antiquarians whose labor, imperfect, and perhaps a bit aimless at first, little by little established a basis for preserving in remembrance those whose lives and accomplishments were worthy but not necessarily pre-eminently distinguished; and so began the long process of development toward dictionaries of national biography. As early as the fourteenth century, however, records of saints had been gathered together in lexicographical form, the Dutch "Eleucidarius Carminum," together with the work of John of Tynemouth, and somewhat later that of John Boston of Bury being notable. John Leland, favorite antiquarian of Henry VIII, moreover, and John Bale who carried out his work, extended the field to include scientists and literary men in general, providing thus a body of information upon which for decades scholarship was to rely.

And the practice begun by them was carried on by Foxe and Parker and led to the work of men like Clark, Phillips, Winstanley, Langbaine, Thomas Fuller, Anthony Wood, and John Aubrey, becoming focused in the contribution of the two last named as clear proof that England was thinking of its own as at least comparable to classical culture. The "Athenae Oxoniensis," published by Wood in two volumes in 1691–1692 was later augmented by the inclusion of Aubrey's "Brief Lives" and remains yet today trustworthy and authoritative. The records are thorough, and their statement in the main is accurate and as complete as facility of research made this possible, even though occasional slips, like calling the notorious Simon Forman "a very able astrologer and physician," do occur. In style the book is concise even to aphorism, with emphasis upon facts, dates, and circumstances — truth beyond the point of sacrifice, for Wood as a result of his work was dismissed from Oxford where he had spent almost the whole of his life and portions of his book were burned by the hangman, only to bring forth the comment: "All good Antiquaries have always been of the same Principle: they all equally sacrificed to Truth." His colleague, John Aubrey, he called "roving and magotieheaded, and sometimes little better than crased"; nevertheless he made invaluable use of him, depending upon his work for additional information but also for characterizing detail. For Aubrey, unlike Wood, was a genial soul and a great gatherer of pertinent anecdote at country-house dinner tables and village ale houses. His notes and jottings — "Brief Lives" is frequently little more — are lively and entertaining as well as informative, and as such lent color to the "Athenae Oxoniensis." As it is Aubrey, under the aegis of Wood, is not without honor in the genre — the chief contribution of both being the significance they accord the seemingly insignificant.

The accumulation of the seemingly insignificant, however, in biography as elsewhere is the approach to reality and involves the massing of less important "lives" in collective biography as well as the piling up of detail in individual life writing; in fact one does not read far before he begins to think of biographical lexicography as applying to a nation as biography itself applies to an individual; both serve to commemorate, and to teach, the one generalizing toward particularity, the other by concentrating upon a single instance. Man reaches toward perfection although he knows that to grasp it is impossible, and biography is a record of his progress. For as society emerged from the old communal patterns to become belligerently nationalistic, and as increasingly men became aggressively individualistic — dependent upon themselves and whatever adjustment they could make with one another — self-knowledge and the assurance of self-worth grew to proportions of necessity; hence biography came to assume something of the characteristics of a grammar of life. But not until its scope was increased to include men of various types and varying degrees of distinction could it function as such. Clerics and their influence sufficed in a pastoral society as did soldiers and rulers with their ideals during a developing nationalism. When complexity arose and power was given to an individual not merely for his understanding in interpreting the ways of God to man or for his prowess in overcoming men with men, but also because of his ability to bend the forces of nature to enhance the common good, then arose the need for an augmented biography so that what men had done all men might know and so "rise on steppingstones of their dead selves to higher things."

This in a manner is the reason for biographical dictionaries — that they provide a record of many men. The renaissance added immeasurably to the complexity of human undertaking, and one of the results was the desire to know what men had been in order to learn what men might be. Therefore the climax in the growth of the form as defined by the origin of the word *biography* in 1661. Once society had grasped the idea, there was no end to biographic inclusion. If the seventeenth century, as a matter of fact, shows a widened scope, the twentieth shows a scope with no limits whatsoever — all men have become all things to all men in the sense that all might learn from each other. Before such condition could obtain, however, much effort and much painstaking thought were required. Anthony Wood and his forebears, antiquarians in general, and scientific methodology all played their part. Then, too, the growth of realism and the ever increasing demand not only to know but to know exactly contributed their influence. So that the eighteenth century, continuing the work of the seventeenth, refining upon it, and multiplying its effectiveness, made straight the paths and prepared for the advent of those who profiting in turn have profited posterity immensely.

Among those who worked in this field and upon whom later lexicographers have depended — for tradition if not for precedent — were Jeremy Collier, whose "A Supplement to the Great Historical, Geographical, Genealogical, and Poetical Dictionary" was issued in 1701; John Downes, who issued "Roscius Anglicanus, or an Historical Review of the Stage" in 1708; Giles Jacob, whose "Poetical Register; or the Lives and Characters of the English Dramatic Poets" was issued in 1719; the "General Dictionary, Historical and Critical," issued by Thomas Birch, John Peter

Bernard, and John Lockman in 1734–1741; the "Biographia Britannica," issued by Thomas Broughton, John Campbell, Andrew Kippis, William Oldys, and Joseph Towers in 1747–1766; Theophilus Cibber, who issued "The Lives of the Poets of Great Britain and Ireland to the Time of Dean Swift" with the assistance of Robert Shields in 1753; Horace Walpole, whose "A Catalogue of the Royal and Noble Authors of England," was issued in 1758; James Granger and his "Biographical History of England," 1769, and Edward Harwood and his "Biographia Classica," 1777. Not all these are of the first order, naturally; the Walpole work is a bit self-conscious, showing in the words of Walter Scott, "Mr. Walpole's respect for birth and rank"; the Collier is something of a hodgepodge; the "General Dictionary" devoted thirteen folio pages to Shakespeare, more than half of which are given over to footnotes; in fact the "Biographia Britannica" is the most satisfying, but even it shows curious omissions and partialities so obvious that Walpole nicknamed it "Vindicatio Brittanica." None the less a tradition was carried on and information which otherwise would no doubt have been lost was preserved.

Collective biography — the best term for such compilations — is usually an alphabetical arrangement of a series of succinctly written "lives" possessing some common denominator. Its purpose is only suggestive of commemoration and only indirectly didactic, being almost wholly informative and striving "to comprise as much knowledge as possible in the smallest compass." For in both style and method it must proceed hampered by the cruelest of shackles. No enthusiasm, no decoration, no color, nothing beyond the directly applicable can be permitted to interrupt the steady progress of names, dates, places, the precise relation of events, and the coldest estimations of personal character — all communicated in accordance with the strictest discipline. There is no room for the "light occasion" or for the allusion to idiosyncrasy unless it be such as, in Plutarch's view, makes

> Men's nature, dispositions, and manners appear more plainly
> than the famous battles won, wherein are slain 10,000 men.

And yet, if one credits Dr. Johnson's opinion, the compiler is a "harmless drudge" who may expect small praise though his work be superb but great censure if he makes the most trivial error.

When one remembers the "Dictionary of National Biography" and Sir Leslie Stephen, its original editor, however, he is tempted to disagree with the Ursa Major. To have guided the destinies of so tremendous an undertaking — 63 volumes comprising 29,108 pages issued at regular intervals between the beginning of 1885 and Midsummer, 1900, containing 29,120 "lives" chosen from 1500 years of English history, and composed by 653 contributors — is to have become anything but a "harmless drudge" and not at all susceptible to censure for trivial error. It is, rather, to have become eligible for a place in the great work itself and even for a full-length "life," as the sequel demonstrates, for Sir Sidney Lee, the second editor, devoted one of the best sketches in the "Dictionary" to his predecessor, and Frederick W. Maitland, one of Stephen's friends and a member of the famous "Sunday Tramps," wrote his "Life and Letters."

Sir Leslie Stephen was the son of Sir James Stephen, an undersecretary for the colonies from 1836 to 1847, later becoming professor of modern history at Cambridge; and brother to Sir James Fitzjames Stephen, a member of the governor-general's council in India, a judge of the high court, and a contributor to "Fraser's," the "Cornhill," and the "Pall Mall Gazette." He himself was born in 1832 and educated at Eton, King's College, London, and at Trinity Hall, Cambridge, where he became a tutor. Never a robust youth, while at Cambridge he developed a decided interest in walking, attaining such endurance that he not infrequently walked the fifty miles into London in twelve hours; and in addition to walking he took to rowing, being responsible in great measure for the intercollegiate boat races during his residence. Even in after life he continued his liking for both sports, gathering fame as a mountaineer and for three years editing the "Alpine Journal," and seldom missing a crew race as long as his health permitted.

Literature was his chief concern, however, and he soon found a place in literary journalism, contributing critical essays to various magazines which he later published as "Hours in a Library." After writing several books, notably "Essays on Free Thinking and Plain Speaking," the "Agnostic's Apology," the "History of English Thought in the Eighteenth Century," "The English Utilitarians," and the "Science of Ethics," he commenced biography, aiding John Morley to establish his "English Men of Letters" series by writing the "Johnson" in 1878, and afterward the "Pope" in 1880, the "Swift" in 1882, the "George Eliot" in 1902, and the "Hobbes" in 1904. Besides these bio-critical "lives," he wrote a "life" of his friend Henry Fawcett in 1885, and one of his brother in 1895.

One reviewing the lives of men like Stephen, and of Sterling and of Froude, for that matter, cannot fail to be saddened by the thought of what they might have accomplished had they not been misled by the confusions of their day into the absurdities of agnosticism. As it is, we may admire them for their gifts although we deplore the fact that they chose to ignore "the way, the truth, and the life," and so fell short of full realization. Who knows, perhaps if they and their coevals similarily gifted had elected to try to stem the rising tide of materialism instead of drifting with it, we might not have been plunged into global war. Surely, the good that men fail to do as well as the evil they actually do lives after them.

Paralleling almost all Stephen's work was his editorship of the "Cornhill," a position which he had accepted in 1871. In this capacity he came in contact with most of the writers that made London in the late nineteenth century the literary capital of the world. Sooner or later he met the best loved figures in the literature of his day — Ruskin, Thackeray, D. G. Rossetti, George Eliot, G. P. R. James, George Meredith, Stevenson, the Brownings, Charles Reade, Thomas Hardy, Matthew Arnold, Darwin, Herschel, Charlotte Bronte, Mrs. Humphrey Ward, all of whom contributed to the "Cornhill" or had some connection with the publishing house of Smith, Elder, and Company whose property it was, and so came within Stephen's orbit.

In 1882, the "Cornhill" beginning to lose some of its previous unprecedented popularity, George Smith, the proprietor, prevailed upon Stephen to undertake the editorship of his projected "Dictionary of National Biography." The first indication of his being involved in the venture appears in the final sentence of a letter to Smith written August 8, 1881: "I have been thinking a good deal about biographies universal and otherwise," an illuminating comment in view of the fact that Smith's original idea had concerned a dictionary of universal biography. Stephen eventually persuaded him, however, that so large a scope was impracticable and the work was accordingly limited. And it was characteristic of George Smith to allow himself to be persuaded on such terms. He was the son of a Scotch bookseller who had founded the firm of Smith and Elder in 1816 as publishers and East Indian agents. As a very young man — he was only twenty-two — George Smith came into control of the business and in but a few years multiplied its activities and its assets. In the end he amassed a fortune through dealing in everything, it seems, from sonnets by Rossetti to munitions of war shipped to quell the Indian Mutiny — not the least of his undertakings being the publication of "Jane Eyre" and the encouragement of its young author. Always, he was open-minded and audacious, willing to listen but anxious to achieve, and a man of the highest integrity. Hence when Stephen showed him how much more effective a dictionary of biography limited to England and Englishmen would be, no time seems to have been lost in launching the project.

And so under the trained and objectively disciplined Leslie Stephen — he was not knighted until 1902 — and the energetically imaginative George Smith as editor and patron, respectively, the largest of all national collections of biography was planned and begun. It appeared in sixty-three volumes issued quarterly during fifteen years, the first twenty-one volumes under the sole editorship of Stephen, the next five under the joint editorship of himself and Sidney (later Sir Sidney) Lee, and the remainder under the guiding hand of Lee alone, Stephen having resigned in 1891 because of failing health. The work as available today, the rights having been acquired by the Oxford University Press, has been augmented by supplements and indices and compressed by improved methods of manufacture to twenty-two volumes. The editorial work was the responsibility of W. H. Carless Davis and J. R. H. Weaver. An extremely interesting statistical description has been added and a memoir of George Smith appears as the preface to Volume XXII — the one indicative of the extraordinary value of the work, and the other, of the extraordinary character of its patron.

But neither would have meant what it does without the contributing genius of Leslie Stephen. He gave the best years of his life to the undertaking, selecting authors — not a few of whom, beginning under his tutelage, later came to distinction — editing their work, and himself composing 378 articles, a total of one thousand pages, including "lives" of Addison, Burns, Byron, Carlyle, Coleridge, Defoe, Dickens, Dryden, Goldsmith, Hume, Landor, Macaulay, Mill, Milton, Pope, Scott, Swift, Thackeray, and Wordsworth. He was ideally equipped for the enterprise. Of sane judgment, wide sympathies, enormous reading, in spite of not being a trained historian and of lacking patience with plodding antiquarian methods of research — which were not infrequently necessary — he diffused his spirit throughout the entire 30,000 pages. Without him to kindle from the spark of Smith's enthusiasm biographical lexicography would not now be the source of national self-knowledge it has become.

And it is such source in high degree. History and its concern with all manner of men *in action* is invaluable; but collective biography and its concern with these same men *in being* is indispensable. We require to know what men have done, naturally, but more essentially we require to know what men have been and so, in a manner, discover our own potentiality — for "great ideas," wrote the English philosopher A. K. White,

> are democratic, not in the sense that everyone in every age can recognize them in a way uniformly the same but that they can be understood in the same way. . . . Thus the soul of the subject [of biography] may be as much mine and yours as his.

Moreover, in reviewing the accumulated accomplishment of 1500 years, or in merely becoming aware that such accumulation has been recorded in order, one develops a new sense of value, realizing that

> As cedars beaten with continual storms,
> So great men flourish.

Hence pride is tempered by self-criticism to a more accurate appraisal of self-worth. In truth, biography, imperfect though it is and no doubt must remain, can be a purge and a motivation.

# 23—Bradford

*The way to find out the truth is by others' mis-taking; for if I was to go to such a place, and one had gone before me on the right hand, and he was out; another had gone on the left hand, and he was out; this would direct me to keep the middle way, which peradventure would bring me to the place I desired to go. — Seldon.*

OF BIOGRAPHERS who have essayed to contribute to man's knowledge of himself one of the most daring is Gamaliel Bradford. Many men have written of triumph and defeat, seeking causes and motives; but Bradford is unique in the directness of his search. A glance at the titles of some of his books reveals his ambition: "The Soul of Samuel Pepys," "Damaged Souls," "Bare Souls," "A Naturalist of Souls." The Christian, however, who here read his own meaning into the word "Soul" would be destined to disillusionment.

But more revealing, perhaps, is his use of the word "psychography" in classification of his work. He explains that he coined it himself and later discovered that the late George Saintsbury had used it in connection with the writings of Sainte-Beuve. He disclaims, however, any intention of suggesting innovation by the term. In fact there is small room within the compass of biography for innovation — even the candid school in which the day just passing seems to take such pride, like the candid camera, records little save the unrepresentative. Nevertheless, Bradford's range and purpose extend somewhat beyond the scope of prior writers, and not any of his contemporaries has equaled either the universality of his choice of subject or the singularity of his persistent stress.

Biography was not his original interest. As a matter of fact, born in 1863, it was not until he was almost fifty years old that he undertook the form. Then, encouraged by the reception of his "Lee, the American," published in 1912, he began the career which made him unique among American biographers. His own attitude toward his success is defined in his essay "On Biography." He says,

> Twenty years ago, after a long period of utter discouragement and as it seemed final abandonment of literary labor altogether, I literally stumbled into the line of biographical work and made a success which, if in no way remarkable, has been more of an astonishment to me than anyone else. I should prefer to write great novels; but we do what we can, not what we should like.*

Writing had been his ambition, from early youth, however, and it became the business of his life to such degree — in spite of his remark that it brought him less than $1,000 a year all told — that when he died in 1932, he had been an author for almost half a century, a period long enough for him to have received a letter of appreciation from Walter Pater and to have inscribed a book to Lytton Strachey.

To be sure, almost every influence contributing to the formation of his character predisposed him to authorship. The old New England traditions were alive in him. A direct descendant through his father from William Bradford, second governor of Plymouth Colony, he was, through his mother, the grandson of Henry W. Kinsman, Daniel Webster's partner at law — and the spirit of the great orator was cherished in his home. Furthermore, in addition to the fortunate circumstances of his birth — which, incidentally, included a not inadequate income — he came early to know Emerson, to make the acquaintance of Matthew Arnold at the home of Charles Eliot Norton through a letter from Oliver Wendell Holmes, and to spend many pleasant days at work in the study of Hawthorne's Old Manse.

* Included by the courteous permission of the publishers of Gamaliel Bradford's "On Biography," the Houghton Mifflin Company.

As a child he was delicate, silent, and retiring—his mother and all her numerous brothers and sisters had died of tuberculosis before middle age, he himself having to be sent at the age of fifteen to the south of France because of the same disease. And illness pursued him during the whole of his life, so that he was seldom able to leave his home and almost never able to spend more than two hours a day at his desk. Of high order intellectually, however, he found compensation in the cultivation of his mind. Too frail for continued residence at Harvard, he left during his freshman year and studied at home with tutors, displaying while still a youth an extraordinary avidity for absorbing not only the best in English literature, but also, as his education progressed, all that came his way in Greek, Latin, French, German, Spanish, and Italian. This interest he retained to the end of his life, commencing the study of both modern Greek and Portuguese, for instance, in 1932! Naturally, with such endowment, he aspired to write.

Slowly he felt his way, beset as it was by discouragements. His father wished him to enter public service and ridiculed his literary efforts, while he himself was almost overwhelmed by failure satisfactorily to "glean his teeming brain" of the imagery within. His Journal records many a lament, and among his first poems is an "Ode to Despair." He followed his gleam, notwithstanding, composing novels, plays, poems, critical essays, everything, in fact, except "lives," but with almost no hint of success until in 1895 when he issued his first published book, "Types of American Character." This work comprises a series of sketches which remind one vaguely of the seventeenth century "character," dealing as it does with abstract types, like "the pessimist," "the idealist," "the man of letters," to indicate a few of the subjects. If not pointedly indicative of the trend of his thought, which seventeen years later was to find expression in the "Lee" and so commence a brilliant career, it at least suggests the presence of the germ, which, coming to maturity, led to his preoccupation with psychography and hence to his attempted contribution to the body of man's knowledge of himself.

For, no matter what his other qualities, by this sign Bradford is shown to have possessed the ethic curiosity, the eternal *why*-quest of human action—the impulse toward which may or may not have been guided by Sainte Beuve's famous *tel arbre, tel fruit!* His first published book suggests his inclination, and his subsequent work connotes the passion of a mind which, to quote a half-sentence written in 1795 by Henry James Pye in a comment upon Horace,

> delights to observe the manners; to investigate the symptoms of character; to infer, from the occasional actions of an individual the predisposing bent or state of his mind.

And so, however short he may have fallen of the artistic and moral ends his intention established, he, none the less, contrived, in no slight measure, to recall past uniqueness. It is an exaggeration, of course, to say with James Field Stanfield that by "the lively description of appearances" he at the same time indicated

> adequately, but not obtrusively, the laws by which these appearances are shaped and governed; sometimes in an interesting, continued series of action; sometimes in delicate circumstances of situation and sentiment; but most of all, in those eventful occurrences, where the soul appears through the actions.

Man's freedom of the will prevents any universal and "adequate" prediction as to his future actions on the part of a Gamaliel Bradford. He may, however, be able to present character in a few sharply drawn lines.

The technique by which he gains his effects he has been at some pains to describe. In his various Prefaces, in the letters and the Journal — a voluminous work in some 1,400,000 words, parts of which are now available through the editorship of Mr. Van Wyck Brooks, who also edited the letters — and in a number of articles in half a dozen periodicals, the reader may find statements of what he tried to do and how he went about it. The chapter called "Psychography" in *A Naturalist of Souls*, however, is perhaps as nearly a summation of his biographic philosophy as he made. There he distinguishes between his own aims and those of the painter of portraits, for instance, by pointing out that the painter must generalize from a single moment while he himself has the records of a life to draw upon. Likewise, he differentiates between psychography and biography by saying that the former selects only the minima essential to design, including nothing for the sake of mere completeness. Moreover, he contrasts his purpose with that of the psychologist in so far as the latter is concerned with individuals as material for the study of behavior, the while he himself attempts to delineate character as distinct from individuality.

Psychography, therefore, he continues, is the artistic presentation of character by exhibiting it as the sum of those qualities which constitute habits of action. In connection with any attempt to proceed on the basis of this definition, naturally enough, complexities develop. It becomes necessary to rely upon the historical record of what the chosen subject has said and done during the course of his life. How accurate is such record? Sometimes it has been left in the form of autobiographical matter. How trustworthy is it? Furthermore, granted the accuracy and trustworthiness of the records, how are they to be interpreted? What a man says depends for meaning, in great degree, upon tone, facial expression, circumstances prompting remark, and the situation in which the speaker finds himself. How is one to tell just what was meant by words spoken, say, two hundred years ago? And what difficulties arise in respect to speech are further complicated by those arising in respect to action. Does one invariably act in accordance with character? Does the cruel man never do a kindness? Is the simple man invariably simple? The answers must always remain inconclusive; the most careful study, the most minute research into the actions and motives of men serve usually only to confuse complexity.

"Of what use, then, is psychography?" he asks. For one thing, it is the most fascinating of studies. Character is the great enigma. Every person is different from every other. The field is inexhaustible; hence there can be no flagging interest. Again, unsatisfactory though psychography is, it is necessary. We require to know about people; we can act only as a result of such knowledge. Whether we are aware of it or not we are all psychographers. The infant learns the rewards of crying. The child learns how to please his parents. The man learns to live with other men, not by trampling blindly over them, but by knowing how to please them in order that they may please him. Such knowledge is the key to ordered living. If it is valuable to an individual in his way through the world, how much more valuable, therefore, is it, in accumulation, to the race in its march toward eternity?

In the great welter of individual activity, some items are vital, others of no significance whatever. The psychographer must discover and interpret what is essentially and characteristically revealing. The long row of Charles Sumner's collected works, for example, serves only to bury him as a personality. On the other hand, every page in Pepys' diary uncovers some new facet. Madame D'Arblay says a great deal about the people among whom she moved, but her diary discloses very little of her own inner life. General Sherman is open to the sky; General Lee but seldom steps from behind the veil of his reserve. "Psychography picks and chooses," Bradford remarks; "in a bushel of chaff it finds only a grain or two of wheat, but treasures that wheat as precious and invaluable."

Sainte-Beuve he refers to as the master of all psychographers, and throughout his work he pays tribute to the great critic. It was Sainte-Beuve from whom Bradford learned the phrase "a naturalist of souls," and he uses it more or less as the *leit-motif* of his work. The Frenchman possessed "insight into the deep and hidden motives and passions of the soul, and the power of distinguishing and defining them," in Bradford's opinion and so became at once model and inspiration. Sainte-Beuve's method of composition was not capable of sufficient variation, to suit Bradford, however. The simple chronological procedure has not the flexibility necessary in a series of sketches. To develop various points of character in connection with different circumstances or periods is to hamper occasions. Bradford's own method, as he points out, is to present qualities of character, "arranged and treated in such logical order as shall give a total impression." Hence, instead of monotonously reviewing the same qualities in the same order, "every individual seeming to suggest and to require a different arrangement, a different emphasis," he seldom uses the same pattern twice, varying his order of presentation as he thinks most pertinent to the effect desired.

A year or two before his death he wrote an article for the *Saturday Review of Literature* called "The Art of Biography" which not only illuminates psychography but comments upon the possibilities and limitations of the whole biographic undertaking as well — as he conceived of it. "But whatever the method, and in all methods," he wrote,

> there are two things chiefly notable about biography; first is its lack of finality, second its charm. Human character is too evasive, too elusive even to be finally portrayed by any one. Perhaps one element of the charm lies in this very thing, and if it were easy to limn souls, the process would lose its attraction. But easy or difficult, the biographer's one object is to catch something of the fluidity, the mobility, the versatility of the human spirit. And thus biography is one of the most fascinating of all pursuits, for by it we are taken out of our own lives into another life which we find is after all very much our own. The pursuit, when it is skillfully carried on, is fascinating for the reader. But for the writer this close, absorbing, enthralling intimacy with another human spirit is the most delicate and delightful of all resources for eluding, if not for solving, the intricate, eternal puzzle of life.*

As a matter of fact, one can find almost at random in his writings remarks upon the delights of his pursuit, even upon the delights of the difficulties he encounters. In "A Clue to the Labyrinth of Souls," for example, appears this revealing question, "How to get at Souls: the inner, hidden, mysterious machinery so cunningly and completely masked behind the solid, compact covering of flesh and blood?" Seldom, however, does he become specific. What he attempts is by its very nature inordinately difficult to explain. It cannot be reduced to formula. And yet in "Biography and the Human Heart" he sets forth something of the process by which he tried "to get at souls," a near approach to a formula that one can perceive in operation in almost all the sketches — more clearly perhaps in the sketches of men, for as applied to women his common denominators are not wholly relevant. He establishes the essential humanity of his subjects as linked through four basic elements, love, ambition, money, and religion — a device based upon Sainte-Beuve's questions concerning

---

* Included by the courteous permission of the publishers of Gamaliel Bradford's "The Art of Biography," the *Saturday Review of Literature.*

a subject's attitude toward religion, women, money, scenery, daily life, friendship, vice, etc. — in terms of which he essays to penetrate "behind the solid, compact covering of flesh and blood." How contributory to successful accomplishment his use of such a device became, one cannot safely judge. At all events the interest that the public took in his work unmistakably signifies, whether justly or unjustly, that he in some wise provided the means by which thousands (for however modestly he remarks upon his success, toward the end of his career his books were in high demand) — might "elude, if not solve the intricate, eternal puzzle of life."

It may be that the subjects he chose are of an enduring attraction; they are, except for occasional obscurities like John Beauchamp Jones, the diarist, and Jones Very, the poet, all familiar figures: Benedict Arnold, John Brown, Charlotte Cushman, John Donne, Flaubert, Madame Guyon, Edward Hyde, Henry James, Keats, Charles Lamb, Madame de Maintenon, Francis de Sales, Mark Twain, James McNeill Whistler, to run an alphabetical gamut. It may be, of course, that such personalities as these, well-known and having some aroma of romance about them, would naturally tend to draw about him a large following of devoted readers, particularly when focused in the light of the appositely illustrative details which he seeks to disentangle and project in a style singularly clear and of an unimpeded simplicity. But it may be, too, that the period during which his maturing talent was brought to bear in the direction of popular taste — as the years 1912–1932 saw biographical undertakings of all sorts and qualities take predominance — played its part in furnishing him with an eager audience. How highly posterity, with the added advantages of perspective, will value him, who can say? It cannot fail to see, as we do, that his work is a crystallization. Having saturated himself with the tendencies of Sainte-Beuve and prior biographical essayists, including Fuller, Johnson and even Walton, he precipitated, so to speak, the residue over the fire of his own enthusiasm, and, calling it "psychography," applied it in definite and practicable form. Moreover, how will posterity judge his quite evident refusal to draw his characters in sharp outlines? For he preferred always to obscure them by an unwillingness either to praise forthrightly or to blame vigorously —

and this in spite of the boldness with which he established himself as "a naturalist of souls."

Bradford's work may or may not survive. None the less, he himself is a subject for psychography. In the books he wrote, in his letters, in the Journal he kept daily for eighteen years, in whatever form he sought expression finally he shines forth an undefeatable soul in the pursuit of his own ambition. Possessed — one almost thinks *obsessed* — by the desire to distinguish himself as an author, he overcame every obstacle he encountered. Not continuous illness, not discouragement to the point of despair, not restricted life-experience, not even meager talent (W. B. Yeats's "will trying to do the work of the imagination" very nearly defines him) could prevail. He is the ideal fulfillment of Froude's

> You can not dream yourself into a character; you must hammer and forge yourself into one.

# 24–Strachey

*The past belongs to us and is far more malleable than the future.* — Maeterlinck.

*Judge not thy stature by thy morning shadow.* — Browne.

T HE clamor for biography is in full voice today. If during the latter years of the Victorian Age the number of "lives" issued exceeded by scores that of any previous period, the mounting lists in our own time bid fair to exceed such totals by hundreds. In that far-off, half legendary day when Adamnan wrote of Columcille, he had more nearly to create a demand for his work than to fill one; in fact, such creation was part of his design — by means of the "life" of a saint to spread the love of God. Through the centuries intervening, however, biography, augmented in range and purpose assumed an ever widening significance as a grammar of life. Its meaning became ever clearer in proportion to the developing awareness of its value as both record and pattern, and the demand for it waxed ever louder; until nowadays, having profited by the contributions of an improved methodology and of the sciences pertinent to its genius, and being subjected to the clamor which popular education and a democratized desire for knowledge have brought about, the form is being exploited to the limits of its present possibilities.

"In the world," Fulke Greville once wrote,
"men must be dealt with according to what they are and not what they ought to be; and the great art of life is to find out what they are and act with them accordingly."

Thus, in a single sentence, he isolated the germ of biographic activity: "the great art of life is to find out what [men] are and act with them accordingly," for biography furnishes a means toward such discovery.

No matter what the age wherein we live or what its dominant conception, one unifying idea obtains: man must understand himself in order to survive. And throughout the history of biography, whether one reflect upon the quest of the middle ages for the things of the spirit, the struggle of the seventeenth century to adjust to an expanding world, the subsidence of the eighteenth into self-sufficiency, the resumed efforts of the nineteenth to balance sense and soul, or the search of the twentieth, impelled by a perfection of means rendered useless by chaotic purpose, for guiding sanctions, — throughout the history of the genre, not to be lost to sight for an instant, appear signs of this same instinctive ambition: survival, and this same unfaltering desire: self-knowledge.

Although the original purpose remained unaltered, when pastoral simplicity with its elementary requirements of conduct disappeared before urban complexity, in the field of biography examples of virtue set forth in primary colors finally diminished in number, superseded by reanimations of personality in all the tints and shades within the compass of radiant energy — the crimson and white abstraction of Adamnan dissolving into the rose and grey of Walton's more concrete virtues; and the earth hues of Boswell's specificity becoming the matrix from which sprang the kaleidoscopic confusions of today.

To think of biography as a form in evolution, however, is to oversimplify. In fact, as pointed out earlier by a quotation from Professor Stauffer, before 1700 all aspects of biography had been established — "the impersonal, political, ethical, malicious, encomiastic, romantic, mystical, satirical, documented, and subjective." It remained for later writers to ring their changes upon these. The differences that developed, therefore, are unrelated except in the most remote of generalities and signify only that as emphases shifted and men viewed their subjects in various lights additions and modifications appeared, sometimes to the improvement, sometimes to the detriment of the form. Hence, what may superficially be thought of as an evolution is, like what is often considered progress, in reality no more than a shift in stress.

In view of the tradition against which contemporary life writing must be focused, no satisfactory comment is possible. That the term "new biography" is entirely justifiable seems difficult to accept. Scholarly "lives" are more accurate today than ever before, valuable additions to earlier accumulations of material having become possible through improved research techniques. It is true also that a wider tolerance has permitted publication of personal traits which formerly would have been glossed over or omitted altogether. And finally, current underscoring of the worth of personality in the struggle for worldly success has encouraged a more intensive analysis in interpreting the characteristics of the subjects discussed. These differences, however, are but matters of degree, to be considered as the results of additional advantages in method — hardly as new or original.

On the other hand, there grew up during the quarter of a century prior to World War II a spirit in life writing comparable in kind to very little that had gone before. For subject, any individual, from racketeer to cardinal, was suitable, the course of whose career and the traits of whose character lent themselves to treatment calculated as appealing to popular taste; and the result varied from sensational journalism to literature of distinction. The novelty lay in motivation, which, in turn is closely related to the attitude of author to subject and the reasons underlying current biographic undertaking. To spend, for instance, twenty years in the preparation of a "life" of Lee, as Douglas Freeman did, for the purpose of making obeisance to one of the greatest of all Americans and, incidentally, of aiding to sustain such obeisance through generations to come — to undertake biography in this spirit is to uphold the best in the tradition. To hit upon some "Cynthia of the minute," however, for the sake of self-aggrandizement is to fall somewhat short even of Thomas Fuller's

> And lastly (which I am not ashamed publicly to profess) to procure some honest profit to myself.

And of much such offering this last seems to be the dominant impulse — a far cry from that earlier day when a "life" was the expression of genuine emotional or intellectual engagement. Such effort, moreover, if it be no more than the exploitation of public craving for titillation, of course, must remain mere novelty. Likewise, if it be an answer to popular demand for informality in treatment, perhaps nothing more than a catering to the pruriginous, it is, again, mere novelty. Dryden, it will be remembered, favored reducing demigods to men, but he stopped short there, content to agree with Shakespeare concerning the survival of evil of its own accord.

Many explanations have been put forth to account for certain recent trends. It is said by some that every age must re-interpret the past in terms of its own predilections. Others say that since the ultimate in democratic processes is the enthronement of mediocrity, the commemoration of distinction is intolerable to the democratic spirit. And still others say that discontent being, as it is, the mainspring of progress, we, having apotheosized discontent and having with Maeterlinck discovered the malleability of the past, are seeking through re-interpretation to allay our self-disgust. Whatever the explanation may be, it is all too early to close our minds. Considering the hundreds of "lives" published in England and the United States during the past quarter century, to say that all are meritless is as absurd as to say that, set apart and labeled "new," they alone are worthy. One may, however, venture the opinion that biography is a study of the inner grace that shapes the outward act, and it retains its integrity only so long as its chief emphasis is upon the spiritually constructive, no matter what the character of the age; it can flatter neither prudery nor prurience and reach the heights.

As has been consistently implied, if not specifically expressed, although the business of literature is primarily to synthesize experience and although biography contributes directly to such synthesis, nevertheless it has come but slowly into recognition as a literary form. As a matter of fact, because of its abiding interest in commemoration and didacticism, its office, like that of criticism, has been held more nearly interpretive than creative. Today, however (and the characteristic is an effect of the desire on the part of biographers for the wider appeal of their work and so is bound up with "redacted purpose"), the balance has tipped, at least slightly, on the side of the creative and consequently the claim of biography to be considered literature has been increased — and the man most obviously accreditable is Lytton Strachey, hailed at his first appearance and complimented by imitators as the prophet of the "new school."

How permanent his appeal is or how lasting his influence will become are questions for posterity. Acclaim was high at his first appearance, it is true; but now, after some twenty-five years, there are indications of declining interest, observable in the decreased demand for his books in shops and public libraries, besides the diminishing effect of his work as a pattern upon the writing of younger men. In fact a recent critic, G. M. Young, remarked that much of Strachey's writing was "variations on a theme for standard biography composed for the piccolo"; and Mr. T. R. Barnes, in "Scrutiny," 1934, wrote that "Incapable of creation in life or in literature, his [Strachey's] writings were a substitute for both." Hence, notwithstanding the plaudits of 1918 and of succeeding years as his later volumes were issued, whether, in view of current trend, his work will "flourish in league with Time," who knows — Churton Collins once said that "the world, like an accomplished hostess, pays most attention to those whom it will soonest forget," and one is not unmindful that ten years were required to exhaust Elia's first edition. At least just now the irony of life has grown so bitter that one's taste for irony has passed.

In the second paragraph of the Preface to "Eminent Victorians," quoted before, Strachey sets forth his philosophy, the salient points of which, if one may repeat, are presented in the following:

> To preserve, for instance, a becoming brevity — a brevity which excludes everything that is redundant and nothing that is significant — that, surely is the first duty of the biographer. The second, no less surely, is to maintain his own freedom of spirit. It is not his business to be complimentary; it is his business to lay bare the facts of the case, as he understands them;

and a "becoming brevity" and "freedom of spirit" are part and parcel of his manner throughout. The first, if one measure it against the

[ 291 ]

vast accumulations — with their sacred wastes — of a Boswell and a Lockhart, or against the interminability of the nineteenth century "Life and Letters" school, is a departure irresistibly appealing at a time when our greatest master of style, George Santayana, can say, "To be brief is almost a condition of being inspired." Moreover, if brevity is an ideal with us, "freedom of spirit" is of our very essence. Hence, equipped with the means, one is tempted to say, of flattering our prejudices — if not of teaching us to see in ourselves what we scoff at in others — he proceeded to capture an audience ready-made.

Unlike many men who have won distinction in life writing, Strachey came early to undertake it — Adamnan was almost 70, Boswell was 51, Trevelyan 48, and Lockhart 44, when their works were finished; in fact, a study of the careers of seventy-seven biographers showed that they began their major work at an average age of 48.75 years. Strachey, however, was only 38 when in 1918 "Eminent Victorians" laid the foundation of his fame. No particular significance, of course, is to be attached to his having turned thus early to biography — unless one chooses to overread the matter. His writing from the beginning in 1903 was concerned with literary criticism and indicates as much interest in the personalities of the authors discussed as in the qualities of their art, a characteristic most apparent perhaps in "Landmarks in French Literature," issued in 1912. There is, however, at least on the surface, a suggestion of the curiously inappropriate, in thinking of the year 1918 as the date of publication for a book so remote in subject from the world as it was. For during the time when Strachey was writing — he spent four years in its composition — the climax of World War I was drawing steadily closer. All about him were men locked in death struggle. Yet, coolly aloof, he cast back into the not distant past and etched in sharp strokes four personalities typical of a vanishing age — a churchman, a nurse, a schoolmaster, and a soldier.

He was indeed aloof from the immediate turmoil, proceeding so far as to undergo an official investigation of his avowed pacifism, but by no means was he untouched by the crescive disillusionment of which such turmoil seems to have been both cause and culmination. For sometimes prose as well as poetry may express the nostalgia of the spirit for a perfect world. Expressive, therefore, of his own discontent — to refer again to the Preface of "Eminent Victorians" — in "attacking its subjects in unexpected places"; and in shooting "a sudden, revealing searchlight into obscure recesses, hitherto undefined"; and in catering to the restless, but less articulate discontent of his audience, his first biographical undertaking, in the phrase of the French critic Charles Du Bos, was accepted as "justified by its day." This comment one may underscore by adding that "Eminent Victorians," far from being at odds with the spirit of its time, as at first sight it would seem to have been, fostered that spirit so sympathetically, crystallized for it so skillfully its own point of view, that it may be taken almost as the definition of a pause in the "whirligig of taste." But considered from still another angle, the book is no less a splendid example of the movement of the governing class — of which Strachey's family had long been members — toward the left. Only, one is mindful that whatever becomes fashionable is doomed, with the certainty of time itself, some day to become old-fashioned.

And the distinctive characteristics of the first work are likewise those of the works that followed. "Queen Victoria," published in 1921; "Books and Characters," in 1922; "Elizabeth and Essex," 1928; "Portraits in Miniature," 1931; and the posthumous "Characters and Commentaries," 1933, are no less relatively brief and free in spirit in their attacks upon their "subjects in unexpected places" and in their searchlight revelations of "obscure recesses, hitherto undivined."

"The biographer is one peering into the dark," wrote Wallace Notestein in an article in the "Yale Review" for March, 1933:

> Yes, but that is, of course, his business, and it must be managed somehow at all hazards. He must be cautious, but not too cautious. He must begin with facts that are evident, but he must go beyond them, and by the skillful use of imagination and reason endeavor to arrive at the facts that are still obscured.*

To begin with evident fact is one thing, but to proceed from such basis toward the more obscure "by the skillful use of imagination and reason" is something quite different. Much of our knowledge

---

* Included by the courteous permission of the publishers of the "Yale Review," the Yale University Press.

of the past has been arrived at in the fashion of this last. Thus, matters of fact are presented as incontrovertibly demonstrable from the most tenuous of clues, like identifying the assailant of Christopher Marlowe, for instance. On the other hand, much has been put forth that is entirely phantasmagorial — Bacon's having written Shakespeare's plays is here a case in point, as is also the hypothesis that a woman wrote the "Odyssey." It is not so much the deduction of error like this, however, that is dangerous, as it is the propagation of false conception, distorted opinion, conjecture offered as authoritative judgment. Examples of this practice, whether proceeding from ignorance or bias or both, have long since, in mounting accumulation, topped Olympus, Pelion, and Ossa. So prevalent is it, so prevalent has it always been, in fact, that the most acescent of all critics, the aphorists, have paid it the compliment of their attention, one of the bitterest, Samuel Butler, once saying, "Although God cannot alter the past, historians can."

When Gamaliel Bradford, to approach the concrete, in reporting Pliny's compliment to Tacitus suggests that Pliny's ingenuousness was really overweening vanity, he is merely in error. When Strachey, however, characterizes Cardinal Manning as a clerical opportunist, Florence Nightingale as a ministering tyrant, Dr. Arnold as a Solomon in grotesque miniature, and Gordon as the victim of Victorianism and the bottle, he is not "by the skilful use of imagination and reason" presenting obscure fact upon a basis of the clearly apparent. After all, Manning did serve not only the church but society also; Miss Nightingale did save countless lives; Thomas Arnold did vastly improve English public schools; and Gordon was emphatically not either a puppet or a drunkard; hence Strachey is deliberately manipulating documentary evidence for the sake of dramatic effect. And what is true of "Eminent Victorians" is true also of "Queen Victoria," "Books and Characters," "Elizabeth and Essex," and "Portraits in Miniature." "To lay bare the facts of the case, as he understands them," means, as applicable to Strachey, laying bare such facts as contribute to his design, and by oblique suggestion and connotative phrase to manipulate such as do not toward the same end.

And of the sharp impress of the design there can be no doubt;

Strachey is one of the few biographers who even begin to shake Hazlitt's dictum that "it is useless to comment upon a man about whom the world has already made up its mind." His attributes, however, are not so readily apparent. From the days of his first coming into fame critics have been at work examining his devices, tracing to its probable origins his style, and looking into his handling of sources. He has been praised by some as a biographic Messiah and condemned by others as a pernicious influence on the basis of the same findings. A list of magazine articles treating of him and his manner shows almost two hundred items — but agreement as to either manner or morals is far to seek except as concerns the broadest principles. The easy solution — and by no means the worst — is to point to "becoming brevity" and "freedom of spirit" as his dominant traits, the last informing the first.

In thinking thus of the source of his effects, one is struck by the keenness of his desire to escape from the past. The great tradition — of which, incidentally, he is not yet free from the risk of becoming a part — was for him a bondage. To escape it he created a past of his own, like the old, but unlike it, real but unreal, substantial but shadowy, factual but true only in his image of truth, a past of old names but new meanings, of characters reincarnated only to be consigned to perdition. What he writes of them can be traced to the documents; nothing less than complete mastery of available record would have enabled him to accomplish his purpose — one must understand profoundly in order effectively to omit or successfully to manipulate. Or, as Walter Bagehot once wrote, "It is only by a rigid adherence to attested facts and authentic documents that original views can obtain even a hearing." Strachey, however, by the substitution of picturesque detail and fascinating preconception for reality very nearly approaches the fantastic. He may, at times, almost be thought of as exemplifying Mark Twain's advice to the young Kipling, "Get your facts and then — you can distort them as much as you please."

If "Eminent Victorians" is illustrative in point, "Queen Victoria" is no less so. Coming three years later it carries on the spirit of the previous work. To be sure, the "Victoria" is more extended; in fact, it is the longest of Strachey's works. Nevertheless, in view of the immense accumulation of material and of the long and momentous life described, proportionately the same "becoming brevity" is maintained and the same "freedom of spirit" indulged, although as one reads he is not unmindful that Edmund Gosse also wrote a study of Victoria, one which makes but little use of the errors of peccant flesh. From the unique circumstances surrounding the childhood of the Princess and the accident of her ascension, to the inevitable end on that January day of 1901, the story extends. The girl, the wife, the sovereign, the widow, the octogenarian, all are shown. But in the showing appears the Victoria of Strachey — perhaps the Victoria of history. Everyone knows that her taste in music, for instance, rose no higher than a liking for Tosti; that her knowledge of political economy was based upon little more solid matter than the stories of Harriet Martineau; and that great credit for much accomplished during her reign was due to the talents of the Prince Consort. There seems, therefore, small need to underscore the obvious. Victoria came to the throne a slim girl, in no wise expected to realize the subtleties of her condition; she left it an empress, the symbol of British complacency, it may be, but the symbol of British might, there can be no doubt — and her name defines an age among the greatest. The 425 widely leaded pages of the book reveal an artist at work with the relics of a personality. Victoria lives among the pages, but one feels the presence of Strachey behind the curtains whether at Windsor or at Balmoral. The famous irony is everywhere in evidence; the mocking grimace — especially in connection with minor characters — never fails. Strachey may in the end have admired Victoria; there are hints now and then that having come to scoff he remained to pray. None the less every chapter discloses, intentionally or otherwise, his ironic attitude toward the age — in pointed allusion, in finessed phrase, in discreet omission. And so the work enhanced the reputation for "manner" established by "Eminent Victorians."

When, seven years afterward, he turned to Queen Elizabeth and the Earl of Essex (having in the meantime issued a collection of writings contributed to periodicals, between 1905 and 1931, "Books and Characters"), he was to treat of an age upon which, in another connection, he had commented,

With few exceptions — possibly with the single exception of Shakespeare — the creatures in it meet us without intimacy; they are exterior visions, which we know, but do not truly understand.

Peopled with "exterior visions" though he thought it, it fascinated him. The mundanity of it, the refinement of its intrigues, the scarlet and gold brocade against which the Queen, Essex, Burleigh, Bacon, Robert Cecil, and the whole host of lesser persons moved, drew from him many pages of his best. Dramatic contrasts develop, violent contradictions, rebellion and subjection, magnificence and niggardliness, lust and piety, barbarism and elegance, youth, age, love, and death upon the block. The impressions are sharp, clearly defined, and dimensional; the characters are full bodied, intensely alive; but the voices and the hands are Strachey — just as frequently they are in the "Victoria."

"Elizabeth and Essex" is not biography in the usual sense; it is drama in chapters. The early life of the queen is shown only in brief, and Essex enters the scene as a courtier of eighteen — the action concerns the turbulent years during which each tried to serve himself at the expense of the other. The outcome is inevitable; the old queen triumphs over the youthful courtier soldier, who could inherit Sir Philip Sidney's best sword but not the spirit it connoted. The triumph is empty, however. Essex's head under the ax becomes the incipience of Elizabeth's mordant melancholy as her last two years draw to a weighty close, and she ruled as "queen of emptiness and death." History the work may be. Strachey knew the period as few men have known it. Only, one finds discrepancies in quotations — words altered and phrases heightened or omitted, a frequent recourse to the "stream of consciousness" device of the novelist, manipulated attitudes on the part of minor persons, overinterpretations of military affairs, and additions of baroque detail, to say nothing of embroidered sophistry. And biography it probably is in so far as "becoming brevity" and "freedom of spirit" permit. But drama created by "subtle strategy," by rowing

out over [a] great ocean of material, and [lowering] down into it, here and there, a little bucket, which will bring up to

the light of day some characteristic specimen, from those far depths, to be examined with a careful curiosity, —
but drama thus contrived it unquestionably is — and as such shares in today's contribution of the creative to the body of biographic techniques.

"Books and Characters," "Portraits in Miniature," and "Characters and Commentaries," the last a collection, for the most part, of early papers, and issued posthumously by the author's brother, Mr. James Strachey, in 1933, complete the list of Strachey books. Personages literary and nonliterary appear in terms of some salient feature, together with critical sketches revealing trenchant insight — if Strachey had never become interested in "lives," he would have achieved distinction as a critic. As it is, however, the critic has emerged as biographer. Of the three volumes, "Portraits in Miniature" is most vital. *Books and Characters* contains, among less noteworthy items, the nostalgically sympathetic "character" of Thomas Beddoes, called the "Last Elizabethan," the reincarnatory "Madame Du Deffand," the uncommon history of Lady Hester Stanhope, and the derisive "Mr. Creevey." It presents for the first time, too, an essay, "English Letter Writers," which Strachey wrote in 1905 in competition for the Le Bas Prize, and which is among the best comments upon the subject to be found, besides an unfinished paper, "Othello," upon which he was engaged at the time of his death. "Portraits in Miniature," however, exhibits his writing at its biographically satirical best, and is highly illustrative of his oft-commented upon "unfeeling sympathy." The essays are in form — although in manner they are as poles removed — suggestive of Walton, of Aubrey, and of the whole "life-essay" tradition. They stress the amusing, the extraordinary and often the trifling. If one depended upon the sketch of Boswell for understanding of that complex personality, for instance, he would be betrayed into paradox; or if he took seriously "The Life, Illness, and Death of Dr. North," he would miss entirely the point of Roger North's purpose in composing the original memoir — he would not, however, fail to be entertained. On the other hand, the "Sir John Harington," the "John Aubrey," the "Madam de Sevigne's Cousin," "The Abbe Morellet," and the "Gibbon," in *Six English Historians,* are from a literary point of view among the finest in the biographical essay genre. A fitting comment upon "Portraits in Miniature" was made by Strachey himself — his inscription "To Max Beerbohm, with gratitude, and admiration" — as a fellow ironist.

Whatever opinion may obtain concerning his treatment of material or the designs into which he wove it, one has nothing but praise for his style. In fact, style, it is not too much to say, is his greatest asset, the distinction of his work, and, justly enough, the despair of his imitators. The veriest tyro can denigrate a subject, but only an artist can so manipulate situation, event, and characteristic that a subject blackens himself. This last is Strachey's proprietary aptitude, its determinate, his style. Seldom, to restress the obvious, have biographers concerned themselves with style. More, Walton, Middleton, Dryden, Goldsmith, Trevelyan, and Froude made it a matter of paramount interest; but Strachey alone seems to have relied upon it as a major instrument; with him it was no badge of "idleness from the sty of Epicurus." Because of it, his work is notable; without it, he would have done no more than justify Tennyson's bitter comment upon the "unofficial" biographers of his day,

> Proclaim the faults he would not show;
> Break lock and seal; betray the trust;
> Keep nothing sacred.

Perhaps its most noticeable feature is its effortlessness. There is never a suggestion of strain either to please or to shock, and never a hint of self-consciousness. The prose culture to which it relates is that of Dryden and Swift, Goldsmith and Newman with occasional echoes from Browne and Gibbon; but without the concise limitation, the precision of advancing phrase, the informing simplicity which he learned from the French, his effects may well have failed of sharp focus. The English of Dryden, Swift, Goldsmith, and Newman is not for the literary craftsman — it is loose, shows little balance, and is of such seeming artlessness that only the artist may safely attempt it. But neither is the French of Saint-Simon, of Voltaire, of Racine — in which the unwary can but flounder confused and astray. Of the first Strachey once wrote that his style was a tropical forest — luxuriant, bewildering, enormous — with the gayest humming-birds among the branches, and the vilest monsters in the entangled grass.

Of Voltaire, in speaking of the "Lettres Philosophiques," he wrote

> The matters treated of are so many and so vast, they are disposed of and dismissed so swiftly, so easily, so unemphatically, that one begins to wonder, whether, after all, anything of real significance can have been expressed. But, in reality, what, in those few small pages, has been expressed is simply the philosophy of Voltaire.

But it is in commenting upon Racine, perhaps, that in terms of admiration for the poet he reveals the ideal of his own accomplishment — the comment having been made as early as 1908:

> His triumph is precisely this — that he brings about by what are apparently the simplest means, effects which other poets must strain every nerve to produce.

This last, one may submit, might stand as a comment upon Strachey himself. "By what are apparently the simplest means," he wrought effects which may, in many quarters, unfortunately, be lasting. One may deplore the effects — as did Sir Charles Firth in saying, "I think Lytton Strachey's style a very bad style in which to tell the truth —" one can, however, do nothing less than admire the means by which these effects are attained. In brief, Strachey's style, in its bright readability, requires the employment of fewer words that at first thought is conceivable. With scarcely an exception — *velleity* in the "Victoria" is notable, however — words beyond the experience of the multitude seem never to be necessary; in fact, words for him are not units of expression so much as, in association reflecting the lights and shades of incisive thought from one to another, they merge into impressions as sentences. But not even the sentence is noticeable as such. Few Strachey sentences, as a matter of fact, are detachable as aphorisms or quotations of wide implication. Almost invariably they have meaning as a group communicating a closely knit paragraph division of the whole. There is no lack of variation, notwithstanding. With a vocabulary consciously limited to bare essentials, and with sentences so enmeshed as to permit no relaxation — in spite of handicaps thus self-imposed, by fresh arrangement and by unexpected interpolation he sustains attention up to carefully contrived conclusion.

A quality of the unexpected is no doubt one of his prime style essentials. "I shall ever remember this day [Coronation Day] as the *proudest* of my life," he quotes from Victoria's Diary, and then adds, "When she returned to Buckingham Palace at last she was not tired; she ran up to her private rooms, doffed her splendors, and gave her dog Dash its evening bath." "Fame," he wrote — "though perhaps it was hardly virtuous — Boswell certainly attained." In writing of Macaulay he remarked, almost aside, "Like Gibbon, like Michelet, like the later Carlyle, he did not — to put it succinctly — understand what he was talking about." And "Every one knows the popular conception of Florence Nightingale," he began what in many ways is his most typical piece of composition. "But the truth was different." The abrupt use of a trite phrase is another essential. "He practiced what he preached," for instance. "And as a conquering hero Victoria welcomed her new Prime Minister." "Horace Walpole had come at a psychological moment." "He spoke, and Lehzen vanished forever." Phrases like these occur not infrequently, always effectively, but never inadvertently.

Simplicity of vocabulary, tightly drawn passages, unexpectedness, and studied triteness, essential characteristics of his style as they are, harmonize by their very nature with his principles of "becoming brevity" and "freedom of spirit," and aid immeasurably in directing "a sudden revealing searchlight into obscure recesses, hitherto undivined." With what success his efforts have been attended, his reputation during these twenty-five years bears witness. How long he will be remembered is not for this generation to say.

# Bibliography

## General

——— Preface, *Dictionary of National Biography* (London: Oxford Press, 1908).

Harry Elmer Barnes, *A History of Historical Writing* (Norman, Okla.: University of Oklahoma Press, 1937).

Hugh H. L. Bellot, *The Temple* (London: Methuen, 1925).

Phillips Brooks, *Essays and Addresses* (New York: Dutton, 1894).

Thomas Carlyle, *Works* (Boston: Brown and Laggard, 1860).

Joseph Collins, *The Doctor Looks at Biography* (New York: Doran, 1925).

C. T. Copeland and F. W. C. Hersey, *Representative Biographies* (New York: Macmillan, 1910).

Wilbur L. Cross, *An Outline of Biography* (Holt, 1924).

Thomas Davidson, "Biography," *Chambers' Encyclopedia.*

Waldo H. Dunn, *English Biography* (London: Dent, 1916).

Edward Edwards and Charles Hole, *A Handbook to the Literature of General Biography* (Ventnor: G. Henry Brittain, 1885).

Havelock Ellis, *Views and Reviews* (Boston: Houghton Mifflin, 1932).

John Foster, *Critical Essays* (London: Bohn, 1856, Vol. II).

Edmund Gosse, "Biography," *Encyclopedia Britannica.*

Frederick Harrison, *Realities and Ideals* (New York: Macmillan, 1908).

Paul Harvey, *The Oxford Companion to English Literature* (London: Oxford Press, 1934).

Edgar Johnson, *One Mighty Torrent* (New York: Stackpole, 1937).

J. C. Johnston, *Biography, the Literature of Personality* (New York: Century, 1927).

E. E. Kellett, *The Whirligig of Taste* (New York: Harcourt, 1929).

Sidney Lee, *Elizabethan and Other Essays* (Oxford: Clarendon Press, 1929).

Sidney Lee, *Principles of Biography* (London: Cambridge University Press, 1911).

Mark Longacker, *Contemporary Biography* (Philadelphia: University of Pennsylvania Press, 1934).

Mark Longacker, *English Biography in the Eighteenth Century* (Philadelphia: University of Pennsylvania Press, 1931).

J. R. Lowell, *Works* (Boston: Houghton Mifflin, 1904).

Andre Maurois, *Aspects of Biography* (New York: Harcourt, 1929).

D. K. Merrill, *The Development of American Biography* (Portland, Me.: Southworth Press, 1932).

J. C. Metcalf, *The Stream of English Biography* (New York: Century, 1930).

Frank Mumby, *The Romance of Bookselling* (London: Chapman and Hall, 1910).

H. W. Nevinson, *Books and Personalities* (New York: Lane, 1905).

Harold Nicholson, *The Development of English Biography* (London: Hogarth Press, 1927).

E. H. O'Neill, *A History of American Biography* (Philadelphia: University of Pennsylvania Press, 1935).

Hesketh Pearson, *Ventilations, Being Biographical Asides* (London: Lippincott, 1930).

Phyllis M. Riches, *An Analytical Bibliography of Universal Collective Biography* (New York: Wilson, 1934).

R. M. Smith, *A Book of Biography* (Garden City: Doubleday, 1930).

James Field Stanfield, *An Essay of the Study and Composition of Biography* (Edinburgh: Sunderland, 1813).

D. A. Stauffer, *Art of Biography in Eighteenth Century England* (Princeton: Princeton University Press, 1941).

D. A. Stauffer, *English Biography Before 1700* (Cambridge: Harvard University Press, 1930).

W. H. Teale, *Lives of English Laymen* (London: Burns, 1842).

W. F. Thrall and Addison Hibbard, *A Handbook of Literature* (Garden City: Doubleday, 1936).

T. G. Williams, *Tradition and Experiment* (London: Oxford Press, 1929).

### Particular

———— *Handbook of the Dyce and Forster Collections in the South Kensington Museum* (London: Chapman and Hall, 1880).

R. C. Beatty, *Lord Macaulay* (Norman, Okla.: University of Oklahoma Press, 1938).

J. Buchan, *Sir Walter Scott* (London: Cassell, 1932).

Frances Burney, *Diary* (New York: Dutton, 1931).

John Butt, *Isaac Walton's Methods in Biography*. Essays and Studies by Members of the English Association, XIX.

Alexander Carlyle and James Crichton-Browne, *Nemesis of Froude* (London: Lane, 1903).

Alexander Chalmers, *A Lesson in Biography* (Edinburgh: Aingervyle Society, 1887).

R. W. Chambers, *Continuity of English Prose* (London: Oxford Press, 1932).

R. W. Chambers, *Thomas More* (New York: Harcourt, 1935).

Andrew Clark, *Brief Lives, Chiefly of Contemporaries, Set Down by John Aubrey* (Oxford: Clarendon Press, 1898).

J. L. Clifford, *Hester Lynch Piozzi (Mrs. Thrale)* (Oxford: Clarendon Press, 1941).

Arthur Hugh Clough, *Plutarch's Lives* (Boston: Little Brown, 1924).

Hartley Coleridge, *Northern Worthies* (London: Moxon, 1852).

Padraic Colum, *The Legend of St. Columba* (New York: Macmillan, 1935).

Austin Dobson, *Eighteenth Century Studies, Wayfarer's Library* (New York: Dutton. No date).

J. W. Draper, *William Mason* (New York: New York University Press, 1924).

Charles Du Bos, *Approximations, deuxieme serie* (Paris: Corres, 1932).

Waldo H. Dunn, *Froude and Carlyle* (New York: Longmans, 1930).

E. W. Emerson, *A Correspondence between John Sterling and Ralph Waldo Emerson* (Boston: Houghton Mifflin, 1897).

J. T. Fields, *Barry Cornwall and Some of His Friends* (Boston: Osgood, 1876).

Charles H. Firth, *The Life of William Cavendish, Duke of Newcastle, by His Wife* (London: Nimmo, 1886).

Percy Fitzgerald, *John Forster and One of His Friends* (London: Chapman and Hall, 1903).

John Forster, *Life of Goldsmith* (New York: Harpers, 1900).

J. T. Fowler, *Adamni Vita S. Columbae* (Oxford: Clarendon Press, 1894).

George Gilfillan, *Galleries of Literary Portraits* (Edinburgh: James Hogg, 1857), Vol. II.

T. R. Glover, *Poets and Puritans* (London: Methuen, 1915).

Stephen Gwynne, *The Famous Cities of Ireland* (London: Maunsell, 1915).

E. V. Hitchcock and R. W. Chambers, *Life and Death of Sir Thomas More by Nicholas Harpsfield* (London: Oxford Press, 1932).

Christopher Hollis, *Thomas More* (Milwaukee: Bruce, 1942).

Walter E. Houghton, Jr., *The Formation of Thomas Fuller's Holy and Profane States* (Cambridge: Harvard University Press, 1938).

R. H. Hutton, *Brief Literary Criticisms* (London: Macmillan, 1906).

Washington Irving, *Oliver Goldsmith* (New York: Putnam, 1864).

Claude Jenkins, *Sir Thomas More* (Canterbury: Jennings, 1933).

J. L. Kennedy, *The Life of Sir Thomas More by Cresacre More* (Athens, Pa.: Riverside Press, 1941).

Elizabeth E. Kent, *Goldsmith and His Booksellers* (Ithaca: Cornell University Press, 1933).

Hugh Kingsmill, *Johnson Without Boswell* (New York: Knopf, 1941).

Andrew Lang, *John Gibson Lockhart* (New York: Scribners, 1897).

T. B. Macaulay, *Critical and Historical Essays* (New York: Everyman Library, Dutton, ......).

W. K. Leak, *James Boswell* (Edinburgh: Famous Scots Series, 1896).

George Mallory, *Boswell the Biographer* (London: Smith, Elder, 1912).

F. W. Maitland, *Life and Letters of Leslie Stephen* (London: Duckworth, 1906).

Stapleton Martin, *Isaac Walton and His Friends* (New York: Dutton, ......).

Harriet Martineau, *Biographical Sketches* (New York: Leypolt, 1869).

James M. Osborn, *John Dryden* (New York: Columbia University Press, 1940).

Herbert Paul, *Life of Froude* (New York: Scribners, 1905).

Henry Ten Eyck Perry, *The First Duchess of Newcastle and Her Husband as Figures in Literary History* (Boston: Ginn, 1918).

Martha Pickens, *John Forster* (a thesis, University of Pittsburgh, 1936).

Hester L. T. Piozzi, *Anecdotes of the Later Samuel Johnson* (New York: Macmillan, 1925).

F. A. Pottle, *Literary Career of James Boswell* (Oxford: Clarendon Press, 1929).

Sir James Prior, *Life of Edmund Malone* (London: Smith, Elder, 1860).

Walter Raleigh, *Six Essays on Johnson* (London: Oxford Press, 1910).

Richard Benton, *John Forster and His Friends* (London: Chapman and Hall, 1903).

Diantha V. Riddle, *Dictionary of National Biography* (a thesis, University of Pittsburgh, 1938).

Sidney C. Roberts, *Doctor Johnson* (New York: Macmillan, 1935).

E. M. G. Routh, *Sir Thomas More and His Friends* (New York: Oxford Press, 1934).

Daniel Sargent, *St. Thomas More* (New York: Sheed and Ward, 1934).

L. P. Smith, *Life and Letters of Sir Henry Wotton* (Oxford: Clarendon Press, 1907).

J. K. Spittal, *Contemporary Criticisms of Dr. Samuel Johnson* (New York: Dutton, 1923).

Leslie Stephen, *Studies of a Biographer* (New York: Putnam, 1907).

C. B. Tinker, *Young Boswell* (Boston: Atlantic Monthly Press, 1922).

G. M. Trevelyan, *Sir George Otto Trevelyan* (London: Longmans, 1932).

Anne Kimball Tuell, *John Sterling* (New York: Macmillan, 1941).

Charles Whibley, *Essays in Biography* (London: Constable, 1913).

Stanley T. Williams, *Life of Washington Irving* (New York: Oxford Press, 1935).

David Wilson, *Carlyle to Three Score and Ten* (New York: Dutton, 1929).

David Wilson, *Mr. Froude and Carlyle* (New York: Dodd, Mead, 1898).

Virginia Woolf, *The Common Reader* (New York: Harcourt, 1925).

### Periodicals

—— "The Biographical Mania," *Lait's Edinburgh Magazine*, N.S., 25:16

E. W. Adams, "On Polishing Windows and Other Matters," *Contemporary Review*, 141:88

J. T. Adams, "Biography as an Art," *Saturday Review of Literature*, 4:297

St. John Adcock, "The Gentle Art of Biography," *Bookman* (London), 75:112

Gamaliel Bradford, "Art of Biography," *Saturday Review of Literature*, 1:769

G. E. Brown, "Goldsmith and Johnson," *Modern Language Notes*, 42:168

G. E. Brown, "Goldsmith's Indebtedness of Voltaire and Justus Van Effen," *Modern Philology*, 23:273

C. J. Campbell, "The Biographical Approach to Literature," *English Journal* (College Edition), 25:292

E. G. Clark, "Mr. Strachey's Biographical Method," *Catholic World*, 129:129

A. Clutton-Brock, "Pleasure of Reading Biography," *Living Age*, 317:89

Elbridge Colby, "Bibliography as an Aid to Biography," *Papers of the Bibliographical Society of America*, Vol. 17

E. T. Cook, "Art of Biography," *National Review*, April, 1914

T. H. S. Escott, "A Literary Cham and His Court," *Fortnightly Review*, 100:900

L. M. Gelber, "History and the New Biography," *Queen's Quarterly*, January, 1930

W. E. Gladstone, "Life and Letters of Lord Macaulay," *Quarterly Review*, 142:1

Ferris Greenslet, "Dictionary of National Biography," *Atlantic Monthly*, 89:270

Frederick Harrison, "Great Biographers," *English Review*, March, 1912

John Hawkesworth, "Of the Different Kinds of Narrative," *Adventurer*, November 18, 1752

Frances M. Haydon, "Oliver Goldsmith as a Biographer," *South Atlantic Quarterly*, 39:50

Francis Jeffrey, "Memoirs of Sir James Mackintosh," *Edinburgh Review,* 62:205

H. M. Jones, "Methods in Contemporary Biography," *English Journal* (College Edition), 21:43

Vicesimus Knox, "Dr. Johnson and Biography," *Winter Evenings* (British Essayists, 42)

Harold D. Lasswell, "Scientific Study of Human Biography," *Scientific Monthly,* 30:79

Sidney Lee, "At a Journey's End," *Nineteenth Century and After,* 72:1155

Sidney Lee, "National Biography," *Cornhill Magazine,* 73:258

Mowbray Morris, "Froude's Carlyle," *Quarterly Review,* 159:76

J. F. Newton, "Romance of Reality," *Homiletic Review,* 90:427

Charles Platt, "The Development of an Attitude," *Century,* 116:318

Sir Charles Russell, "Johnson, Gibbon, and Boswell," *Fortnightly Review,* 125:629

Goldwin Smith, "Froude," *Atlantic Monthly,* 97:680

Lytton Strachey, "One of the Victorians," *Saturday Review of Literature,* 7:418

D. R. Stuart, "From New Biography Back to Old," *Princeton Alumni Weekly,* March 9, 1928

W. R. Thayer, "Biography in the Nineteenth Century," *North American Review,* 211:632; 826

Leonard Whibley, "William Mason," *Blackwood's,* October, 1927

A. K. White, "The Philosophical Significance of Biography," *Journal of Philosophical Studies,* 1:320

Frances Winwar, "Biography Today," *English Journal* (College Edition) 27:7

Virginia Woolf, "The Art of Biography," *Atlantic Monthly,* 163:506

# Index

Burke, Edmund 177, 231
Burleigh, Lord 297
Burman, Peter 125
Burnet, Gilbert 79
Burns, Robert 217
Burrows, Lieutenant 183, 184
*Bury Fair*, Shadwell 97
Bute, Lord 126
Butler, Samuel 79, 294
Byron, Lord 194
Bysshe, Sir Edward 68

Cadell, Thomas 127, 130, 201, 205, 210
Calais 52
Calous 190
*Cambridge History of English Literature* 40
Cambridge University 80, 85, 107, 114, 214, 216, 218, 219, 225, 249, 274
Cambusnethan 203
Campbell, Thomas 192
Cann, Sir Robert 120
Canterbury Convocation 81
Carlisle, Earl of 82
Carlyle, Jane Welch 262, 263, 265
Carlyle, John 107, 212, 262, 265
Carlyle, Thomas 11, 17, 89, 113, 137, 158, 160, 161, 171, 172, 181, 182, 189, 199, 211, 213–222, 237, 238, 242, 251, 252, 254, 256–267, 268
Carnan, Thomas 130
Casaubon, Isaac 59, 79
*Cases of Conscience*, Sanderson 75
*Castle Dangerous*, Scott 208
Castlemaine, Lady 100, 120
*Catalogue of Royal and Noble Authors*, Walpole 273
Catchpole, Ezakial 114
*Catholic Encyclopedia* 42
Cave, Edward 125, 126, 135
Cavendish, Sir Charles 100
Cavendish, George 4, 5, 34, 50–56, 92
Cavendish, Margaret, Duchess of Newcastle (see Newcastle)
Cavendish, Thomas 51

Cavendish, William, Duke of Newcastle (see Newcastle)
Cecil, Robert 297
*Censura Literaria* 103
*Chaldee Manuscript* 202
Chambers, Professor R. W. 32, 37, 38, 40, 41, 42
Chancery Lane 58
*Character of a Grave Divine*, Earle 62
*Characters and Commentaries*, Strachey 293, 298
*Charles at Tunbridge*, Forster 225
Charles I 32, 61, 86, 92, 99, 100
Charles II 97, 99, 100, 102, 117
Charlotte, Queen 163
Chatham, Earl of 163
*Chartism*, Carlyle 222
Chaucer, Geoffrey 107
Chelsea 39
Chetwood, Knightly 107
Cheyney, Francis 126
Chitty, Thomas 225, 226
*Christ, Reading* 151
*Christian Magazine* 151
*Christian Morals*, Browne 126
Christie, J. H. 202, 204
*Chronicle*, Harding 30
*Church History of Britain*, Fuller 82
Churchyard, Thomas 50
Cibber, Colley 139, 148
Cicero 106, 142
*Citizens of the World*, Goldsmith 150
Clare, Lord 156
Claremont, Lord 175, 176
Clarence, Duke of 32
Clarendon, Earl of 79, 98, 99
Clark, Andrew 270
Clement family 42
Clonard 18, 24, 25
Clonmacnoise 18
*Clue to the Labyrinth of Souls*, Bradford 284
*Cockney School* 194
*Coeur-de-Lion*, Sterling 218
Colburn, Henry 226, 228
Colchester 94
Coleridge, Hartley 138

[ 311 ]

[ 319 ]